D0918171

# Rockets

# ABOUT THE AUTHOR

Peter Macinnis is a science writer who lives and works on Sydney's northern beaches, where he was also raised. He and his wife Christine (a science teacher who understands him) have three adult children, all with a taste for things scientific. He has been a teacher himself, as well as a bureaucrat, management consultant and museum educator, among other things, but he works mainly in things related to education, writing, science and number-crunching. For the past four years he has been writing on science, technology and mathematics for WebsterWorld.com, an Australian online encyclopaedia.

For amusement, he maintains a science Web site called Science Playwiths, which seems to draw a fair amount of critical acclaim (and traffic) and he is an enthusiastic member of the Gateway to Educational Materials, a project of the US Department of Education.

He says that he is, at heart, an essayist, but that some of his essays go on for quite a while and when a temporary obsession takes over his life, that is where his books come from. His last book for Allen & Unwin was *Bittersweet: The Story of Sugar* (2002) and he is currently working on a history of poisons and poisoners for release in 2004.

His admitted hobbies include ambulatory plant taxonomy, wandering up small hills slowly, sitting on top of small hills and wondering how to get down, listening to classical music and watching ballet and opera, reading, argument, rocks, invertebrates and red wine. He holds an MCSE in iambic mechanics and was recently the William McGonagall Fellow in Scansion Adjustment at the University of Anson Bay, where he gave master classes in designing stoppers for Klein bottles, using mistaken identity matrix theory.

# Rockets

Sulfur, *Sputnik* and Scramjets

## Peter Macinnis

ALLEN&UNWIN

First published in Australia in 2003
Copyright © Peter Macinnis 2003

All rights reserved. No part of this book may be reproduced or transmitted in any form or by any means, electronic or mechanical, including photocopying, recording or by any information storage and retrieval system, without prior permission in writing from the publisher. The *Australian Copyright Act 1968* (the Act) allows a maximum of one chapter or 10% of this book, whichever is the greater, to be photocopied by any educational institution for its educational purposes provided that the educational institution (or body that administers it) has given a remuneration notice to Copyright Agency Limited (CAL) under the Act.

Allen & Unwin
83 Alexander Street
Crows Nest NSW 2065
Australia
Phone:    (61 2) 8425 0100
Fax:       (61 2) 9906 2218
Email:    info@allenandunwin.com
Web:      www.allenandunwin.com

National Library of Australia
Cataloguing-in-Publication entry:

Macinnis, P. (Peter).
Rockets: Sulfur, *Sputnik* and Scramjets.

Bibliography.
Includes index.
ISBN 1 86508 794 7

1. Rocketry—History. I. Title

621.4356

Typeset in 11/14.5 pt Garamond 3 by Midland Typesetters, Maryborough
Printed by Griffin Press, South Australia

10 9 8 7 6 5 4 3 2 1

*This book was being written when the* Columbia *was lost, with all its crew. They were not the first and they will not be the last.*
*This book is respectfully dedicated to all those who have lost their lives in pursuit of a dream.*

*Husband, McCool, Anderson, Brown, Chawla, Clark, Ramon, Komarov, Grissom, White, Chaffee, Dobrovolsky, Volkov, Patsayev, Resnick, Scobee, Smith, McNair, McAuliffe, Jarvis, Onizuka.*

*These names will be written under other skies.*

*Ken MacLeod*

CENTRAL ARKANSAS LIBRARY SYSTEM
ADOLPHINE FLETCHER TERRY BRANCH
LITTLE ROCK, ARKANSAS

# CONTENTS

# PROLOGUE
# ON THE
# FUTURE

... in our passage from thence to the East Indies, we were driven by a
violent storm to the north-west of Van Diemen's Land. By an observa-
tion, we found ourselves in the latitude of 30 degrees 2 minutes south.

Jonathan Swift, *Gulliver's Travels*, part I, chapter 1

describing the location of Lilliput, 1726

To save you getting the map out, that puts Lilliput in the dry
north of South Australia, a long way from the sea. To get
there, you head north from Adelaide on the coast, and you drive
on, north and west, and then you drive some more. The first
couple of hundred kilometres are green and pleasant, but just
past Port Augusta everything gets brown and flat, the soil
becomes soft and dusty, dotted with stones, tussocky plants and
the occasional sheep. Occasionally there is a richer patch with
eucalypts straight off a Hans Heysen canvas, but the trees get
fewer and the dry gets drier as you go north.

This isn't really desert, just the arid zone of Australia, where
novel ecosystems are wedged in tiny niches between rocks and
a hard place. It is wonderful country, and part of it is a rocket

range called Woomera. Of course, it wasn't always dry like this:
the range area at Woomera is littered with rounded quartzite
pebbles, reminders of an ancient past when rivers ran through
here. These were perennial flows, not the rare gully-washers generated when a large part of today's annual 190 mm of rain falls in
a short time.

Given the right conditions, you might be able to drown here
—if you were a Lilliputian—and Swift's Lilliput lies just north of
Woomera township, well inside the Woomera Exclusion Zone. But
whatever else the place is or isn't, the land around here is no
farmer's delight. Benjamin Herschel Babbage discovered that.

He was the clever son of Charles Babbage, inventor of the
mechanical computer (although he called it a difference engine),
and named for astronomer Sir John Herschel, his father's good
friend. It seems everybody called him Herschel, and he was, for
want of a better term, a highly original polymoth. All his life, he
fluttered from one thing to another, working on his father's
difference engine, assisting Isambard Kingdom Brunel in building the Great Western railway in Britain and in surveying the
Genoa–Turin railway in Italy, acting as local chief engineer for
the Port Adelaide railway, then becoming Government Assayer
for South Australia.

Herschel Babbage also became the colony's Geological and
Mineralogical Surveyor, before pioneering the use of photo-
graphy to record exploration in the 1850s. After his exploring
stint, he transformed into a winemaker and writer on that art—a
Renaissance Man born out of his time, it seems, somebody who
would be more at home in Peter Carey's pages.

Herschel Babbage went into the Woomera area in 1856,
looking for gold and good agricultural land, but found neither,
much to the disappointment of the young colony that was
paying his expenses. He went equipped for months of parched

travel, taking drilling equipment to sink wells, four stills to pro-cess salt water, eight pounds of filter paper to clear muddy water, and an 1100-gallon water cart. He probably also carried some rockets—most explorers did, in those days—but there seems to be no mention of that.

When Police Commissioner Peter Warburton was sent to ride out and recall him, Babbage apparently got wind of this unwelcome plan, and took off, covering a creditable twenty miles a day with all his baroque equipment, and Warburton had to pursue him all over the parched landscape. It struck me when I was there that I had covered, between lunch and a rather early dinner, what Babbage would have traversed in a fortnight's seri-ously hard slog. I had a couple of litres of water in the car, just in case, but that was it. I travelled lighter and much faster.

I wondered as I drove what Babbage would think if he could see how fast we travel now. Then it struck me how appropriate the thought was, given that I was in Woomera to see a scramjet test—the Australian Hyshot project. The hype for these devices always tells us how future scramjetliners may take us from Sydney to London (or sometimes New York to Tokyo) in two hours, going much faster than I was travelling.

At the end of World War II, people had realised that 'these rocket things' had a reality beyond the covers of lurid science fiction pulps. This was largely courtesy of Wernher von Braun's V-2 missiles, though bazookas and other shorter-range rocket weapons had also impressed. This was the way of the future, and everybody had to have rockets.

The USA had desert areas in New Mexico for testing, and Russia had vast plains from which people could be shifted, but Britain had nowhere to test missiles. Luckily, one of the former colonies was available and willing, so Babbage's dry landscape became a late bastion of the British Empire, an exclusion zone where most of the Australian people were prohibited from visiting or travelling, where mostly British rockets could be allowed to rain down in the wasteland, which was all that Eurocentric eyes could see in the dry, flat plains set about with remarkably tenacious plants. It was only good for an exclusion zone, they thought.

Then, to show their cultural sensitivity towards the Aboriginal people who had been shoved rudely off a place where they had made a perfectly adequate living for millennia, the authorities named this patch of land, roughly the size of Greece, Woomera. This name commemorated the ingenious spear-launching stick used by Aborigines across Australia to throw spears further and harder.

Everybody started with sounding rockets which 'sounded' the upper atmosphere, devices made of a small tactical rocket strapped onto a V-2 or a close simulation of it, but as rockets got bigger the V-2 design was quickly left behind. As Britain fell behind in the space race, Woomera became less and less a site where breakthroughs were likely to happen. It remains today an exclusion zone, and works well as a place to test various technologies, mainly with small rockets, but none of the really big devices used to launch today's satellites and space missions are fired there.

The only way really to understand today's monster rockets is to go and see them being made, as I had done at the Aerojet plant in Sacramento, California, some six weeks before I drove to Woomera. Today's rockets come in two main types: simple tubes filled with solid fuel and oxidiser that blaze across the sky in a single burn that ends only when the fuel runs out, and complex liquid fuel rockets with the potential to be stopped and restarted by controlling the pumps that deliver the fuel and oxidiser to the combustion point.

The Titan 4 booster is a long tube filled with hydroxyl-terminated polybutadiene (HTPB). It is basically a high-explosive firecracker, 50 feet long and five feet across (in the USA, that is; others would call them 15 metres long and 1.5 metres across). Either way, these are seriously big fireworks, with a carefully crafted hole right down the middle. It is a firework for Brobdingnag, Swift's land of giants, not for Lilliput.

The boosters are fired at the top of the hollow. Flames roar down the hole so the entire length of the tube burns at once, with the fires eating away outwards and enlarging the hole until all the solid fuel is gone—in just a few minutes. By then, if all goes well, the rocket is a long way away from where it began.

To be filled, though, the rocket tube must first be stood on its nose, while vat after 6000-pound (2700-kilogram) vat of the fuel mix is brought in and poured around a set of shaped pieces that define the central hollow where the fires will roar. The hole is cylindrical at the top and star-shaped near the bottom, precisely calculated to give the right burn profile. The continuous pour takes 31 hours to fill the tube, and then the propellant has to cure for almost a week, after which the booster is ready to use. Solid-fuel rockets like this are easy to store until needed, but all they provide is mindless muscle, with no hint of control. There is no subtlety in a Titan 4 booster, just immense power.

These boosters are great for lifting a spacecraft. They can be strapped to the outside, and they get the craft up through the denser air at the bottom of the atmosphere. Their furious blaze burns out in two or three minutes then they fall away, their duty done, leaving the spacecraft to carry on. Later stages of the spacecraft use liquid fuel, often hydrogen and oxygen, with complex pumps and mazes of tiny holes that the gases pass through, mixing as they go; even a simple rocket engine for liquid fuels will cost several million dollars.

All rockets since the first known gunpowder rockets, fired at Kai-fung fu in China in 1232, have carried both fuel and an oxidiser. Rocket chemistry in the twentieth century was mainly about finding more energetic fuels and more efficient oxidisers, fearful brews like red and white fuming nitric acid and fluorine, as well as less exotic chemicals like liquid oxygen and hydrogen peroxide. The fuel components included aniline, benzene, methanol, ethanol, gasoline, butyl mercaptan, acetone, ethyl mercaptal and even roofing-tar.

Solid fuels now tend to use gentler oxidisers like ammonium perchlorate, but the chemistry has always been rather macho. So have the workers with that chemistry—I asked one of the pourers at Aerojet if he was ever worried with all that high explosive around. 'No, we tested it,' he said with a slow smile, pointing over a five-storey drop to a concrete floor below. 'The engineers said it was safe, so we filled a gallon bucket with the mix and threw it over that drop. It didn't go bang, so then we knew it was safe.'

After World War II, scientists knew that the mixed acid oxidiser, red fuming nitric acid or RFNA, containing a certain amount (10–17 per cent) of sulfuric acid, was 'magnificently hypergolic' with many fuels. That is to say, if the oxidiser and a fuel came in contact, they would spontaneously ignite. This meant that some rockets could ignite simply by having fuel and oxidiser mix in the chamber. For other oxidisers, if there was a delay in ignition for any reason, there would be a glorious explosion, known in the trade as a 'hard start', but this was no problem with hypergolic mixes.

One of the substances that would react with mixed acid was rubber, and in the best hairy-chested tradition, pioneer rocket chemist John Clark would employ that knowledge in a test:

I used to take advantage of this property when somebody came into my lab looking for a job. At an inconspicuous signal, one of my henchmen would drop the finger of an old rubber glove into a flask containing about 100 cc of mixed acid—and then stand back. The rubber would swell and squirm a moment—and then a magnificent rocket-like jet of flame would rise from the flask, with appropriate hissing noises. I could usually tell from the candidate's demeanor whether he had the sort of nervous system desirable in a propellant chemist.

John Clark, *Ignition: An Informal History of Liquid Rocket Propellants*, 1972

The first generation of spacecraft, from *Sputnik* to *Apollo*, and even most of today's Mars missions, relied and rely on straightforward single-use rockets, while second-generation projects like the International Space Station rely on reusable vehicles like the space shuttles. Now I was off to see the start of the third generation, scramjets that do away with the need for on-board oxidiser.

In today's rockets, the oxidiser has to be carried and accelerated to high speed, but it provides no energy to make the rocket go faster. The air around us contains a very useful oxidiser, oxygen, but how do you make use of it? A jet engine compresses air with a fan before fuel is added and burned, and this provides the thrust to keep the plane moving. When you get to supersonic speeds, though, those fans tend to overheat, imposing a natural limit that turns us back to rockets that carry their oxidiser along with them. But if you could pick up the oxygen as you go, then you would be looking at much cheaper space travel, because all that weight left on the ground becomes available for extra payload.

The idealists say a scramjet has the potential to increase lift efficiency a hundredfold. That, says one of my NASA informants, is ambitious, but it makes a fair enough goal for the future. All the same, we must walk before we run, and the first step has to be taken. With luck, it was taken at Woomera on 30 July 2002 by Australian researchers, using off-the-shelf components to such an extent that they called their creation a 'scrounge-jet'.

A scramjet is a supersonic combustion ramjet, basically a very high-speed scoop that gathers up air and forces it into a combustion chamber, where the fuel (usually hydrogen) is burned, generating thrust. The real trick is to get a scoop which has a low enough drag that the scramjet generates a thrust greater than the drag caused by the scoop. This will always be a difficult balancing trick.

Carrying an oxidiser cuts down on efficiency, because it could be replaced by payload. One of the most efficient rocket fuels is hydrogen, but to burn one gram of hydrogen, you need eight grams of oxygen. You also need a second container to carry the oxygen, and it is all waste—some of the oxygen becomes reaction mass, but scooped-up oxygen will do that just as well. If the oxygen can be left out, or even just drastically reduced in mass, and if the oxygen fuel pumps and metering and other gear can be left out or reduced, that makes a huge difference.

In the strict sense, the Hyshot project is about a 'hcramjet', since anything faster than Mach 5, five times the speed of sound, is hypersonic, not supersonic, but it is probable that only speakers of Icelandic could wrap their tongues around the word, so it remains a scramjet.

The real challenge is to get the scramjet travelling very fast, with all its components untested. You might have everything right but for a single key control surface, and all your excellent work could be lost when that weak link fails. Ideally, you would test as many items as possible separately, under controlled conditions. It would make sense to test the components in a wind tunnel first—but a wind tunnel is no use in this case. Wind tunnels have fans that blow air along them, but the speeds needed to test rocket parts are more than any fan can stand. When the V-2 rockets were being tested in Peenemünde during World War II, the Germans solved the problem by having a large vacuum chamber that could be pumped out. When valves were opened, air screamed down a tunnel past the test models into the empty chamber. That was good enough for a supersonic V-2, but it isn't enough to test scramjets.

NASA has been trying to build and fly a complete scramjet craft, getting everything right if they are lucky. They are putting all their eggs in one basket, but the Australian team has been trying another way. Engineers at the University of Queensland in Brisbane have been using the T4 shock tunnel. This holds back hot helium as a piston hurtles into it, until the massive pressure bursts what they amusingly call a 'diaphragm'. To anybody else, it is a piece of 3 mm steel plate, but in Brobdingnag, the inverted Lilliput that is brutal rocket engineering, this plate is a mere tissue that bursts to let a torrent of supersonic gas howl down the tunnel. This scream of hot helium lets the researchers test many design principles under high-speed conditions, but there remains the problem of linking what is seen under artificial conditions to reality.

In simple terms, you can learn a great deal about how a scramjet behaves in a shock tunnel, but the absolute proof only comes when you fly all of the bits; if the tunnel was unrealistic, all the money you put into trying to save time and cash by using it becomes money wasted. So the Hyshot launch was mainly about gathering real data to compare with shock-tunnel data.

All the television footage, all the stuff that will be shown as historical footage in the future, has the Orion-Terrier rocket taking off, but that signifies very little, for the rocket was just a means to an end, a grandparent giving a start to a grandchild.

This primitive two-stage rocket used aluminium powder and ammonium dichromate, solid fuel with a burn-hole through it, just like the fuel casting in a Titan 4, but far smaller, to send the third-generation payload 314 kilometres up into space—so high that the launch could not take place in one small period, as its projected path was within a few thousand metres of the orbit of an American satellite, too close to take any risks. But that part was easy—the schedule just had to work around it, by flying before or after the satellite passed by.

On the day, everything went to plan. Where the first trial had failed some months earlier, due to fin problems on the rocket, there was nothing like that this time. The first-stage rocket burned for six seconds, accelerating the craft to Mach 3.6, or 3.6 times the speed of sound. It ran up the sky, leaving a white trail behind it, and then the roar reached us, standing out on the plain several kilometres away. We were a motley crowd including a group of Harley-Davidson riders, elderly campervan tourists making their traditional big retirement trip around Australia, and several busloads of schoolchildren who appeared on the range road, having somehow talked their way in.

It was peculiar, because we saw the white streak of exhaust rise and stop, halfway up the sky, before we heard the roar, and then silence. This was a 16-second pause while the second stage and the payload slipped free of the spent initial stage, using a difference in drag. That is the secret, one of the engineers told me later: keep it simple, and the chances of failing are reduced.

The second stage sat on top of the first stage, and drag made the first stage fall behind, aided by some dry graphite in the sleeve between the stages to ease them apart. The business end, the slimmer second stage and its payload hiding behind a nose cone, rushed on, losing speed from Mach 3.6 back down to 3.2, stabilising any flutters from the first blast, but also getting through the worst of the atmosphere before the second-stage rocket kicked in, high in the sky.

The second blast finished at a height of 56 kilometres, a mere 39 seconds after take-off, and then the rocket just coasted to the top of its parabola. In rocket jargon, correctly applied, it had gone ballistic, following a path that depended only on a previously applied force and the pull of gravity. The second blast accelerated it up to about Mach 7.7 and, as the rocket stopped burning, it was almost out into space.

The nose cone was ejected at 47 seconds, and then the rocket was turned slowly around, ready for re-entry, levelling out after a little more than four-and-a-half minutes. At that point, it was still travelling down-range at a horizontal speed of Mach 2.7, but as it tilted and began to plunge back to the atmosphere, it was accelerated by the force of gravity. By the time the turn was completed, three minutes later, it was almost halfway down to the ground again.

At 497 seconds, it was travelling at Mach 7.7 again as it re-entered the official edge of the atmosphere at 100 kilometres, but there would be another 30 seconds before its moment of fame was reached. As the air thickened, the rocket and the passenger scramjet slowed to Mach 7.6, and more oxygen began to pass through the system. At 35 kilometres, about three times the height that jetliners fly at, the scramjet kicked in, just as it disappeared over the horizon as seen from the control block.

That is to say, we hoped it had kicked in. Preliminary telemetry from the control block before the rocket sank below the horizon showed a drop in fuel pressure in the hydrogen tank, indicating that fuel began to be pumped into the chamber, where (all going well) it ignited and produced more thrust than drag. In just 6 seconds, the scramjet and its rocket casing were down to 23 kilometres, travelling at about Mach 7.4, but the end would be (hopefully) a few seconds of glory, before a crunch into the arid soil of Woomera.

As one of the defence people said to me when we had only the skimpiest data, 'Whatever happens, we've certainly learned something.' With luck, though, we agreed that the launch did something more, that we had both been present at a milestone in space history. That certainly was the consensus on the roof of the control centre afterwards, where Royal Australian Air Force media personnel had to call repeatedly for quiet as they tried to get interviews out of the way, where every conversation was interrupted time and again as the key players fielded phone calls. Even here in the desert, mobile phones work, and these days recalling and dismissing a straying explorer would be easy.

The rocket flew as it should, and the scientists tracked it down-range to 320 kilometres, the same distance a German V-2 could travel in 1944. The remote listening stations were in contact with base by satellite phone, so they knew where to point their equipment in order to find the craft as it hurtled towards them. We knew soon enough that the listening stations had caught the data, now it was just a matter of careful analysis—but we had to wait for that.

The Hyshot project has a large number of partners who will be able to share in the results, NASA among them, with Japan, Germany, Korea and other nations involved in the project. If it all worked, the team would have data to compare with what they get from the T4 shock tunnel; if the two sets of data match up, NASA will be delighted, for they can then fast-track development. All we could do was stand around, hug ourselves, and hope it would all come good.

So what does the scramjet mean, I asked one of the engineers? For starters, he said, forget the hype about aircraft flying from Sydney to London in two hours. Ronald Reagan started that with a line about flying from New York to Tokyo in two hours that was later translated for Australian conditions. Even if somebody did build a scramjetliner, a ticket would cost millions of dollars, and the passengers would stay away because there would not even be time to open the second free bottle of champagne before the flight ended. There might just be a niche for space tourism, but the clear future for the scramjet lies in getting humanity into orbit and out into space.

Then again, if twenty-second-century humans are routinely going into space, there are going to be pollution problems, because many of the fuels and oxidisers are ferociously unfriendly. Red fuming nitric acid is not nice, and neither is ammonium dichromate. Scramjets burn hydrogen to produce water—the scramjet is our friend.

History will be the judge. History, aided by a painstaking analysis of telemetry data gathered in the desert, number-crunching work performed by machines as mindless as a Titan 4, electronic marvels that are lineal descendants of the simple gears-and-cogs device Herschel Babbage once helped his father with. These computers outdo Babbage's mechanical device in power and complexity, just as a Titan 4 outdoes a skyrocket—but we had to await the analysis. Certainly, as John Simmons, the University of Queensland engineering dean told me over dinner when I mentioned the Jonathan Swift connection, the achievement was by no means Lilliputian.

By the middle of August, the telemetry data had given the right results. This now-destroyed craft had shown us the first successful trial of what may be the third generation of launch vehicles to lift payloads into space. So from a first generation of toxic fuming rockets to a generation of slightly less toxic reusable craft like the shuttles, we are now turning to the third generation of space lift, in the form of a scramjet. If the scramjet flew, it did so for just 6 seconds—but the first flight by the Wright Brothers only lasted 12 seconds, and Robert Goddard's first rocket flight in 1926 lasted just 2.5 seconds, which would seem to place the scramjet in the middle of the duration span for historic space and flight exploits.

I did not wait for the results. In fact I drove out of Woomera that night, well before sunrise. Appropriately, the CD in the player was Handel's triumphal *Royal Fireworks Music*. I turned up the volume, and drove on. Two hours and 190 kilometres later, as the sun began to lighten the eastern sky, I ran into a kangaroo, but that's another story. My research phase was over, and it was time to tell this story instead.

I was there at Woomera, as I had been at Gallipoli, in Istanbul, Prague, Cracow, Auschwitz, Berlin, Dresden, Dublin, Washington, in Goddard's home town of Worcester, Massachusetts and in Aerojet's home near Sacramento, California and many other places, gathering information to allow me adequately to pursue a long-term interest that began when I was a small boy and *Sputnik* flew across our skies. It is a long and tangled tale of invention and brilliance, foolishness and stupidity, and now it is time to unravel it.

# 1
# *SPUTNIK* AND THE 50-YEAR RULE

I shall always remember seeing the pin-point light of 'Sputnik I' crossing the sky, man's first artificial satellite, as we sat at dinner in the open air on the harbour mole at Valencia in Spain in 1957.

Joseph Needham, *Science and Civilisation in China*, Volume 5, Part 7

Never before had so small and so harmless an object created such consternation.

Daniel Boorstin, *The Americans: The Democratic Experience*, 1984

In my youth, every month was special. The warm nights of a Sydney October would often see me led willingly out into the garden to see something. It might be a cicada bursting from its juvenile prison into adult form, a spider weaving a web, or just an owl that turned its head to follow those who walked around it. Most of the time the wonders of the night were natural, but one October night in 1957 I stood in the garden waiting to see an amazing and novel sight, a Russian satellite in the sky.

At thirteen, I was full of enthusiasm for science and things scientific. My father started it off, but most of my enthusiasm was a direct result of the work of Penguin Watson, a science teacher without parallel. By the time he took our class Penguin was an old man, but in his younger days he had been 'south with Mawson', on Australian expeditions to Antarctica early in the twentieth century. His nickname commemorated that time, and the way he sometimes drew on his experiences there in his teaching. What we boys did not know or realise was that he was a special teacher who had been a headmaster before coming out of retirement as a 'retread' to follow his joy in teaching science.

Penguin inspired us, of course—and knowing no better, we thought he was just the norm for science teachers—but we responded well. In my second year under Penguin's tutelage, I was listening one Saturday morning to the radio when the program was interrupted to tell us that Russia had launched its first *Sputnik*. I was impressed—not so much by the science as by the fact that the ABC would interrupt important comedy like 'Take It From Here' to share the news with us.

Now I knew right away that *Sputnik* would have been launched on a rocket, because I and my fellow students had been drawing plans of space rockets for years—it seems to be one of those things little boys like. No doubt Mr Freud could explain it all, but to us they were just a normal part of the future. We knew rockets would one day take humans into space, long before Penguin Watson introduced us to the idea in a rather more scientific frame. Our laboriously drawn plans fitted into the outline of a German V-2. They had work and living space, and no room for fuel, those early drawings, but Penguin told us a bit more about the practicalities of getting somebody into space, about escape velocity, the need for stages, and much more. We began to comprehend the problem.

Of course, some people doubted the whole thing, like the Astronomer-Royal who snapped at reporters in 1956 that space travel was impossible, but Penguin knew better, and he prepared his students for the Space Age. We gained at least an inkling of how it all worked, slipped in when the rigid curriculum wasn't looking.

So there my family was, in our suburban garden on a still October night. All around us, voices could be heard as other families stood in their yards, waiting to catch a glimpse of the first human construct to appear among the stars. We had no idea what to expect, but there was a feeling of anticipation and excitement in the chatter we could hear in the night air. Television in Australia was just a year old and still a rarity, so most of us knew from the radio when to look and where to look, and as the time got closer, so the voices in the darkness grew more excited. Then something traced a fiery arc across the sky, prompting shouts of amazement. The wonder soon turned to laughter as we realised that this was a mere firework rocket, powered by gunpowder, launched by some suburban wit. People clapped and cheered.

At the dawn of the Space Age, the old fireworks could still steal the scene and turn the satellite's appearance a scant minute later into an anticlimax, but it was the last gasp of gunpowder, and the age of the serious rocket was upon us. All the same, if rockets and rocket science would shape our world during the rest of the twentieth century, the old gunpowder rockets had blazed the trail, and had not been without influence themselves.

This is the story of the rockets, old and new—and of the Space Age they brought, something which turned out, when I looked into its origins, to be rather older even than Penguin Watson. It took time, because all technologies need time to mature, and quite a few were needed for space travel, each of them needing time, and some of them depending on others.

... while poor Mr. Huskisson, less active from the effects of age and ill-health, bewildered, too, by the frantic cries of 'Stop the engine! Clear the track!' that resounded on all sides, completely lost his head, looked helplessly to the right and left, and was instantaneously prostrated by the fatal machine, which dashed down like a thunderbolt upon him, and passed over his leg, smashing and mangling it in the most horrible way.

Lady Wilton, an eyewitness to the accident, to Fanny Kemble, 1830

In 1830, William Huskisson MP permanently marred himself, and temporarily marred the opening of the world's first serious passenger railway, the Liverpool–Manchester line, by being run over by a locomotive. As a consequence, he was the first injured person ever carried to hospital by a railway system, but it was the end of him, and it happened mainly because he had no sense of the new speeds that locomotives might reach, no sense of the new technology.

Trains really began, tentatively, in 1804, when Trevithick used a locomotive to haul iron, and the Stockton and Darlington railroad was carrying freight in 1825, but it was a passenger line that brought about the age of rail travel and linked whole nations. This new railway set many standards, like the 4 foot 8½ inch standard gauge that most railways would adopt, the idea of having two parallel tracks (one 'up', one 'down'), and stations where passengers could alight on a platform.

At the time, not even the inventors had much idea of what was involved in shaping a new technology. Franz Anton von Gerstner's first railroad passenger cars looked much like the horse-drawn coaches that were then in use, and these items of rolling-stock are called carriages or coaches to this day. By 1840, the first dining car was running on an American railroad. Many other lines had been built by the fiftieth anniversary of

Trevithick's first operation, including one that Herschel Babbage oversaw in Adelaide. By 1880, countries and even whole continents were spanned, just 50 years after Huskisson's death.

Curiously, this time pattern of a 20-year development phase and a 30-year expansion phase to maturity appears in many developing technologies. It probably reflects the human working life span, but it is remarkable how many technologies only begin to have their real (and generally unanticipated) social effects about 50 years after they were first introduced.

The surprise bound up in those social effects is central: people cannot quite see the promise and the opportunities, cannot see what the social effects of the new technology will be at the time, and most new technology brings surprising changes with it. The first 50 years of printed books generated 40 000 titles and perhaps 20 million volumes, which are known collectively as *incunabula*, from the Latin word for 'cradle'. The typeface used was commonly one based on the chancery script, a style of handwriting used in the Vatican, while legend has it that Aldus Manutius based his italic font on the handwriting of Petrarch.

At the end of 50 years, or two human generations, the technology and format of the book had settled into a stable pattern, with accepted sizes, binding standards and typefaces, and most developments since that time have followed a similar path. New forms like the novel and the coffee-table book may have emerged more recently, but the books of today would make sense to somebody who first became familiar with them at the end of the incunabula phase, even if their content did not. The first e-books now emerging are little more than printed pages reproduced on a screen, but that will change in time.

Later in the nineteenth century, the railway began to shape the nature of warfare in unexpected ways by allowing troops to be transported rapidly into a war zone. Where Blücher had to march his Prussians for days to get to Waterloo, his descendants two generations later could pour in fresh troops from a hundred leagues off, at the drop of a flag on a platform. In Prussia, Moltke had foreseen this as far back as 1839, but rail transportation of troops became a key element in Europe in the 1860s and 1870s.

The telegraph began with the first workable systems in Britain and Germany around 1835, and there was large-scale cabling of individual countries by 1855. One of the 'advances' of the Crimean War was that members of the infant profession of war correspondent could get news to the home government (and worse, thought the government, to the home population) so fast. The world was largely linked by submarine cables by 1885.

The telephone was invented in 1876. It was being accepted in some offices around 1900, but had apparently led Sir William Preece, the chief engineer in the British Post Office to say, some years earlier, when asked if the new device would be of any value: 'No, sir. The Americans have need of the telephone—but we do not. We have plenty of messenger boys'. By 1914, people in New York could talk to people in San Francisco by telephone, and it became common in homes in the Western world around 1930.

'Wireless telegraphy', as it was revealingly called, began when Hertz discovered radio waves in 1888; by 1908 it was in effective use, and by 1938 most homes in the developed world had a radio receiver. Morse code lasted longer than one might expect, its use largely dying away in the late 1990s, kept alive now by a few keen amateurs. Radio did away with the use of signal rockets on the battlefield much earlier.

The first projected motion pictures were shown to the public in 1895, and by 1915 movies had progressed from short scenes to complex features, cinematography had become an art, and California had become a centre for film-making. By 1945 the

Hollywood system was in full swing, and many of the classic films that we know and revere had already been made, although later advances in computerised special effects would make most of them seem amateurish by modern standards.

From another viewpoint, feature movies started around 1909; *The Jazz Singer*, the first 'talkie', was filmed in 1927, and 1959 saw that standard 'biggest movie', *Ben Hur*, released in cinemas. Al Jolson said in *The Jazz Singer*, 'You ain't seen nothin' yet, folks,' but from today's perspective the same line could have been used in *Ben Hur* to alert us to the changes still to come, even though those changes did little to alter cinema's social impact, well and truly with us even in 1959.

Television began with the first successful transmissions in 1925; it took off in Britain and America in 1946, and by 1975 most homes in the developed world had a television set. But who, in their right mind, would have thought that television and cinema would bring home to the Third World just how much it was missing out on? I spoke to a geophysicist in Washington while working on this book—he had just come from West Papua, where people one generation away from headhunting watched *Seinfeld*—and that just has to have an impact on how they think, he said.

Computers were once seen only as glorified adding machines, which explains their name—the original 'computers' were people who carried out arduous and repetitive calculations in dreary offices. This explains why, when the Sydney Observatory was built in the 1850s, just when Herschel Babbage was exploring arid South Australia, the plan featured a 'room for the computer'.

Most computer buffs would say modern computing really began with the Fortran language, invented in 1956. In 1975, the first floppy discs were being sold, the Altair 8800 computer was on sale and Microsoft was founded. By 2005, when the half-century is up, most homes in the developed world should have a computer—but few of them will be used for the arduous calculations done by the original human computers.

Then we have the Internet, which started as ARPANET in 1969, created to maintain communications in the event of any rain of nuclear missiles—launched, of course, by rockets. It came into wider use around the world twenty years later, in 1989, when Tim Berners-Lee created the World Wide Web. We are now near the halfway mark in the adoption phase, and we are beginning to have some ideas about what the Internet is, and how it should work, the functions it may fulfil. Certainly the Internet is an essential tool for anybody trying to stay abreast of the latest in rocket developments.

In the late 1980s I was working in a museum of science and technology, where I had to plead to get a second computer for a staff of 50; now we take it for granted that each work-station will have a computer, and that these will be networked; even homes have networks. In the early 1900s, a telephone on each office desk was a ridiculous idea, and the notion of a teacher in a class-room having phone and Internet connections is *still* seen as remarkably wasteful—in most schools, anyhow—but this may change one day.

Equally, school students must still complete public examinations with pen and paper, even if the examination involves essay-writing, a task these students habitually do, and will do in real life, using an entirely different medium, the keyboard and screen. Is this because the people who make the decisions are from the pre-computer era? Like those who argued in the 1980s against the use of calculators in examinations, they may burble about the risks of cheating, but the problems are not insuperable, and to hide behind such excuses is to ignore a coming reality. It is like demanding that students revert to quill pens and write in copperplate script, or use slide rules marked up in cuneiform.

Clearly, many of the opportunities presented by a new technology are not apparent at the start. Technologies continue to progress after their development and adoption phases, but the further changes they make to society may be muted as their use becomes a part of the background. Jet airliners began in 1952, and matured with the flights of the first Boeing 747 and the first Concorde, both in 1969—and by the end of the century had changed the way people in the developed world made business trips and took their holidays, and terrorists waged war.

Who could have predicted in 1952 that today's holiday-makers would quite probably have booked their flight over the Internet, having found out about their destination on the Web, or that they would use Internet cafés in Third World villages to maintain links with the folks at home?

Who would have predicted that their expectation of swift communications would lead to the Internet penetrating all sorts of odd places in the Third World, letting local people gain access to facilities started up for travellers, and this at a time when downtown Washington DC is almost entirely lacking such facilities—and those that exist are exorbitantly overpriced? Who would have predicted that the poor of Anatolia or Cracow would be better endowed with public Internet access than the poor people in the capital of the world's most prosperous nation?

The story of rockets is the story of a technology that grew, how it grew, some of the side tracks it has taken, some of the unexpected results it has produced and some of the directions it may diverge into. The technology of rockets will probably go somewhere entirely different before it is finished, but if we understand a little of what makes it tick, we may just have an inkling of why it took off in that unexpected direction.

Many of the people we meet in this story approached rockets with a blinkered viewpoint, seeing only old uses for a new idea. To us, with the benefit of hindsight, this may seem ludicrous, but it is worth considering how rarely the scramjet is mentioned today without the obligatory and equally blinkered reference to a scramjet journey around the world in just two hours, a journey that will never happen.

Rockets and space research have brought a few gadgets and materials to improve how we live. At the same time, however, rocket-launched satellites have linked nations and made us more aware, just incidentally, that we have just one world and that we are fast destroying it. If the material effects are sparse, the social effects have been significant, and will be even more so.

飛鎗箭　裂刀箭

# 2
# THE FIRST ROCKETS

On the seventh day of the attack, a very high wind having sprung up, they began to discharge by their slings hot balls made of burned or hardened clay, and heated javelins, upon the huts, which, after the Gallic custom, were thatched with straw. These quickly took fire, and by the violence of the wind, scattered their flames in every part of the camp.

That is how Julius Caesar, in Book 5 of his commentary on the Gallic wars, described how a group of Gauls called the Nervii attacked Cicero's camp. Fire in warfare is an old trick—in the *Book of Judges*, Chapter 15 tells us how Samson fired the fields and vineyards of the Philistines with burning foxes. The Gauls were quite good at variations on the fiery theme, and in Book 8 Caesar describes another method they used when they were being besieged:

Alarmed at this calamity, the townsmen fill barrels with tallow, pitch, and dried wood: these they set on fire, and roll down on our works. At the same time, they fight most furiously, to deter the Romans, by the engagement and danger, from extinguishing the flames. Instantly a great blaze arose in the works.

Of course, the Romans knew all about throwing firebrands, a practice which is mentioned in Book IX of Virgil's *Aeneid*, and there was even biological warfare in ancient times. Cornelius Nepos tells us how Hannibal used snakes while supporting the Bithynians against Pergamum, a Roman client-state:

> [Hannibal] gave orders to collect the greatest possible number of venomous snakes and put them alive in earthenware jars . . . When the other Pergamene ships began to press their opponents too hard, on a sudden the earthenware jars of which I have spoken began to be hurled at them. At first these projectiles excited the laughter of the combatants, and they could not understand what it meant. But as soon as they saw their ships filled with snakes, terrified by the strange weapons and not knowing how to avoid them, they turned their ships about and retreated to their naval camp. Thus Hannibal overcame the arms of Pergamum by strategy.

The mysterious substance known as 'Greek fire', when it was used at some hazy time not too many centuries away from 600 AD, was part of a long tradition, although the 'Greeks' who invented it would in fact have called themselves Romans or eastern Romans. Their city, once Byzantium, then Constantinople, and later to be Istanbul, was the centre of the eastern Roman empire. The people who lived there were Greek in their culture and their language, and Greek fire was a weapon used by these people in their constant wars.

It seems to have included naphtha and sulfur, perhaps with quicklime or nitre, or even charcoal. Nobody really knows, and the recipes we are offered today seem to owe as much to speculation and to what people know of gunpowder as to what they know of Greek fire, but sulfur is a fairly constant item. Whatever it was, thrown and hurled Greek fire gave way to guns, and occasional rockets.

These rockets relied on gunpowder, a powdered mix of salt-petre, charcoal and sulfur. Powdered charcoal burns in air or oxygen, and so does sulfur. When it is heated, saltpetre gives off oxygen, so when charcoal, sulfur and saltpetre are combined, the whole mixture burns very fast, forming carbon dioxide and sulfur dioxide, smoke and heat. When the mixture is confined, the pressure of the hot gases can be used to fire a bullet or drive a rocket, or it can burst a paper casing with a loud bang, or break rock in a quarry. That leaves us with an interesting question: what was somebody doing, mixing these three substances together for the very first time?

Perhaps some would-be magus was just dabbling, mixing powders of different colours. Maybe the idea was that white salt-petre, yellow sulfur and black charcoal would drive away the blues? Possibly our experimenter tried to make pills of the mix, and one fell in a fire, but somehow I doubt it. We need a more probable scenario.

It involves fairly complex chemistry, some of it biological, but urine and ashes can produce quite good quality saltpetre on a dung heap. It happens as urea turns first to ammonia and then to nitrates that combine with metallic ions in the ash. Saltpetre, or potassium nitrate, forms when a dung heap dries out. As fluid seeps to the surface and evaporates, it leaves white crystals of saltpetre behind. Now imagine a time of drought, when the surface organic matter is dry, and all the fibres have been covered and filled with tiny crystals of potassium nitrate.

Youthful pyromaniacs of my generation all knew that cotton string, soaked in saltpetre solution and dried, made an excellent slow fuse for setting off firecrackers in the toilets at school, infuriating our teachers, who could never find the boy responsible for the outrage of an explosion when the headmaster was pontificating at assembly. So if somebody, perhaps in China, walked outside and dumped ashes from the hearth on a dried dung heap, and those ashes had glowing coals in among them, it would have been noticed that the surface of the dung heap sometimes erupted into flame when there was enough saltpetre around.

Once people knew that saltpetre promoted burning, they may have started to think of using it to invigorate life. Soon alchemists would have been experimenting, mixing it with charcoal, perhaps using it in pellets to get a fire started on a wet day. And while it is one of the things we can never know, the sulfur probably came later. Which raises the question: why would it be used at all?

Sulfur dioxide, $SO_2$ to the chemists, is evil, stinking stuff. You can smell it around volcanoes, which were obviously related to the Underworld—so it was hardly surprising that the smell was generally associated with the Devil and other unpleasant characters, who mostly lived in the nether regions accessible through the yawning gaps that are volcanic craters. In such places, hydrogen sulfide, $H_2S$, and sulfur dioxide react to form elemental sulfur and water, with the sulfur deposited around the edges, the brims, of vents and pools, giving it the name brimstone.

Strangely, it was the Creator, not Satan, who rained fire and brimstone down on Sodom and Gomorrah in *Genesis*, and on other transgressors at the end of the Bible. Nonetheless, sulfur is usually associated with the darker power. The *Revelation of St John the Divine* mentions lakes of molten brimstone in Hell, indicating in passing the maximum possible temperature of Hell as 444.6°C, since this is the point above which sulfur would be a vapour (at any pressure). Incidentally, the Franciscan friar Roger Bacon was probably only experimenting with gunpowder when people claimed that their sense of smell revealed he was in touch with the Devil.

So perhaps our would-be magus added some sulfur to his mix to persuade an audience that he had contact with the spirits, but we might be wiser to look at the more common Biblical references to brimstone, which relate more to a rain of fire. If there was a tradition of throwing burning sulfur at the enemy besieging your town, then adding saltpetre to the brimstone to promote its burning would make great sense. There is no need to drag in hypothetical mages if people were able to find practical uses for the stuff like driving off invaders.

Joseph Needham takes a different view. He traces gunpowder to an earlier practice than any actual use as gunpowder, when the main need was to fumigate the house, citing a Chinese song that goes way back to the seventh century BC, or maybe even earlier:

> In the tenth month, the crickets
> Chirp, chirp beneath our beds.
> Chinks are filled up, and rats are smoked out,
> Windows that face north are stopped up
> And all the doors are plastered . . .
> The Changing of the Year requires it . . .
>
> *Shih Ching (The Book of Odes)*

Many different plant materials found a use in fumigation, he says, and later Chinese scholars would fumigate their books regularly to keep down bookworms. In a side note, he adds that about 980 AD, Tsan-Ning reports that the Chinese were using steam to sterilise the clothing of the sick to prevent infection when there were fevers in the house—rather earlier than Pasteur and Lister. That does not advance our gunpowder enquiry very much, but it reminds us that Chinese scholars were accurate observers of cause and effect, just the people to discover and develop something like gunpowder.

Before or around the time when gunpowder was first used to fire projectiles (either in fire-arrows or rockets, or in primitive guns), it and other substances were being used in smokebombs, and it is likely that the chemical warfare tradition against vermin fed into the use of chemical warfare on human vermin as well. Then again, Needham suggests that the Chinese tradition was one of action at a distance. Rather than ramming or boarding an enemy ship, you flung things at it, and that is why the Chinese provided the bombard, gun and cannon to the rest of the world, somewhere around 1300, and the rocket soon after.

When we look at warfare since 1300, we see an alternation of rockets and guns, with guns generally in the ascendancy, forcing rockets to occupy small and special niches on the battlefield. It was only in the twentieth century, with better control and guidance systems in place, that the rocket became an important element of military armaments. One common theme in the story of modern warfare is the way rockets and guns vied for dominance, another is the way military leaders commonly failed to see the importance of new technology.

To recap briefly, gunpowder was generally made from a mix of powdered charcoal, powdered sulfur and saltpetre, with a fair amount of variation in the proportions. Charcoal, of course, is easy to obtain, and sulfur is found around volcanic areas, but a chemical such as saltpetre is only of use if it can be obtained in pure form, and if it can be distinguished from other white powders and crystals. And before such a substance finds a regular new use, it is likely to have been applied in other ways.

Needham traces one of these other applications back to around 604 AD, noting that about that time, a Buddhist monk wrote of saltpetre being used as a flux in the smelting of ores. Significantly, there is a reference to the material burning with a purple smoke, which Needham takes to be the diagnostic purple flame of potassium salts. So at the start of the seventh century, people not only knew about saltpetre, they knew how to test it for purity, and had known about the flame test perhaps as far back as 500 AD.

The Chinese named the substance *hsiao shih*, the purple-violet colour seen when it was placed in a fire ruling out other nitrates. From 500 AD to around 1240, when a book in Arabic first mentions 'Chinese snow' (*thalj al-Sin*), the Chinese tried *hsiao shih* out in all sorts of mixtures. Somewhere along the way, somebody, for some medical or alchemical or other reason, mixed white *hsiao shih*, yellow sulfur and black charcoal and, either in grinding the mixture or in gently heating it, made an interesting discovery.

Needham says gunpowder first had a military use in China in 919, but he cites a work probably written earlier, called (in translation) *Classified Essentials of the Mysterious Tao of the True Origins of Things*, which offers us an interesting insight into how its military potential may have been discovered. The author warns that some alchemists had heated realgar (a sulfide of arsenic), saltpetre, honey and sulfur, and had suffered scorched faces and hands, or even had their houses burn down! Violent explosions in the laboratory and on the launch pad are yet another recurring theme in the story of rockets. They go with the territory, given the energetic chemicals used.

Much of our understanding of the very first rockets must rely on guesswork. Infantry may well have been supplied with fearsome flame and smoke tubes on their spears, and perhaps somebody felt the backward push, and did some thinking. More likely, gunpowder was put in bamboo tubes for throwing into fires, where a few, rather than exploding, burned at one end, and vipered across the surface as primitive ground rockets.

The Chinese firework called *ti lao shu* (which we can translate as 'ground rat' or 'earth rat') was a length of bamboo crammed with low-nitrate powder, so a jet of flame, coming out of a hole in the septum, would make it run around on a flat surface. This may be an ancestor of the rocket, since a few ground rats would do nothing at all for the composure of the horses in a cavalry charge. They did very little for the empress Kung Sheng either—in 1264, when rockets must have been well known, the mother of the then emperor was alarmed when a ground rat came straight at her during a courtyard display of fireworks. She withdrew in all haste and high dudgeon, but after a tense night, all was forgiven between her and her son.

Perhaps somebody then had the bright idea of tying a tube with a wick to an arrow, lighting the wick and hurriedly firing the arrow—even such a primitive rocket would have flown further than a conventional arrow, catching an enemy beyond normal bowshot, perhaps even setting fire to the tents of nomads or upsetting cavalry.

It is just possible that the first use of rockets took place around 969, since there is a hint in a record that the Sung emperor at that time rewarded officers who had invented 'a new fire arrow', but this is unlikely. China's Sung dynasty ran from 960 to 1279, and their forces mainly used defensive strategies, fighting their enemies from behind walls. The first guns were seen mainly as weapons for battering down walls, so there would be no real need for Sung boffins to make cannon, even if they had thought of the idea, but they *might* have made rockets.

The Sung fire arrows are likely to have been no more than incendiaries, and it is probably safer to set the date of the first rocket at about 1180. A gestation period of 50 years is more likely than one of 250 years, and our first definite record of the 'arrows of fire' comes from their use in 1232 against the Mongols who were besieging the Chinese city of Kai-fung-fu—primitive rockets propelled by black powder. Now that the secret was out, the idea of rockets moved fairly quickly.

In 1240, the Tartars were making good use of the trebuchet (a military engine for casting heavy missiles) to batter their way into Kiev, although in 1241 they are said to have defeated a group of Polish knights led by Henryk Pobozny when they carried a 'dragon head' that spewed smoke and fire. Certainly, on 25 December 1241, rocket-like weapons were used by the Mongols against Magyar forces at a battle on the banks of the Sajó river, just before they captured Buda (half of modern Budapest). We know that the Mongols used lengths of bamboo filled with gunpowder as incendiaries to attack the timber gates of fortified towns, and these also may have given people the idea of making rockets.

There is a tantalising glimpse of Islamic forces just possibly using rockets around 1268 against French crusaders. Jean, Sire de Joinville, wrote an account of this in his *Vie de Saint Louis*, written around 1309. Given the dates, however, while some of the description makes the missile sound rocket-like, it could just as easily have been a pot of flammable stuff hurled by a trebuchet.

> This is what Greek fire was like: it came straight at you, as big as a vinegar barrel, with a tail of fire behind it as long as a long spear. It made such a noise as it came that it seemed like the thunder of heaven; it looked like a dragon flying through the air.

In time, gunpowder changed the balance of power and the way wars were fought, because bullets went right through armour, and cannonballs made holes in walls that soldiers could pour through, unless a cannon loaded with grapeshot could be fired by the defenders at the right time. Rockets did very little wall-smashing, and so in the field were really only seen as useful against humans or maybe horses that were unfamiliar with them.

After about 1940 rockets would come into their own as real weapons rather than specialist tools favoured by a few enthusiasts. But while there are those who claim that the modern rocket was developed as a purely military object that was later converted to more peaceful uses, the opposite may also be true. There may just have been a few civilians who hijacked military needs in the 1950s, and perhaps even before, to further the development of space rockets. The world needed rocket science, all of a sudden, but we will come to that later.

Our understanding of rockets has always been subjective. Some people saw (and see) rockets just as amusing things to play with, little more than skyrockets. Others saw (and see) them purely as an alternative to guns, employing them to deliver explosives at a distance, to harpoon whales or even carry a line to a foundering ship.

The third group to consider the rocket, which has flourished since around the end of the nineteenth century, consists of the dreamers about space travel, who saw (and see) rockets as a way of getting into space. Early dreams of space, however, had to wait until there was some prospect of getting a rocket to go beyond the edge of the atmosphere. The first rockets had only a small range, just a few thousand metres at best, but without those short-range versions, we might never have got to the massive space vehicles that have been commonplace now for nearly half a century. They were first steps.

The first rockets were hideously inaccurate, things that you pointed, lit and prayed about or, if you were wise, hid from. In the absence of any way of controlling the flight or the force of the burning fuel, the early rocket was very much an unguided missile, for without any quality control in its making, the fuel would burn unevenly and the rocket might even turn around and come back at the people launching it. Serious rockets demanded serious control.

Notions of control and guidance grew slowly, and even into the twentieth century most rocket enthusiasts thought only in terms of stabilisers to cajole the rocket into travelling in something close to a straight line. Robert Goddad wrote to Robert Esnault-Pelterie in 1920, suggesting that a moon rocket might home in on its target with 'photosensitive cells . . . the guiding of the device toward a source of light, automatically'. So long as rocketry was a matter of point, hope and shoot, dreams of space travel would have to wait.

On Jan. 13, 1920, 'Topics of the Times', an editorial-page feature of the *New York Times*, dismissed the notion that a rocket could function in a vacuum and commented on the ideas of Robert H. Goddard, the rocket pioneer, as follows:

'That Professor Goddard, with his "chair" in Clark College and the countenancing of the Smithsonian Institution, does not know the relation of action to reaction, and the need to have something better than a vacuum against which to react—to say that would be absurd. Of course he only seems to lack the knowledge handed out daily in high schools.'

Further investigation and experimentation have confirmed the findings of Isaac Newton in the 17th Century and it is now definitely established that a rocket can function in a vacuum as well as in an atmosphere. The *Times* regrets the error.

New York Times, 17 July, 1969, p. 43

Rockets are easy to understand, but they are harder to understand correctly. To a simple mind, a rocket cannot operate in a vacuum, and many people once held that view, including that earlier writer at the *New York Times*. The retraction was a long time coming, appearing as a small box inserted in a larger article providing background on the first Apollo moon landing team that even then was approaching the moon. It came just six months short of the fiftieth anniversary of the 1920 editorial sneer.

The rocket principle was clearly understood by early science fiction writers, who often used plots involving a spacesuited figure drifting away from a spaceship. The solutions included firing a six-shooter away from the spaceship to impart a small momentum towards it, and throwing tools away. (Every well-dressed spaceman would have a six-shooter in those days, though spacewomen apparently did not, perhaps because there was nowhere in their traditionally scanty attire to conceal it.)

In fact such solutions are fairly unworkable in space. They might work if you were trapped in an oarless boat on the middle of a pond with an elephant gun, but there is no friction in space, and without very careful planning the force will not act through your centre of gravity. Without planning, part of the energy would be converted into rotation of the hapless spaceperson, who will then cartwheel out of control past the spaceship and disappear, screaming in the confines of the spacesuit, into a cold and lifeless eternity.

One way of explaining a rocket is to think of a sealed balloon. This will stay where it is, even though compressed gas molecules are slamming into its inner surface at some 330 metres per second (a speed that, not coincidentally, is the speed of sound). The balloon does not move in any direction because the gas molecules bounce off the inner surface in every direction and so the forces balance out. But if we open the balloon, and let some air escape, the gas molecules are bouncing off one part of the inner surface but not the rest of it, and so the balloon begins to travel away from the place where the hole is, making the classic noise characteristic of released balloons everywhere.

In the simplest terms, a rocket is just a tube with a hole at one end, and some means of producing very energetic particles that stream away from the hole, heading in a direction opposite to the way the rocket is meant to go. And the opinion of the 1920 *New York Times'* editorial writer notwithstanding, rockets actually fly ever-so-slightly better in a vacuum.

The first serious suggestion for using rockets in space came from Konstantin Eduardovich Tsiolkovsky in 1883; he recalled his idea some years later, in 1911, saying:

> For a long time, like everyone else, I viewed the rocket from the standpoint of amusements and small applications.
>
> I do not remember exactly when the idea came to me to do calculations relative to the rocket.
>
> It seems to me that the first seeds of the idea were cast by the famous fantasy writer Jules Verne; he awakened my mind in this direction. Then desires arose and they were followed by the activities of the mind, which of course would have led to nothing had they not encountered the aid of science.
>
> Konstantin Tsiolkovsky, *Investigation of World Spaces*, 1911

The intuitive (and incorrect) view is that a rocket moves something like a boat pushed off from a wharf. This is not quite correct, but imagine yourself stranded in a boat in the middle of a pond. This is an imaginary boat, so it can contain whatever we want, and out of consideration I have chosen to have a large supply of smallish bricks, just the right size for you to throw. This is lucky for you, as it is what you need to get back to dry land.

One way to save yourself might be to pelt me with the bricks in revenge for stranding you in the hypothetical boat, but whether you behave maliciously or not, so long as you keep firing off bricks in one direction, your boat will drift in the opposite direction, simply because momentum always remains constant. (If I want to be malicious in turn, I move around the pond, so that you keep firing off your missiles in all directions, with the result that you have no net gain in momentum, and end up still stranded at the centre of the pond.)

If you know your physics, you will know to postpone your revenge until you are ashore, and you will throw all the bricks in one direction. Momentum is what we call a vector quantity: it has a direction as well as a value (or magnitude), and your system (you, the boat and the bricks) has an initial momentum of zero, using the planet Earth as your frame of reference. (If you wanted to assess yourself against the centre of the Milky Way, or the Sun, you would have considerable momentum, but that has nothing to do with getting to shore with dry feet.)

Staying with the realistic scenario at the appropriate scale, you have zero momentum, and your *system* must retain the same total momentum, so when you change the momentum of a brick (that is, when you heave it), the momentum of you, the boat and the other bricks must also change, but with the reverse sign. You throw a brick to the west, and you, the boat and the diminished pile of bricks will begin to drift to the east.

The brick will hit either the water or the mud, and transfer its tiny momentum to the planet, making a negligible difference to the planet's rotation, but your brick-boat-you system will retain its new momentum until frictional effects slow you down. In space, of course, there is almost no friction at all, so when you throw bricks, or fire a rocket in space, the momentum you gain lasts a very long time—but while friction from a boat's keel stops the boat from spinning, spacecraft need some form of attitude control to keep them facing the right way.

This was the brilliant insight that Tsiolkovsky had on the morning of 28 March 1883, when he wrote in his notebook:

Suppose we have a barrel filled with a highly compressed gas. If we open one of its minute stopcocks, the gas will stream out of the barrel in a continuous jet, and the elasticity of the gas (it is this elasticity that pushes the gaseous particles into space) will likewise continually repel the barrel . . . By means of a sufficient number of stopcocks (six) it is possible to control the exit of the gas so that the motion of the barrel or an empty sphere will depend entirely on the will of the stopcock operator, which is to say that the barrel will execute any desired curve and in accord with any law of velocity whatsoever.

Konstantin Tsiolkovsky, *Notebook*, 1883

Making a good rocket, then, was a matter of finding better ways of generating fast-moving material in a tube, and finding ways to make the tube larger. There was just one other problem: steering and controlling the rocket's forces so they passed through the rocket's centre of gravity, and so kept the rocket on a straight and true path.

The western world was familiar with the notions of reaction propulsion, the rocket principle, long before rockets were seen there. Some time in the fourth century BC, Aulus Gellius suggested making a mechanical pigeon, powered by steam jets in its tail. The first practical use of action and reaction came with the aeolipile of Hero of Alexandria in the first century AD, a sort of steam-driven rotor which had amusement value but no real practical purpose. In the absence of gunpowder, rockets remained unknown to the western world until they were brought from China by the Tartars and the Mongols.

Most of the dispersal of rockets seems to have come from the Mongols, who used rockets when they captured Baghdad in 1258 AD and, as we have seen, Islamic forces *may* have used rockets against the Seventh Crusade of King Louis IX of France in 1268. Certainly we know that by 1280, al-Hasan ar-Rammah was writing in Syria about the importance of saltpetre in making fireworks and rockets, suggesting that these were no imported novelties or captures. Gunpowder must have already been known in the West, given the tradition that Roger Bacon, who died in 1284, introduced it into Britain.

It is fairly clear that when Bacon wrote 'no thunderclap can compare with such terrifying noises, nor lightning playing among the clouds with such frightening flashes' he had encountered a firecracker of some sort. The Franciscans had been visiting the Mongol court at Karakorum since 1245, so it is by no means improbable that he had the chance to experience a firecracker that somebody had brought back.

Bacon is said to have developed a better form of gunpowder that gave rockets an increased range, but at a time when the longbow and the crossbow dominated warfare, roads were few and wagons were primitive, it was unlikely that large numbers of rockets would ever make it onto the battlefield. There were other traditions in siege warfare, with dead animals and other noxious items being fired in, while the besieged, safe on their walls, had more leisure and a better position from which to fire rockets and flaming arrows or pour hot liquids on the attackers. They may even have still known how to make Greek fire, or some form of it, and that sort of knowledge would probably have made them dismiss rockets as poor sorts of things, with little more than shock value and none of the lasting nastiness of ripe, dead cows and smoking, boiling oil.

Gunpowder was power, but to get your share of that power, you needed to be able to make the stuff; in time, you needed to be able to make good gunpowder, and that meant pure ingredients and careful measurement of amounts. It needed chemistry, the grandchild of alchemy, but even the old alchemists had something to contribute.

# 3
# THE
# ALCHEMISTS

Unslekked lym, chalk and gleyre of an ey,
Poudres diverse, asshes, donge, pisse and cley,
Cered pokkets, sal peter, vitriole,
And diverse fires maad of wode and cole;
Sal tartre, alkaly, and sal preparat . . .

Geoffrey Chaucer, 'Canon's Yeoman's Tale', *Canterbury Tales*

The early alchemists show many signs of a perhaps unfortunate fixation with human waste, but it delivered them a number of useful chemicals. In the Scots tradition, for example, wool was treated with urine, perhaps after somebody noticed that wool can be stained with sheep urine. 'Waulking of the wool' in the Hebrides involved first soaking tweed in stale urine that neutralised the dogfish liver oil that had been used to dress the wool, and then generally handling it to 'full' the cloth, to make it more airtight.

Before that, Egypt and Rome knew all about stale urine as a treatment for cloth, and the emperor Vespasian even placed a tax on the urine collected in the street urinals of Rome. This fluid was used by the guild fullers to clean cloth, once it had aged and the urea of the urine had turned to ammonia. According to the Roman historian Suetonius, Vespasian's son Titus disapproved of the tax, and said so. Vespasian handed him a coin, asking if it had a bad smell. Titus said it did not, and Vespasian, knowing the coin to be part of the proceeds of the tax, is said to have commented, 'That's odd, it comes straight from the urinal!'

The emperor Augustus may have found a Rome made of brick and left it made of marble, but Vespasian did better. Coming after Nero, he found a bankrupt Rome and left it solvent. He also left the French with a name for the small pissoirs of Paris, still called *vespasiennes*, which was probably the sort of posterity that would have pleased an emperor who, as he was dying, made light of the habit the Romans had then of making dead emperors into gods. 'Dear me,' he quipped, 'I must be turning into a god.'

The use of human waste was a long-lasting alchemical tradition, and the excerpt above from the *Canterbury Tales* offers the first reference in English to the chemicals used by the alchemist. If you try reading it out loud, you may be able to make out the sense of it, but here is a literal translation to help you along:

> Unslaked lime [quicklime], chalk and white of an egg,
> Diverse powders, ashes, dung, urine and clay,
> Wax-sealed bags, saltpetre, vitriol,
> Assorted fires made of wood and coal,
> Salt of tartar, alkali and prepared [common] salt

Keep this list in mind in what follows. Chaucer obviously knew what substances a good alchemical storehouse should contain, but urine must have been one of the oldest. It was also used in dyes, and the standard red, yellow and black dyes used in tartan are all urine-based (though this should probably not be mentioned to members of certain clans).

The tradition of tapping urine for its concealed riches ran on into the time when science really began to be science, about the time of the discovery of phosphorus. In 1677, Daniel Kraft arrived in London, demonstrating the marvellous phosphorus which Hennig Brandt in Germany had recently discovered. Kraft had paid Brandt 200 thalers, quite a large amount, for the secret of making it. Kraft was hardly likely to give his expensive secret away for free, certainly not to that famous London chemist Robert Boyle, who was known to have purchased other 'secrets' from other people, and who might be persuaded to pay for this one as well. If that was his hope, Kraft was foolish to have offered an enigmatic hint: that phosphorus derived from 'somewhat that belonged to the body of man'.

Brandt (and Kraft) had been using large amounts of human urine. When this is boiled and evaporated, urea reacts with a phosphate salt to produce phosphorus vapour, which can be condensed under water to form white phosphorus. Boyle and his assistant Ambrose Godfrey deduced that urine was the starting point, though we are not told how they came to that conclusion. Perhaps they learned that Kraft had been collecting urine on a large scale—it might be hard to keep that sort of thing secret.

It must have been disappointing when their efforts to get phosphorus from urine met with no success. Undeterred, Godfrey went and asked the right questions in Germany. Once he learned that very strong heat was required, the two could make the phosphorus that Boyle called *noctiluca*, or night light.

Boyle wrote down the recipe, of course, and sealed it in an envelope, to be opened only on his death. In the meantime, Ambrose Godfrey was doing very nicely, selling phosphorus as a novelty in Covent Garden for £2 10/- an ounce, using animal dung and urine as his raw material. So while Godfrey made a profit, Boyle took the credit, and they were both happy.

The storage and processing of human waste was, and still is, essential in an agricultural society, even more so when guns became more common, giving the saltpetre that crystallised on the manure heaps a special value over and above its applications in medicine and in food preservation. While there were also places where saltpetre could be mined from caves, for the most part it had to be made. At a pinch, gunpowder could be made without sulfur, and charcoal was always available, but saltpetre was an essential, and that made it the main problem.

It may help to stop and look here at how saltpetre comes to be found in caves, the result of some peculiar natural chemistry. It appears as a white crust on manurial soil, soil which has a high proportion of organic material, in particular, nitrogen-filled animal wastes like bat guano. Dropping to the floor of the cave, the guano is absorbed into the soil, where bacteria go to work, oxidising the proteins and any urea to nitrate ions. These then combine with metallic ions in the soil, yielding a family of nitrate salts: sodium nitrate, potassium nitrate and calcium nitrate, depending on the minerals present.

In a limestone cave, calcium nitrate is the main product in the mixture of nitrates. The trick is to convert all the material to the most useful form, potassium nitrate, and the answer is simple: use saturated solutions! Those who have undergone high school chemistry will generally recall some apparently useless rote learning about solubility and solubility rules, but nothing is ever truly useless—it is just harder to find a use for the facts, especially these days, when we buy our chemicals in jars. Back when people had to make their own chemicals, such knowledge was of practical and everyday importance.

Calcium carbonate is almost entirely insoluble, but sodium carbonate and potassium carbonate are soluble, and easy to get. 'Potassium', by the way, is just a Latinised form of potash, the ash produced by certain woods when they are heated to complete combustion in a pot. In Arabic-speaking cultures, this was called *al kāli*, and it was added to fat to make soap (among other things), but while we adopted the soap idea and took the name as a generic (alkali), the actual material became potash, with the *kāli* recalled only in the chemical symbol of potassium, which is K (for *kalium*, the Latin form of *al kāli*).

Now back at the saltpetre works, the addition of potash to calcium nitrate puts calcium and carbonate in the same solution, but not for long. They fall to the bottom as a precipitate of calcium carbonate, leaving the potassium nitrate and a small amount of sodium nitrate in solution, ready to be decanted. Then a bit of tricky recrystallisation can produce almost pure potassium nitrate for the powderworks.

Sulfur in the days when gunpowder ruled came mainly from mines in Sicily, although, at a pinch, it could be made from sulfide ores. Roast some metal sulfide to get sulfur dioxide, treat more of the mineral with acid to produce hydrogen sulfide, then react the two, producing elemental sulfur and water. Saltpetre remained the problem, especially when you were cut off from easier sources.

The French learned all about this after Britain gained control of the saltpetre production of Bengal, certainly as C. Northcote Parkinson saw it:

> Naval history has recently been written in terms of timber. Sooner or later it will become necessary to write it again in terms of gunpowder. For there can be no doubt that one factor in the English success at sea was the good quality of the powder used. It was pointed out in a letter to the *Moniteur* that the powder burnt in the French fleet at the Battle of the Nile was adulterated by more than 25 per cent. This was naturally, perhaps rightly, attributed to the dishonesty of the contractors and the venality of the commissaries. Yet an exhaustive experiment at

Bombay in 1808, with the powder used on each side in the action between the *San Fiorenzo* and the *Piedmontaise*, proved that the English powder was better . . . It is hard at least to believe that all of the dishonest contractors were on one side. And this suggests, again, that English powder may have owed its quality to the purity of Bengal saltpetre, of which England had a complete and permanent monopoly. The raw material was peculiar in the ease with which it was prepared for export, and perhaps it had other merits.

C. Northcote Parkinson, *Trade in the Eastern Seas*, 1937

In all probability the difference lay in the level of nitrate impurities, which in turn was determined by the soil or, in some cases, the nature of the ash that was used. Ash is the mineral part of the plant left after all else is completely burned away; while this can vary somewhat in the relative amounts, typically there is ten or eleven times as much potassium as sodium. There is even more calcium, but this quickly changes to insoluble calcium carbonate when the ash cools. The real problem lies in the residual sodium nitrate.

The French had other sources of saltpetre open to them, as did other people cut off from normal supplies. Writing at another time of wartime blockade, of the need for saltpetre in South Carolina during the US Civil War, Joseph LeConte described the 'Swiss Method':

The method practiced by the small farmers in Switzerland is very simple, requires little or no care, and is admirably adapted to the hilly portions of our State.

A stable with a board floor is built on the slope of a hill (a northern slope is best), with one end resting on the ground, while the other is elevated, several feet, thus allowing the air to circulate freely below. Beneath the stable a pit, two or three feet deep, and conforming to the slope of the hill, is dug and filled with porous sand, mixed with ashes or old mortar. The urine of the animals is absorbed by the porous sand, becomes nitrified, and is fit for leaching in about two years. The exhausted earth is returned to the pit, to undergo the same process again. This leached earth induces nitrification much more rapidly than fresh earth; so that after the first crop the earth may be leached regularly every year. A moderate-sized stable yields with every leaching about one thousand pounds of saltpetre.

Joseph LeConte, *Instructions for the Manufacture of Saltpetre*, 1862

Whatever saltpetre might be obtained in France, the quality was apparently not the best, even though at that time the French had some of the world's best chemists. Of course, the Revolution had unwisely done away with Antoine Lavoisier in May 1794, after Jean Baptiste Coffinhal gave the order, observing that '*La République n'a pas besoin de savants*' (The Republic has no need of scientists). Lavoisier had started work on the saltpetre problem as early as 1776, and continued to work for the new régime after 1789, but he still lost his life to the guillotine during the Terror.

In the end, all the French effort was insufficient, but there was an interesting spin-off in 1811, when Bernard Courtois was extracting potassium carbonate from seaweed ash. Treating the ash with acid to get rid of sulfur compounds, Courtois noticed a purple vapour which condensed to make crystals. He later told Sir Humphry Davy of this and Davy proposed the name iodine, from the Greek word for the colour violet, *iodes*. Courtois also discovered that major fascination for undergraduates of a certain kind, nitrogen triiodide, which forms tremendously unstable crystals that will even explode when hot water falls on them.

I have no intention of revealing how I discovered this, as I know now that I had a lucky escape; Pierre Dulong lost three fingers and an eye investigating the substance—which may explain why, when he was formulating what is now called 'Dulong and Petit's Law', he chickened out and did not investigate tellurium, fraudulently manufacturing the data for that and several other elements. The reason is probably that when you handle tellurium, it is absorbed, and you get 'tellurium breath'. Not to mince words, you stink of stale garlic for months after working with tellurium compounds. Dulong either feared that, or perhaps was attached to his remaining fingers and wished to stay that way.

The nature of gunpowder is such that it is not a perfect explosive by any means, and this, paradoxically, is what makes it perfect in guns and rockets. To pyromaniacs, nitrogen triiodide is a brilliant explosive for destroying things (if you can put up with the iodine fumes) because it is viciously unstable and is consumed in an instant. Gunpowder burns more slowly, so instead of bursting the cannon or the rocket casing, it either pushes a projectile out of the barrel, or pushes the rocket along as the hot gases and residues go hurtling out of the rear. Gunpowder is perfect as powder for a gun because it is an imperfect explosive, especially if the saltpetre level is a bit low, so that it burns slowly and launches the projectile rather than breaking something like the breech or barrel. The best explosive gunpowder is about 75 per cent saltpetre, but incendiary and rocket powder is more like 60 per cent.

Of course, if the powder is contained in a strong enough sealed casing, there is time for the gases to build up, and there will be an explosion when the casing eventually bursts. It is possible that rockets began as sealed sections of Chinese bamboo filled with gunpowder to be thrown in a fire. One day, in this version, a tube was poorly sealed and flew away but it is more likely that arrows with tubes of gunpowder attached were fired off at the enemy. This would not have happened unless there was some sort of wick in the gunpowder payload, a wick that could ignite the arrow in mid-flight or after it landed, because there would be nothing so damaging to an archer's aim as an eyeful of rocket exhaust. So the original idea would have been to launch the arrow, which would then be carried further by a primitive sort of rocket effect; sooner or later, some archer, tired of being singed, may have tried launching rockets from a stand. It matters little how it started—over time, people worked out a method, and ways of launching many rockets in a short space of time. Then the secret was out, and in places where saltpetre was used to preserve meat or to smelt ores, and where sulfur could be obtained, rockets were suddenly all the rage.

The problem with gunpowder made with sodium nitrate, or Chile saltpetre, is that sodium nitrate is deliquescent. It slurps up moisture from the atmosphere, which makes the powder damp. So it is important to use only the potassium salt, and this is why the Chinese used the same test that chemists use today, the flame test.

If you heat glass in a gas flame, or sprinkle salt in a gas flame, the burning sodium gives off a characteristic yellow colour; it is no coincidence that sodium lamps produce exactly the same colour. Needham quotes from the alchemical text *Chin Shih Pu Wu Chiu Shu Chuëh* (or *Explanation of the Inventory of Metals and Minerals According to the Numbers Five and Nine*), which he dates to about the seventh century, where one section describes the travels of some Buddhist monks. Here is Needham's translation and annotation:

Later they came to Tsê-chou, where they found a mountain covered with beautiful trees. [The monk] said once again 'Saltpetre should also occur in this region. I wonder if it will be as useless as [what we came across] before?' Whereupon, together with the Chinese monk

Ling-Wu they collected the substance and found that upon burning it emitted copious purple flames [literally smoke]. The foreign monk said 'This marvellous substance can produce changes in the Five Metals, and when the various minerals are brought into contact with it they are completely transmuted into liquid form . . .'

*Chin Shih Pu Wu Chiu Shu Chüëh*, 7th century

Here, the Chinese alchemists were using saltpetre as a flux to melt other minerals, and identifying the pure product by the flame test. As Chinese saltpetre or *hsiao shih* goes back in the literature to the fourth century, it seems it was made in a pure form for at least six centuries before it reached the Islamic and European societies that would take up gunpowder with such enthusiasm.

The bombard, the earliest form of cannon, suddenly appears in European records in the form of an illustration to Walter de Milamete's Bodleian manuscript of 1327; give or take a few decades, it cannot have come to Europe much before 1310. Of course, illustrations are not always entirely reliable: *De nobilitatibus, sapientiis et prudentiis regum* (*On the Majesty, Wisdom and Prudence of Kings*) shows arrows being fired from a curious cannon as four knights stand immediately behind the unrestrained barrel, setting it off with a hot poker.

The artist's ignorance of the recoil effect means that we cannot infer too much from the illustration, but at least we know that some sort of gun was in use in Europe by that time. Oddly, the basic principle behind the gun, the idea of a blowpipe, which originated in Indonesia, had already arrived. The Indonesian and Malay *sumpitan* had reached the Arabs by the twelfth century as *zabatāna*, and was called a *cerbottana* in Italian by 1425. Once you have the principle of the blowpipe and the gunpowder effect in the one place, the gun cannot be far behind. In Europe, guns had a head start because there were so many Christians around—not

This illustration from Walter de Milamete's MS shows one of the four knights on the left applying a heated rod to the rear end of a bombard, which appears to be lying on a sort of table. An arrowhead is visible at the muzzle of the bombard.

because they were more war-like, but because of the way Christians had of summoning other Christians to prayer.

In Asia, traditional bronze drums and gongs were thin-walled objects that could not compare with the ponderous thick metal of the bells that Christians made and hung in their church steeples; Muslims used neither in their call to worship, preferring the voice of the muezzin. The technology that made excellent church bells relied on large continuous pours of metal, and now it also made possible the thick-walled cannon that could withstand the force of the gunpowder blast.

The actual users of the guns were not necessarily Christians, but they needed access to Christian metal-workers who were willing to hire out their skills. When Constantinople fell in 1453, a key factor in the Turkish victory was the 8-metre cannon that Transylvanian Christian metal-workers had made for Sultan Mehmed Fatih, Mehmed the Conqueror. This monster fired stone cannonballs weighing half a ton; it would have been a challenge to transport, and so was cast on the spot.

In Renaissance times, the Turkish guns were commonly far smaller, and usually transported by wagon until they were needed, when they were unloaded and mounted on their carriages. This proved to be the Turks' undoing when they arrived at the gates of Vienna in 1559 for a siege. They found that their artillery was not up to the task of toppling the walls, and they wandered off again, never to return.

Around the time that Constantinople fell, the French were mopping up English holdings in France as the Hundred Years' War came to a close. John Talbot, the Earl of Shrewsbury, is usually said to have been killed by a stray cannonball at the battle of Castillon, also in 1453. A generation earlier, in 1428, the French had equal luck when Thomas Montacute, Earl of Salisbury, was killed by a stray cannonball during the siege of Orléans.

*The walls that served Byzantium and Constantinople still stand in modern-day Istanbul.*

In fact, neither was directly killed by a cannonball. Rather more recently, Hugh Talbot, a descendant of the Earl of Shrewsbury, investigated the matter further and found that John Talbot was actually killed after his horse was knocked over by a roundshot. Horse and rider both survived the impact, but Talbot's left leg was pinned beneath the horse, and as his men gathered around to defend him, one by one they fell to the superior numbers of the French, and in the end Talbot died of an axe blow to the back of his head, as confirmed by an examination of the skull when his tomb was opened during reconstruction in 1873.

Thomas Montacute, Earl of Salisbury, was also an indirect victim, struck down as he was examining the French defences from a tower on a bridge over the Loire. He had timed his inspection to coincide with the French gunners' dinner time, and the cannon in question was apparently fired by a small boy, the son of one of the gunners, when he saw the English. They ducked, but the cannonball struck the lintel of a window, dislodging an iron bar which struck Salisbury and removed half his face. He died eight days later, in terrible pain.

Such indirect deaths were also a characteristic of fatalities from cannonballs in eighteenth and nineteenth century naval battles, where many were maimed or wounded by the splinters thrown out by cannonballs crashing into wooden ships. Spalling of the inner surface of armour plate would also kill many German tank crews in World War II, when the outer surface was hit with shaped charges, most of them delivered by rocket.

Whether as direct or indirect killers, fifteenth-century cannon proved their worth, and they also caused changes in warfare. City walls were made lower and thicker, and thus more resistant to the battering of cannon. This would have made it easier to lob incendiary rockets over the wall, but these would have made warfare less attractive to the rough soldiery with their hearts set on a bit of looting and pillaging, since ashes and embers make poor loot and pillage.

Some writers claim that rockets as well as cannon were used by the defenders at Orléans with Joan of Arc, but I can find no real justification for this. There is a problem with evidence from this time, in that rocket enthusiasts are inclined to read into a text what they wish to see. Just as de Joinville's description of Greek fire may or may not be a rocket reference, other old accounts may be taken to mean rockets, especially by an eager and enthusiastic mind. In short, I suspect that a variety of other incendiary and explosive devices were actually mentioned, but all have been dragooned into fitting the label of 'rocket'. Rockets may have taken a back seat for a while, but they never entirely went away.

In China, where rockets were still being used in the nineteenth century, at least against boats, western guns had long been accepted. In 1675, Father Ferdinand Verbiest, a Belgian Jesuit missionary, was called upon by the Manchus to set up a foundry to make bronze cannon. The Manchus' problem was that their existing cannon were of iron, and too heavy for troops to carry into position over steep and rocky ground.

After first refusing on religious grounds, Verbiest was coldly informed that his whole religion would, in the words of Louis Lecomte, another Jesuit who told the story some years later, be 'utterly rooted out' if he did not cooperate. Faced with that threat, Verbiest undertook the work, and sought to use the guns as instruments for the conversion of the Manchus. In all, he cast some 340 guns, each being duly blessed and given a saint's name. The Chinese were still using some of these weapons in the nineteenth century as they fought off European invasions. Two of Verbiest's saintly guns were captured at the Taku Forts in 1860, and are now preserved at the Tower of London, a reminder of one of the drawbacks of guns: once a gun is captured, its ammunition is of no further use.

Oddly, a western version of eastern technology had been returned to the East even earlier. A western design of breech-loader cannon, known in southern China before the fall of Malacca to the Portuguese in 1511, must have been carried there by Muslim traders. The guns were called *Fo-lang-chi*, which probably meant 'the machine of the Franks', the Fo-lang or Franks being any and all western Christians as seen by Muslims—just as all Muslims are perceived in the west as 'Arabs'.

The main difference between eastern and western shipping and armaments at this time was that while Asian countries also had guns, European ships needed to be tough enough to weather Atlantic storms and the long voyage to the East. They had stronger hulls and decks that were better able to withstand the recoil of larger guns, and also better able to withstand the small cannonballs thrown by Asian guns. That may have been enough to make rockets less attractive to the Europeans when armaments were being chosen.

Whatever the reason, rockets in Europe were largely relegated to the role of fireworks, a trend that seems to have developed as early as the fourteenth century. The first celebratory fireworks display in England seems to have been at the wedding of King Henry VII in 1486. They gained popularity during the reign of Henry VIII and by Elizabethan times there was a Fireworks Master in charge of all royal fireworks.

There were a few warlike exceptions, appearing as traces in occasional books. Kazimierz Siemienowicz, a Polish general under Wladyslaw IV, published *Artis magnae artilleriae* (*The Complete Art of Artillery*) in Amsterdam in 1650 which included, among other things, plans for a multi-stage rocket. The Dutch were experimenting with rockets at the same time, and there were rockets in Germany as well. A translation of Siemienowicz into German in 1676 was followed by an English version in 1729.

Other records of rockets appear after 1650, but the increase in publishing activity may be evidence not so much of an increase in research rather than a reflection of the fact that with the end of the Thirty Years' War people were free to write up developments which had been wartime secrets. In addition, Siemienowicz provided many recipes for pyrotechnics in general, which must have encouraged minor experimentation.

The alternative may be that as science began to flourish in the seventeenth century, the attractions of playing with rockets may have been seductive to those of a military mind and with a tendency to curiosity. Certainly there was more rocket work happening: in 1696, the Englishman Robert Anderson published a two-part treatise on how to make rocket moulds, prepare the propellants and perform the calculations, and in 1730, a German field artillery colonel, Christoph Friedrich von Geissler, was manufacturing rockets weighing 55 to 120 pounds.

We can tell that rockets were around in other places because of musical effects like the 'Mannheim rocket' being used by composers like Stamitz and Gossec (although this trick owed more to the greater musical ability of orchestral players and the larger orchestras of the eighteenth century than to any fireworks). This particular 'rocket' was a combination of arpeggio and crescendo which people regarded as similar in sound to the rockets that were set off to accompany Handel's *Royal Fireworks Music*.

Handel's work was first performed in April 1749 to accompany a fireworks display celebrating the peace of Aix-la-Chapelle (signed the previous year to end the war of Austrian succession). There were two performances. The first, a rehearsal in London's Vauxhall Gardens, drew 12 000 people a week before the real thing in Green Park, where the fireworks proved to be somewhat unpredictable. Something, generally said to be a stray rocket, set fire to some wooden scaffolding that is often described as 'a wooden pavilion' but was, in fact, a part of the display.

Several things made the event memorable: a rainshower stopped many of the fireworks going off, then there was the fire in the scaffolding. As a finale, the Italian stage designer and pyrotechnical virtuoso, the Chevalier Giovanni Servandoni, drew his sword and threatened to skewer Charles Frederick, Comptroller of the Ordnance and Fireworks, whom he blamed for the fiasco. They don't seem to put on shows like that any more.

War rockets were enticing to all who saw them. They hissed, they sparked, they set fire to what they hit, with any luck—and with any luck at all, they hit the enemy and not the troops who fired them. While rockets were at first more useful as frighteners, there seem to have been several stages of enthusiasm for them on the battlefield, most probably representing a seesawing between cannon and rocket technologies, and perhaps the seesawing of what passed for military thinking. The evidence that rockets could turn on their owners was all too clear, however, and most of Europe kept them as items of celebration, mere toys to be played with. In Asia, on the other hand, there was an old-established Mongol tradition of rocketry—but at some distance from their usual haunts on the plains of central Asia.

We know the later Mongols as the Mughals or Moguls. The first Mughal ruler in India, Babar by name, was a descendant of Genghis Khan and Tamerlane. Babar came through the mountain passes in 1526 and settled in northern India, having a remarkable military advantage: access to the tough little horses of central Asia. It was somewhere between hard and impossible to breed horses in India, but Babar could not only draw on horses from the north, he could also find trained cavalry, and men like himself, as skilled with the bow as they were in the saddle, and sharing a delight in Persian poetry.

Those might not seem like a set of useful traits for conquerors, but coupled with local infantry the Mughals had a distinct advantage in the field, and perhaps the poetry gave them the insights to rule successfully when they made a conquest. Babar's son Humayun, driven out in 1530, later swept back in, but a stabilised Mughal reign only came about when Humayun's son Akbar took over the throne, which he held from 1556 to 1605.

The Mughals took a leaf out of the book of Mehmed Fatih when they had their cannon cast locally rather than hauling them over and through the mountain ranges. It was one thing to sweep all before you in the field, but if an enemy could retreat behind city walls, then that enemy could hope to rise again. If you knocked down their walls, the enemy could entertain no such hope. So successful were the Mughals in building an empire in India, that when a later Mughal emperor's wife died in 1631, the lady, known as 'the Chosen One of the Palace' or *Taj Mahal*, was commemorated by a mausoleum that remains one of the wonders of the world to this day. It took 20 000 workers to build it, over some 22 years, a clear indication that here was a well-run empire, with resources to spare.

There was one small problem: the Mughals were the Muslim overlords of a Hindu population, and while they managed a level of cooperation and accommodation with the middle classes, unrest was always lurking among the less wealthy Hindus. In particular, the Mughals had problems managing the population in steep terrain, where cavalry and artillery found the going difficult. Perhaps this explains why rockets remained a part of the Mughal armoury, since rockets are far more useful in hilly areas.

Then again, rockets were pretty much endemic in eighteenth century India. Quintin Craufurd was a Scots traveller who wrote on the 'Hindoos' in 1790, with an engraving of a cluster of bamboo-stick rockets as part of the title page of his work. In each case, the sharpened end of the bamboo protrudes past the iron tube which holds the powder.

> It is certain that even in those parts of Hindostan that never were frequented by Mahommedans or Europeans, we have met with rockets, a weapon which the natives almost universally employ in war. The rocket consists of a tube of iron, about 8 in. long, and one and a half inches in diameter, closed at one end. It is filled in the same manner as an ordinary sky-rocket and fastened toward the end of a piece of bamboo, scarcely as thick as a walking-cane, and about 4 ft long, which is pointed with iron. At the opposite end of the tube from the

iron point, or that towards the head of the shaft, is the match. The man who uses it points the end that is shod with iron, to which the rocket is fixed, to the object to which he means to direct it, and setting fire to the match, it goes off with great velocity. By the irregularity of its motion, it is difficult to be avoided, and sometimes acts with considerable effect, especially among cavalry.

Quintin Craufurd, *Sketches Chiefly Relating to the History,*
*Religion, Learning and Manners of the Hindoos,* 1790

All in all, the Mughals had a fairly good empire under fairly good control. There was a weak spot, however, because they had no thoughts of controlling the seas. Thus Europeans, in particular the British, were able to gain access to the ports of the subcontinent, and having established their toeholds were able to move in—and in, and in—and since by 1707 the Mughals ruled most of India, a clash with Britain became inevitable. Europe was about to encounter rockets of war.

Would-be-Imperial Britain first encountered Mughal rockets when they clashed with the forces of the Mysore empire in 1798, in the latest in a series of fights that had been going on for more than 30 years. Haidar (or Hyder) Ali was the victor in the war of 1766–69 and for most of the war of 1780–83 (until his death in 1782), when he had the assistance of a French naval squadron that was operating in the Indian Ocean. His son Tipū Sultan, sometimes called Tipū Sahib, then took the throne, but Tipū made a bad decision when he invaded the British-protected state of Travancore, starting the Third Mysore War of 1789–92. In the end, he was forced to cede half his territory to the British, and that was the beginning of the end for the Mughals.

Without the ceded territory to draw troops and taxes from, the Mughal ruler was short of resources, especially troops, when the fourth and final war began, and he ended up dying in the battle to defend his capital, Seringapatam. All the same, Tipū Sultan had one nasty surprise for the British and their allies: a force of 6000 rocketeers, able to move swiftly from place to place, laying down a fire that was new to most of the soldiers. A young English officer named Bayly wrote: 'Every illumination of blue lights was accompanied by a shower of rockets, some of which entered the head of the column, passing through to the rear, causing death, wounds, and dreadful lacerations from the long bamboos of twenty or thirty feet, which are invariably attached to them'.

These were small rockets, about $6\frac{1}{2}$ pounds (3 kilograms) according to reports of the time, and they certainly unsettled the enemy, but in the end Mysore fell to the British forces. A few of the missiles were captured, and found their way back to London, but the rockets of Tipū Sultan had not impressed a British colonel in Mysore, a 30-year-old who had just changed his name from Arthur Wesley to Arthur Wellesley. Today, we recall him as the Duke of Wellington.

# 4
# CONGREVE'S RICOCHET ROCKETS

'The rocket,' to use the words of Congreve, 'brings into operation the power of artillery every where, and is nowhere embarrassed by the circumstances limiting the application of artillery.' It imparts to infantry and cavalry the force of artillery, in addition to the power of their own respective arms. Thus, a foot-soldier might, on particular occasions, carry several 12-pound rockets, each having the propulsive and penetrating effect of a 12-pound cannon-shot, without the embarrassment of the 12-pounder gun. The rocket, as we shall hereafter discover, may be discharged on many occasions without the aid of any apparatus; but even the corresponding rocket-tube, by which its accuracy of flight is promoted, weighs only 20 pounds, whereas the weight of a 12-pounder gun is no less than 18 hundredweights.

*Harper's New Monthly Magazine*, 'What is a Congreve Rocket?', 1851

We move from Wesley/Wellesley/Wellington, a man with three names, to three men with but a single name. In the study of history, it is important never to confuse William Congreve with either William Congreve or William Congreve. William Congreve (1670–1729) was a dramatist and poet, best remembered for his play *The Way of the World*. Lieutenant-

General Sir William Congreve (1741–1814) was Comptroller of the Royal Laboratory at Woolwich, responsible for all matters relating to British artillery, and most famous for being the father of his eldest son (1772–1828), the important William Congreve from our present point of view. (It is also important that we distinguish between the various Wesleys, but we will come back to them later.)

William Congreve the father was made a baronet in 1812, gaining a hereditary knighthood. This meant the son also became Sir William when his father died, and because he spent many years at Woolwich tinkering with rockets, many accounts accord him a military rank that he did not really possess—but he was the first person to whom the title 'rocket scientist' might be given.

Our rocket-conscious William took his Master of Arts degree at Cambridge, then moved to London, where he read law and edited a newspaper and, more importantly, was befriended by the Prince of Wales, later to be the Prince Regent and then King George IV.

This is a key point when we look at patterns of acceptance and rejection of the rocket in Britain. There appear to be those whose poor opinion of rockets may have derived in part from their poor opinion of the Prince, who associated closely with the Whigs in the early days of the nineteenth century. There were undoubtedly those, perhaps of a Whiggish persuasion, who admired rockets solely on account of their patron, and no doubt there were some on both sides who formed an opinion based on what they had actually seen of Congreve's rockets. (But that assumes that military leaders had the ability to make decisions on a sensible basis.)

Arthur Wesley was already a lieutenant-colonel before he saw active duty, and this was typical of army officers in his day. It was probably lucky that warfare in those days was so bloody—it acted to select the less inadequate officers for promotion by leaving them standing. When you look at Britain's officers in the eighteenth and nineteenth centuries, it is a wonder anybody took so long to come up with the label that Herbert Spencer would later graft onto Darwin's evolutionary model, 'survival of the fittest'. Perhaps it was because even the survivors were commonly uncommonly unfit and inept.

Wesley was a survivor, and it seems he was almost certainly one of the rare ept ones, but his military assessments might still be clouded by other considerations. As the Duke of Wellington, he might dismiss the Prince and his brothers as millstones, but that was a politician speaking. Prinny, as the Prince of Wales was usually dismissively called, was a patron of architecture and art, and had someone persuade Jane Austen (who detested him) to dedicate *Emma* to him—though she took her revenge in *Mansfield Park*, her third novel, where a thinly veiled 'regency' in the Bertram family is held up for distasteful consideration. Even the dedication in *Emma*, 'by His Royal Highness's dutiful and obedient humble servant, the Author', reflects her annoyance at the Royal demand transmitted to her.

The Prince was also interested in science. He was President of the Royal Institution and encouraged a number of scientists, endowing readerships in mineralogy and geology at Oxford, as well as conferring knighthoods on Humphry Davy, William Herschel—and William Congreve. In short, Prinny wasn't all bad.

Young Congreve was something of a dabbler and inventor all his life. Among his inventions we find an elegant clock, operating on the principle of balls running down an inclined plane, a canal lock, unforgeable banknotes and, of course, the Congreve rocket. It is not all that surprising that Congreve turned to rockets—they were exciting and spectacular, and the specimens captured at Seringapatam were kept at Woolwich, under his father's control, so he had access to them.

Young Congreve went out and bought the best rockets the London fireworks sellers could offer, and found they had a range of just 600 yards, far less than the reported range of the Indian products. Being a wealthy young man, he was able to spend 'some hundreds of pounds' of his own money to produce a rocket with a much greater range.

There is more to making a rocket than poking powder into a tube: the powder needs to be shaped, moulded to have a hollow up the centre and rammed, so that it does not crack. When there are cracks, flame eats into them, causing uneven burning. So the powder needs to have the right proportions, be well mixed and be rammed into the tube under high pressure.

Congreve used his father's connections to get access to the facilities and the firing range at England's Royal Arsenal at Woolwich. Here he worked out the correct firing angles for different distances and created the 'Congreve rocket system', which used various sizes and different models for different purposes. His system originally included rockets weighing 3, 6, 9, 12, 18, 24, 32, 42, 100 and 300 pounds; the last two were too large to be practical in the field and were quickly dropped. By 1844, there were just four sizes—3, 6, 12 and 24 pounds—but that was later. First, the rocket system had to be accepted.

The next step was political, and it is about this time that people begin according Congreve a military rank. He still did not have a genuine military role, but in 1810 or 1811 he became equerry to the Prince Regent, and in 1811 was elected a Fellow of the Royal Society and gazetted a lieutenant-colonel in the Hanoverian artillery. This was effectively an honorary rank, but people were quick to use it, and he was Colonel Congreve ever after.

The Congreve rockets lacked the fins we see in modern military rockets, and had instead a stick, rather like a skyrocket has today. These long, stabilising guidesticks were used to balance the rockets as they hopefully traced mathematically precise arcs in the sky, or flew directly across the ground, hissing and snorting, skittering and spitting. At first, the guidestick was attached to the side of the rocket, but after 1815 it was screwed to the centre of a metal baseplate in a threaded ferrule, surrounded by five equidistant exhaust holes.

In 1805, Congreve demonstrated his rockets to the Prince Regent and others, and they were greeted with great enthusiasm. Here, it seemed, was a way to hit the French threat of invasion. To explain this, we have to understand something of the nature of warfare in the Napoleonic era. A cannon could be used to hurl cannonballs over considerable distances, but these were solid balls. When fired from a ship at sea, they could not do a great deal of damage to masonry, not to mention that a heaving, rolling ship was not the best of platforms to aim from. In a contest between a stone fort and a wooden ship, the fort usually had the advantage.

The bigger the cannon, the greater its range, and the really large cannon with the greatest range were far easier to work on land. As well as that, a land-based cannon high up on a cliff or tower would have a greater range than the same cannon on a ship, close to sea level. That meant a fort's defenders could strike a ship before the naval guns were yet in range. Even a shore battery with protective stonework, sandbags or just barrels for fortification was a much more difficult target than a timber ship. Damage a mast, punch a hole in the hull or just cut a key piece of rigging, and the ship was in trouble. In the fort, a splintered flagpole or a hole in the wall meant nothing, there was no rigging and forts did not sink.

Forts could also use heated shot, cannonballs kept in a furnace until they were hot enough to set fire to the hull and masts of any ship they struck. A furnace might be used safely in a stone fort, but on a wooden ship with tarred rigging, the risk of the furnace being struck, or a heated shot rolling loose on the decks was too great, and it was usual to dowse even the galley fire before a ship went into action, the only fire left aboard being the slow match, a sort of fuse, used by the gunners to set off the cannon. Of course, inside any fort there would be plenty of flammable material, but an attacking ship had no way of setting it on fire, and was at risk of being converted to matchwood, possibly even flaming matchwood.

All of this meant a superior naval force had no safe way of getting at shipping sheltered in a fortified harbour other than by sending in fireships on a favourable wind, or by cutting-out expeditions mounted from boats rowed with muffled oars, each of them a risky operation. Even before October 1805, when the Battle of Trafalgar against combined French and Spanish forces gave Britain complete control of the seas, Britain had the upper hand on the oceans of the world, but Napoleon held much of Europe. Just as Napoleon was never able to invade Britain, so the British navy had trouble inflicting damage on the French and their allies.

Even though Britannia ruled the waves, all it would take to leave the country open to invasion would be a shift in the weather. A gale might blow the Royal Navy's blockading fleet away, giving the French a chance to launch an invasion, using the boats and barges that filled the harbour of Boulogne. A strong wind that blew away from France and towards Britain might well scatter and disperse the British fleet far from the shores of France, while giving a downwind run to sluggish French invasion barges laden with cannon, horses and soldiers.

To prevent this sort of disastrous break-out, it was necessary to risk the fire of the French shore batteries, to get in close enough to damage or destroy that fleet of barges. Here, all of a sudden, the navy realised they had Congreve's rockets as a way of raining fire down on the enemy from a safe distance; better still, the rockets could be fired in large numbers from small boats controlled by oars, able to navigate against wind and tide, far harder to hit than ships, and free of recoil problems.

While Admiral Gambier would later have little kind comment to make about the newfangled Congreve rockets at Copenhagen, Admiral Nelson could certainly see their potential, and on 1 October 1805, not long before his death at the Battle of Trafalgar, he wrote a despatch to Viscount Castlereagh, Secretary for the War Department:

> My Lord,
>
> The far greater part of the Combined Fleets is in the Harbour, and indeed none can be called in the Bay of Cadiz; they lie in such a position abreast of the Town, and many entirely open, over the narrow strip of land, that Congreve's rockets, if they will go one mile and a half, must do execution. Even should no Ships be burnt, yet it would make Cadiz so very disagreeable, that they would rather risk an Action than remain in Port. I do assure your Lordship, that myself and many thousands in the Fleet will feel under the greatest obligations to Colonel Congreve. But I think, with your Lordship's assistance, we have a better chance of forcing them out by want of provisions: it is said hunger will break through stone walls—ours is only a wall of wood.

It was this sort of consideration that saw Congreve travel to Boulogne with a British flotilla on 21 November 1805, just a month after Nelson died. His intention was to try his new rockets as a way of destroying the invasion boats, but the weather was too poor, and the exercise was called off. Then, almost a year later, on the night of the 7–8 October 1806, eighteen boats were rowed into range of the invasion fleet and some 200 rockets were launched in just half an hour from frames mounted on the boats. There was apparently some minor success, though it seems most of the rockets struck the town rather than their intended targets. In 1807, the Congreve rockets were used with very great success against Copenhagen.

By this time, the art of making gunpowder had become both an art and a science, and rockets were carrying a double charge of black powder: one for propelling the rocket, and one as a warhead of sorts, set off to burn after the rocket landed. That was what Copenhagen had to contend with.

The rockets had two sorts of 'head': the largest rocket, the 32-pounder, could be fitted with either an explosive warhead for use against fortresses or an incendiary warhead for use against wooden sailing ships and other burnable objects like towns. The incendiary-carcass rockets had conical heads, which would penetrate the targets and then burn, while those with explosive warheads had rounded heads. The incendiary rockets also had large cloth-covered holes equally spaced around the warhead. The cloth held the incendiary powder in, but allowed the flames to break out once the rocket had landed.

The attack was not entirely a secret: the Danes had a large and flammable fleet, and *The Times* published a report on 6 August 1807, in rather unhelpful terms, though there is a degree of care shown at the end of the story:

MR. CONGREVE, the inventor of the inflammable arrows or rockets, embarked at Yarmouth on Tuesday, on board the *Claudia* cutter, having three sloops, laden with these formidable implements, and fitted up for discharging them, under convoy. Nothing had transpired respecting their destination.

There were probably 25 000 rockets launched against Copenhagen. A few reports say there were as many as 40 000, but the contemporary accounts are a little confusing. In August 1807, the *Gentleman's Magazine* recorded that Admiral Gambier was bombarding Copenhagen as the magazine went to press, while the September issue features a letter dated 23 August, which indicated in passing that a fleet including five bombs (strengthened vessels used to lob explosive shells at an enemy) and 'ten launches fitted as mortar boats' was going into action. The letter continues, describing Danish fire from gunboats and a shore battery: 'The fire was returned with great spirit from the squadron, and some attempts were made to throw Mr. Congreve's rockets, but the distance was too great to produce much effect from them.'

In fact, while we tend now to think of the Congreve rocket mainly as a naval weapon (due in large part to a famous ship-launched rocket bombardment described in the next chapter), the main rocket bombardment of Copenhagen was land-based, and it was quite effective, as we can read into news from Denmark in the December 1807 issue of the *Gentleman's Magazine*:

> It appears that the trial of Gen. Peymann, for signing the Capitulation of Copenhagen, is merely a matter of form. Had he protracted the siege 48 hours longer, the whole of the town must have been laid in ashes. The heads of the thirty Corporations have a right, by charter, to dictate to the military power in cases of emergency or any attack against the City.

*The Times* had a slightly different slant, reporting on 5 October that Congreve had been to Copenhagen to see for himself:

> This Gentleman, we are informed, was two days in the town of Copenhagen, in disguise, for the purpose of ascertaining what damage had been done by the new weapon which through his means has been

employed in this siege. We understand that in the quarter where the fire was most violent, there are whole streets in which not one house is left standing . . . The inhabitants have indeed suffered most grievously in this bombardment; but they can, *and in fact do*, only accuse the Governor of it; who instead of enforcing precaution, as he should have done, after having been most fully and generously apprised of the extent of the preparations made by the English, lulled the inhabitants into a false sense of security, which by inducing them to undervalue, and even ridicule, the means of annoyance prepared by the British, kept them in their houses till the dreadful storm burst over their heads.

The *Gentleman's Magazine* had no doubts about who was to blame: 'The Crown Prince of Denmark . . . forced the command of Copenhagen on General Peymann, who in vain urged his advanced age as an excuse for his retirement from so weighty a responsibility, and now punishes him for the natural consequences of that imposition'.

Ships' crews were generally as concerned about fire as townspeople. In February 1814, Sergeant Thomas Morris was outside Antwerp, under fire from French gunboats which were supporting a man-of-war in attacking a fort. His regiment sheltered behind a river bank, he recalled later, where men of the regiment were safe 'except when they had to assist the artillery-men in superintending the furnaces, and getting the red-hot shot ready for them', but the soldiers were fairly well pinned down until relief arrived.

At about three o'clock two men belonging to the Rocket Brigade arrived at the fort, and immediately commenced operations. The first rocket fell just astern of the enemy: the next one was sent with greater precision, and fell on the deck about midships. The greatest confusion prevailed on board, and they were shouting and running in all directions: of course, they expected some more to follow, and they were so evidently afraid of them, that they took advantage of the flood tide, slipped their cables, and made the best of their way back towards Antwerp.

Thomas Morris, *The Recollections of Sergeant Morris*, after 1815, published 1845

Here we see the limitation of cannon, which could only smash what could be seen, while rockets were launched from behind an embankment, and could cause fires wherever they landed.

Arthur Wellesley was very much a landsman with little need to attack ships at sea, and no time for rockets on land. When he was offered rockets during the Peninsular War in Spain, he wrote to Earl Bathurst in November 1813:

I have received your letter of the 11th, regarding the Rocket Brigade. The only reason why I wished to have it was to get the horses; but as we are to have them at all events, I am perfectly satisfied.

I do not want to set fire to any town, and I do not know any other use of the rockets.

His reasoning here was quite sound: Wellesley was fighting a war far from the resources of home, where he had to rely on the friendly support of the Portuguese and Spanish, both civilians and guerrilla allies. The people of the Iberian peninsula had been thoroughly alienated by Napoleon's armies, who lived off the land and the people, taking what they needed, both at home and abroad. The British forces, on the other hand, paid for what they needed. Later, when he moved into the south of France, Wellesley used the same approach to win over the locals, making his troops far more secure against guerrilla attack. Burning towns was not an option under this approach, though it was an acceptable, even desirable stratagem in some events.

*The Times* on 26 September 1807, outlined the effectiveness of Congreve's rocket in just such terms:

Nor can we doubt for a moment that the surrender of the Danish
capital has been accelerated, and the effusion of blood prevented, by its
employment; for it is calculated to operate rather as an instrument of
conflagration, than as an engine of personal destruction; and though it
widely and rapidly extends the afflicting scene of extreme distress, it in
a great measure spares the valuable lives of those whose property it
destroys. The ruin of their homes could not fail to produce in the
inhabitants of the town a disposition to an early capitulation; and
when no prospect presented itself of successful resistance, such a disposition must evidently have made a just impression on the garrison
and hastened the termination of the siege.

Their fiery destructiveness may not have been Wellesley's only
objection to rockets, though. As far back as 1805, the serving
soldier Arthur Wellesley was also a member of parliament. He
had accepted the post of Chief Secretary for Ireland, and after
that, was identified as a member of the Tory party, the party
that supported King George III against that friend of the
Whigs, the Prince Regent. So we might speculate that the
soldier Wellesley rejected the ideas put forward by a political
enemy's protegé.

One thing is certain, Wellington clearly had real respect for
the rockets as town-burners, as we might expect, given that he
had been in the thick of the Copenhagen campaign. This may
explain why he commanded on 11 November 1810 that some of
the rockets brought ashore in Portugal be taken back on board
the ship they had landed from:

I observe that the officer of artillery has taken on more rockets than I
intended . . . I desired that he would take one carriage drawn by four or
six horses, and I understand that he has taken four carriages drawn by
twenty horses and twenty loaded mules. In case it should be necessary
to bring you back across the Tagus, it might, in the existing state of
the roads, be very difficult to draw off this equipment; and we should

then possibly be obliged to leave in the hands of the enemy the means of burning the town of Lisbon.

Perhaps Wellington disdained rockets because he had defeated Tipū Sultan, in spite of his rockets? That would seem to be part of the explanation as well, given this revealing letter to Admiral Berkeley, written a few days earlier, on 6 November 1810:

> I have received your letter of 11 AM , the 5th instant. I assure you that I am no partisan of Congreve's rockets, of which I entertain but a bad opinion, from what I recollect of the rockets in the East Indies, of which I believe those of Congreve are an imitation. It is but fair, to give everything a trial, more particularly as I have received the orders of Government to try these machines.

There was, however, one senior European military figure who regarded rockets as effective weapons, a man who was responsible for the only British presence at the pivotal Battle of Leipzig in 1813, when Napoleon's forces were soundly defeated. The victory was helped by a rocket troop attached to the forces commanded by the Crown Prince of Sweden, who would later become Charles XIV of Sweden.

The Crown Prince was born Jean Baptiste Jules Bernadotte at Pau in France, and he entered the French army in 1780. An ardent revolutionary, he rose rapidly through the ranks, commanding a division by 1794, and gaining his marshal's baton in 1804. He was highly successful in the field, but that just earned him Napoleon's jealousy, and he returned to Paris. Elected heir to the Swedish throne in 1810, the diehard revolutionary transformed into the Crown Prince. He took his duties seriously, even becoming a Protestant to qualify himself better. When Napoleon's demands proved to be contrary to the interests of Sweden, the two men broke, and Bernadotte, who had once

*Larger rockets were often fired from a bombarding frame, using a lanyard to ignite the rocket's fuse from a safe distance.*

accepted the surrender of Blücher himself, now became an ally of the forces aligned against France.

In his earlier role, Bernadotte had commanded French troops in northern Germany and Denmark, so he would have known what marvellous uses could be made of rockets. Napoleon, trained as an artillery officer, thought little of rockets, and those two factors were probably all it took to inspire Bernadotte, or Crown Prince Charles John, to seek the attachment of a troop of rocket artillery to his forces.

Of course, there might have been another cause. Congreve was, as we have seen, a favourite of the Prince Regent, and the commoner-Prince of Sweden would have been politically wise to take the Royal Horse artillery rocket troop.

Whatever the cause, the results were outstanding. For once, the rockets flew truly, straight at an advancing French division. The French, of course, had no expectation of attack, having seen none of the traditional earthworks that typically surrounded a battery of cannon that fired about once every 90 seconds if the guns were well served.

All of a sudden, a flight of six 32-pounder rockets flew over the division and exploded, sending canister through the dense formations. The Russian General Wittgenstein wrote later of the rockets: 'They look as if they were made in Hell, and surely are the devil's own artillery. It was beyond any hope to expect these Frenchmen to advance into this unholy barrage.' Warfare had suddenly lurched forward a pace, and it had done so in full view of the Russians and Prussians.

In the south, as Wellington emerged from Spain into France, he found himself well supplied with rockets, at the insistence of the Prince Regent, it seems, and they proved useful several times. One of these was in February 1814. When Sir John Hope transferred six companies of the Guards and two of the Sixtieth, some 600 men, across the Adour River in rowing boats, the British forces found themselves confronted by 14 000 Frenchmen. If there was ever an occasion for the rockets to work, this was it. According to that arch storyteller and reminiscer, Captain Rees Howell Gronow, witness to the action that followed:

> The first operations of our corps were to throw over the 3rd Guards, under the command of the gallant Colonel Stopford; this was not accomplished without much difficulty: but it was imperatively necessary, in order to protect the point where the construction of the bridge of boats would terminate. They had not been long on the French side of the river before a considerable body of men were seen issuing from Bayonne. Sir John Hope ordered our artillery, and rockets, then for the first time employed, to support our small band. Three or four regiments of French infantry were approaching rapidly, when a well-directed fire of rockets fell amongst them. The consternation of the Frenchmen was such, when these hissing, serpent-like projectiles descended, that a panic ensued, and they retreated upon Bayonne. The next day the bridge of boats was completed, and the whole army crossed.

> Captain Gronow, *Reminiscences of Captain Gronow*, 1862

This was how rockets ought to be used: in a situation where the artillery needed to be light and effective—and we have evidence from British lieutenant George Gleig that they definitely disturbed the recipients, though it seems they disturbed him as well:

> I saw and conversed with a French sergeant who was taken in this affair. He assured me, that he had been personally engaged in twenty battles, and that he had never really known the sensation of fear till today. A rocket, it appeared, had passed through his knapsack without hurting him; but such was the violence with which it flew, that he fell upon his face, and the horrible hissing sound produced by it was one which he declared that he never could forget. It skips and starts about

from place to place in so strange a manner, that the chances are, when you are running to the right or left to get out of the way, you run directly against it; and hence the absolute rout, which a fire of ten or twelve rockets can create, provided they take effect. But it is a very uncertain weapon. It may, indeed, spread havoc among the enemy, but it may also turn back upon the people who use it, causing, like the elephant of other days, the defeat of those whom it was designed to protect. On the present occasion, however, it proved materially serviceable, as every man can testify who witnessed the result of the fire.

George R. Gleig, *The Subaltern*, 1821

Just outside Toulouse, William Beresford found his artillery unable to cross the boggy ground, so he left his field guns behind and took the light equipment of the Rocket Troop through with him. After struggling for several miles through mud, Lowry Cole's Fourth Division faced a French charge, and showed once more that the British line was superior to Napoleon's columns. Then, with any threat from the French cavalry reduced by the lay of the land, they launched their rockets at the French infantry, who were put to flight.

As William Napier described it, these were weapons 'whose noise and dreadful aspect were unknown before', yet some Frenchmen at least must have known about rockets, since Tipū Sultan's crack troops in India, the ones defeated by Wellington in 1798, had been trained by French forces. The difference was that the English had paid attention, taken a good idea, and used it. The tradition of using rockets to frighten inexperienced troops lived on—and at least in Leipzig, they demonstrated that there was indeed something to be frightened about.

Part of the surprise for the French troops probably stemmed from Napoleon's own propaganda machine. *The Times* for 27 October 1809 thunders at an alleged analysis of English rockets gleaned from *Le Moniteur*, a French newspaper, which had suggested that the French were now ready to make their own rockets:

> Thus, the Rocket they pretend to have analyzed is said to have been made with '*brown paper*'. Now we are authorised boldly to assert, that the CONGREVE Rocket is absolutely made of *no such material, nor anything like it*. So the diameter of this rocket is stated to be one centimetre, but the *smallest* of our war Rockets *is more than ten times that diameter*.

The main thrust of the article was to prove that the French were unable to make Congreve rockets themselves, but as the average French soldier was far more likely to hear what was reported in *Le Moniteur* than in *The Times*, they could be forgiven for expecting a mere firework, magnifying the effectiveness of the Congreve rocket when it was brought to bear on their lines.

If there was any general military doubt on any side about the effectiveness of rockets, it evaporated when the Emperor of Russia, Tsar Alexander, arrived in London, along with King Frederick William of Prussia. Their two nations took most of the credit for the victory in Leipzig, but in the delight of putting down the Corsican upstart they were more than ready to celebrate the rockets crafted by the favourite of the Prince Regent of England.

It was England, after all, whose forces had harried the Corsican from the south, even if rockets were less popular down there. The *Gentleman's Magazine* gave a full account of their arrival, starting like this:

> *Monday, June 6.* The two Sovereigns, the Emperor of Russia and the King of Prussia, to whom Europe is so deeply indebted for their share in the overthrow of the general Disturber of the civilized world, and in the restoration of the blessings of Peace, landed, from the *Impregnable* and *Jason*, on British shores at Dover, this afternoon at half past six.

The foreign sovereigns were there to help celebrate the over-throw of Boney, a little prematurely as we can see now, because Napoleon's escape from Elba and his final defeat at Waterloo were still in the future. All the same, when Blücher arrived, the magazine assures us that 'Colonels Bloomfield and Congreve came out and received the General uncovered, and in that state, conducted him to the principal entrance of Carlton House'.

Two pages on in the same issue, we read of a demonstration of Congreve rockets on 13 June. At that time the word 'experiment' had more of the sense of 'experience', hence its use here:

In the model-room they inspected the curious model of Quebec, and went from thence to the Rocket-ground, where several experiments were prepared to show the effect and strength of Col. Congreve's rockets. A superb tent was erected on the mound for the Illustrious Visitors and their suite; and after they had taken their station, a most interesting exhibition ensued. On a signal given by Colonel Congreve, who superintended the rocket-department, a demonstration was made of the power of the rocket-composition. At about two hundred yards North-east of the mound, where the Royal Visitors were stationed, a quantity of the composition placed on three pieces of timber exploded, producing columns of flame awfully grand. The discharge produced a volcanic appearance, attended by a tremendous roaring; but the burning property of the material was most remarkable. After the discharge, the timber remained in flames, and actually consumed to a cinder. The next operation was a display of the rockets as used in besieging. They shot upwards to a considerable elevation, carrying a tube filled with burning material a considerable distance.—They were larger than any used on a former occasion, and made a tremendous roaring. The next experiment was a proof of the havock [sic] these engines occasion in a field of battle. They were fired from the opposite bank of the Thames horizontally over the low grounds, to the distance of 800 or 1000 yards. It is impossible to describe the effect produced by these discharges. Wonder was expressed by the beholders. The shells thrown by the rockets flew to the distance required, and exploded with horrible sounds. There can be little doubt that a single volley would disunite a body of cavalry. Against that description of force they are peculiarly operative, as they not only kill, but spread terror among the horses. The foreign officers were struck by the effect of this new engine in the art of war.

According to the *Gentleman's Magazine*, the Royal party then went to view another marvel of the modern age, a steam-powered sawmill cutting logs of fir, elm and ash to planks in no time at all. Then there was a public celebration, described by *The Times* in these terms:

> At ten o'clock a loud and continued discharge of artillery announced the commencement of the fireworks, which were, certainly, if not the most tasteful, yet on the grandest and most extensive scale that we have ever witnessed. From the battlements of the castle, at one moment, ascended the most brilliant rockets: presently the walls disclosed all the rarest and most complicated ornaments of which the art is susceptible: the senses were next astonished and enchanted with a pacific exhibition of those tremendous instruments of destruction invented by Colonel Congreve. Some notion of their terrible power might be formed from the display of last night, and their exceeding beauty could be contemplated divested of its usual awful associations. Each rocket contains in itself a world of smaller rockets: as soon as it is discharged from the gun [sic], it bursts and flings aloft into the air innumerable parcels of flame, brilliant as the brightest stars: the whole atmosphere is illuminated by a delicate blue light, which threw an air of enchantment over the trees and lawns, and made even the motley groups of universal London become interesting as an assembly in romance. These several smaller rockets then burst again, and a shower of fiery light descends to the earth, and extends over many yards. Such was one of the beautiful fire-works which, during the space of two hours, amused and astonished the people. But the public, who had

been on their legs all day, and were not sufficiently accommodated
with seats, began at length to be tired with the endless repetition even
of the most striking beauties, and became impatient . . .

There was more celebration with and of rockets, with fireworks
and a musical celebration of rockets as well, and this came from
the pen of a distant relative of Arthur Wellesley, who was, we
must recall, born Arthur Wesley.

Samuel Wesley was one of the famous religious Wesleys, the son
of Charles Wesley and the nephew of John Wesley. Where the
elder Wesleys preached and Charles also wrote hymns (more than
5500 of them!), Samuel Wesley was an organist and composer.
Arthur Wesley's father, Lord Mornington, was a professor of
music in Dublin, and he met Samuel as a child, though it seems
Arthur never did so, as the two family branches were not close.

By the time of the battle of Seringapatam, Arthur's older
brother Richard, who had inherited the title, was looking to
move up in the world, and elected to change the family's name
to the more antique form of Wellesley. Richard was made Baron
Wellesley in 1797, and was appointed as Governor-General of
India. Arthur was advised by his brother of the change in the
family's name just before the battle, and so won his first major
victory in new plumage.

There is at least a hint in the records that the name change
was in part to distinguish the descendants of Lord Mornington
from the 'Methodists', as the Wesleys and their followers were
known, but whatever the reason, it happened. Distant cousin
Samuel Wesley would write a number of compositions related to
the Duke, including 'The Siege of Badajoz' and later, a 'Waterloo
Battle Song', but that lay in the future.

Samuel kicked over the traces in a number of ways, so far as
his Methodist family was concerned. He became what was then

termed a 'Roman Catholic', he fathered a son out of wedlock, the famous nineteenth-century organist Samuel Sebastian Wesley (whose second name, of course, was for J. S. Bach), he generally irritated his family and had to live in part by his pen, and in part by performances. Samuel was a passable composer, and his works can be found today in the company of other known but lesser composers like Clementi, Dussek and John Field. But while his classical pieces might please the academics, the real money came from compositions that could be played in drawing rooms.

In the days before radio or gramophone, people had to make their own music, and were forever looking for new works to play. Some would prefer technical brilliance, but most would go for something that allowed the player to appear more brilliant. There was money in generating stuff like that, and many composers did quite well that way, even as the academics turned up their noses. Thekla Badarzewska was born the year after Samuel died, and she took a real pounding, almost a century after she died, when Percy Scholes described her output:

> Born in Warsaw in 1838 and died there in 1861, aged twenty-three. In this brief lifetime she accomplished, perhaps, more than any composer who ever lived, for she provided the piano of absolutely every tasteless sentimental person in the so-called civilized world with a piece of music which that person, however unaccomplished in a dull technical sense, could play.
>
> Percy Scholes, *The Oxford Companion to Music*, 9th edn, 1955

An earlier victim to this robust school of musical criticism, Samuel Wesley fared little better when Hodsoll brought out 'The Skyrocket, a new Jubilee Waltz for the Pianoforte; composed and inscribed to Colonel Congreve', by Samuel Wesley. In September 1814, the *Gentleman's Magazine* offered something of a backhanded review:

It is certain that the ingenious Colonel has been more successful in sky-rockets than the composer. It is lamentable that this very learned musician should not find it more advantageous to employ his distinguished talents on their proper objects than in unmeaning trifles, like the present, that do him no credit. But to the generality, wealth is preferable to fame; and *il n'ya rien de tel pour se défaire de sa marchandise, que de savoir tourner au gré de l'acheteur*. This waltz will amuse those who are partial to the easy trick of sliding the fingers up the keys of the instrument. In these slides, we find consecutive perfect fifths, which some composers would avoid; they are, however, very inoffensive. In Mr. Wesley's trifles there is always harmony, never sentiment-expression. For the sake of young organists, we wish he would continue his organ voluntaries, abandoning trifles to composers of inferior knowledge.

Samuel Wesley had earlier shown a sort of general awareness of rockets. In an 1809 letter to Benjamin Jacob, he writes of a performance in Tamworth near Birmingham:

> The Choruses went off *spank*, slap bang, like a Cannon, or Mr Congreve's Rockets. Notwithstanding I sat at a great Disadvantage, for the New Choir Organ completely obstructed all Possibility of seeing any Part of the Orchestra but a Violin or two on my right & left Wing, so we were obliged to have a Mirror in Order that I might see Frank Cramer . . .

Wesley's works are rarely heard of today, but on the other side of the Atlantic, a rather earnest young lawyer was soon to write a rather ordinary poem mentioning rockets that, set to an old English drinking tune, is today one of the world's better-recognised national anthems. The tune probably lacked the elegance of Wesley's waltz, but it worked to keep rockets in the American people's memory and imagination.

# 5

# THE ROCKETS' RED GLARE

Oh, say can you see, by the dawn's early light,
What so proudly we hailed at the twilight's last gleaming,
Whose broad stripes and bright stars, through the perilous fight,
O'er the ramparts we watched were so gallantly streaming?
And the rockets' red glare, the bombs bursting in air,
Gave proof thro' the night that our flag was still there.
Oh, say, does that star-spangled banner yet wave
O'er the land of the free and the home of the brave!

Francis Scott Key, The Star-Spangled Banner, 1814

No history of rockets could be complete without the story of the only rockets to gain a place in a national anthem. In the War of 1812 (it ran from 1812 to 1814), the British made highly effective use of rockets against the generally untrained militia that they confronted, close to the port of Baltimore.

Whatever else you might say about George Calvert, the first Baron Baltimore, he demonstrated an exquisite sense of timing when he organised to leave Ireland for America in the 1620s. Calvert was a Yorkshireman who took his title from Baltimore

House in County Leitrim, not from the fishing hamlet on one of the most south-westerly points of Ireland, but there are some curious parallels between the two ports called Baltimore.

Ireland's Baltimore was a nest of English pirates. Just as the baron was finalising a land grant in what was to become Maryland, trouble hit the small West Cork town, which had just a couple of hundred residents and 47 cottages. The tiny port gave shelter to small boats, but even though there were (and are) castle remnants there, the town had no real defences.

Algerian pirates came in the night on 20 June 1631, seizing 107 townsfolk, taking them off into slavery. It was pretty much the end of the first Baltimore, as the remaining English settlers withdrew to Skibbereen, a more easily defended area about 10 kilometres away, and hopefully safer from sea raiders. There, they established a Protestant centre for oppression of the Catholic Irish, while remaining safe from the oppression of being enslaved by corsairs.

Baron Baltimore was an English Catholic who would never have been acceptable in Ireland's Baltimore. Part of the attraction of the Americas was no doubt to get further away from religious intolerance, but he died before he could actually take up his new grant. That mattered little, since the second Baron, his son, found that the patent passed to him, and so a new Baltimore was founded in the colony of Maryland, far across the ocean, and far better defended by geography than the little town in West Cork.

There was a cheerful viciousness in the religious relations of West Cork. Bandon, a ferociously Protestant walled town close to Baltimore, had a sign over the gate: 'Turk, Jew or atheist may enter here, but not a papist'. A Catholic wit is said to have retorted: 'He who wrote this wrote it well, the same is written on the gates of hell'. All in all, Ireland seemed no more and no less religiously advanced then than some parts of it are today.

Maryland was to be different. To help make it so, a list of words not to be used about those of other religions was set out in the *Maryland Toleration Act* of 1649. Here, in the original spelling, are some of the forbidden terms: 'heritick, scismatick, idolator, puritan, independant, Presbiterian popish prest, Jesuite, Jesuited papist, Lutheran, Calvenist, Anabaptist, Brownist, Antinomian, Barrowist, Roundhead, Separatist, or any other name or terme in a reproachfull manner relating to matter of religion'.

Many of these words have entirely lost their sting, but would legislators today be willing to provide a checklist of useful pejoratives to hurl at opponents? Still, if Maryland was to be a place of greater religious tolerance, it was also to be a great place of maritime trade, and that brought mercantile intolerance, but so long as people were making a profit they tolerated competitors, and when they were taking a loss their intolerance was directed at the outside forces that caused the loss.

By the early nineteenth century, the behaviour of the British was arousing the wrath of Baltimore merchants and sailors. In large part, it was the fault of the British, who controlled the world's sea lanes after their victory at Trafalgar in 1805, but we need to look at power balances and trade to see why the folk of Baltimore felt so aggrieved.

In 1812, Baltimore was the third largest city in the United States, riding a boom that centred on shipping and shipbuilding—it was the home of the remarkable Baltimore clipper. Napoleon controlled most of Europe and, with only Britain standing against his tyranny, tried to cut off Britain's trade by the Continental System. This was a bold plan to deny Britain access to trade anywhere in Europe, because without trade, Napoleon thought, the 'nation of shopkeepers' would crumble.

There was, however, a third and smaller national interest involved, one that perhaps did not see itself as a power yet, but one that had some degree of kind feelings, and some less kind feelings, to each of the major powers. This was the fledgling United States.

France had supported the Americans in the revolution of 1775–83, but Britain and America had blood ties and the link of language. French privateers taking American merchant ships provoked a quasi-war between 1798 and 1800. British vessels were in the habit of stopping and searching American merchant vessels, to 'press' crew and, all too often, to capture the ships, even though they were neutral vessels sailing to and from neutral ports. They also outraged American sentiment by seizing several deserters from the frigate *Chesapeake* in 1807. American sailors were killed, and one of the deserters was later hanged, which infuriated the American public.

More to the point, Britain issued Orders in Council that banned all trade with Napoleon's empire other than on Britain's terms. It was something of a standoff, with Britain controlling the seas and Napoleon the land, but there were gaps in Spain and in Russia, which explains why Napoleon attacked Spain in 1808, sparking the Peninsular war, and Russia in 1812, setting the scene for his eventual defeat. Britain just held on, and the end result was that America bore much of the burden of a war being fought out on the other side of the ocean, a month or more's sailing time away.

While patriotic fury about a few hangings will not always ignite wars, economic loss commonly will, and a combination of Jeffersonian bungling and British blockading and ship seizures placed the costs squarely on sailors and shipowners alike. So when the War of 1812 broke out, the merchants and sailors of Baltimore were only too happy to take to sea, now carrying letters of marque as privateers, to prey on British shipping. As 1813 slipped into 1814, they harried the western approaches to the British Isles, and Glasgow merchants complained of losing 800 ships in two years to the Americans.

Mercantile intolerance was alive and well and living in Baltimore, well-protected by the long run up Chesapeake Bay and by fortifications and booms. So long as Britain was busy dealing with the Corsican upstart, the folk of Baltimore had an easy time of it, but in 1814, the day of reckoning arrived. Britain now had battle-hardened troops and a battle-hardened navy ready to deal with the colonial upstarts, to show them what sort of harvest mercantile intolerance reaped.

In London, *The Times* thundered in an editorial for the parricidal Americans to be punished for their ungrateful attacks on Britain when she was at war; it was the government's intention, declared Wellington, 'to give Jonathan a good drubbing'. As it has largely disappeared from the language, it may be worth noting that 'Jonathan' meant 'the Americans'.

Where Arthur Wellesley had feared setting fire to towns in Spain, his compatriots had no such qualms in America. Moreover, the Iron Duke, with his dislike of rockets, was nowhere to be seen. As the British land forces approached Baltimore, General Robert Ross was cut down by what is usually called a stray shot from a final American volley as the defenders retreated. In fact an officer, any officer, on a horse, would make a tempting target for a backwoods rifleman, and while many later claimed to have been aiming at him, London's *Morning Post* saw it as another damn Yankee trick, referring to 'the assassin-like manoeuvre of *marking their man*, under the security of their impenetrable forests'. It was thought to be typical of the colonials that they would not stand and be shot at like well-trained soldiery.

Ross's men commandeered a rocket wagon to carry him back to the British fleet, but Ross would have none of it, saying that he would not deprive his men of a weapon so important to their success. In the end, he was carried back on a farm cart, but died before he reached the beach. The rockets went forward.

Ross was not alone in his views. The British expectation (out of earshot of the Iron Duke) of rockets on the battlefield is perhaps best summed up by Rifleman Harris, who also saw action against the Danes at Copenhagen. Later, as a London shoe-maker, he told his story to Henry Curling, who seems to have faithfully recorded his words about Copenhagen:

> I rather think this was the first time of Congreve rockets being brought into play, and as they rushed through the air in the dark, they appeared like so many fiery serpents, creating, I should think, terrible dismay among the besieged.
>
> 'John Harris, *The Recollections of Rifleman Harris*, 1848'

Of course, Harris was wrong there, in that he was unaware of, or had forgotten, the earlier trial at Boulogne, but he knew well what caused deaths on the battlefield, at least from his perspective, having served in the same areas as Wellington. Here he speaks of cannon balls:

> Indeed we caught it severely just here, and the old iron was also playing its part amongst our poor fellows very merrily. I saw a man named Symmonds struck full in the face by a round shot, and he came to the ground a headless trunk. Meanwhile, many large balls bounded along the ground amongst us so deliberately that we could occasionally evade them without difficulty.
>
> John Harris, *The Recollections of Rifleman Harris*, 1848

Among disciplined troops, fighting in the proper way in tight formations where they made nice targets, cannon seemed to have it all over rockets, but that was largely a matter of perception, and troops in the field sometimes saw it differently. Sergeant Morris later recalled the little-known Battle of Göhrde in Hanover, where Hanoverians, Swedes, Russians, Britain's 73rd Regiment and half a British rocket battery defeated a French army, taking 15 000 prisoners and killing about 2000, just a month before the far greater victory at Leipzig, at the Battle of the Nations. Even so, rockets had a part to play in this battle as well, and Morris takes up the story as some of the French units began to break and run:

> The square of French infantry on the left . . . were still firm; but there happened to be two or three of the Rocket Brigade in the field, and the first rocket fired, fell directly in the square, putting them in the greatest confusion; and while they were so, the German Hussars, who had been previously repulsed, charged them again, and influenced by feelings of revenge, cut among them, right and left, giving no quarter.
>
> Thomas Morris, *The Recollections of Sergeant Morris*, 1845

When it came to cowardly colonials, hiding behind trees and generally skulking about, cannon and muskets might not be able to get at them, but rockets were the thing to instil some fear into them. That was what the British believed, and it certainly seemed to hold true at Bladensburg in 1814. At that battle, untrained militia were more than a little disturbed by the noise that the rockets made and they fled, leaving the road to Washington open. Rockets were something new, something they had not experienced before, but the effect did not always last. Lieutenant Gleig is often quoted as saying of Bladensburg that 'never have men with arms in their hands made such good use of their legs'. It is a pretty line, which probably explains why it is so often repeated, but I have not so far been able to locate it in any of his books.

Captain Mercer of the Royal Horse Artillery described the rockets he saw a little earlier in France, showing how rockets could be a problem for both sides:

> . . . the Rocketeers had placed a little iron triangle in the road with a rocket lying on it. The order to fire is given—a port-fire applied—the fidgety missile begins to sputter out sparks and wiggle its tail for a second or so, and then darts forth straight up the chausee [sic]. A gun stands right in its way, between the wheels of which the shell in the head of the rocket bursts, the gunners fall right and left, and, those of the other guns taking to their heels, the battery is deserted in an instant. Strange; but so it was. I saw them run, and for some minutes afterwards I saw the guns standing mute and unmanned, whilst our rocketeers kept shooting off rockets, none of which ever followed the course of the first: most of them, on arriving about the middle of the ascent, took a vertical direction, whilst some actually turned back upon ourselves—and one of these, following me like a squib until its shell exploded, actually put me in more danger than all the fire of the enemy throughout the day.
>
> Cavalié Mercer, *Journal of the Waterloo Campaign*, 1870

After a while, the French noticed the rockets' erratic paths, and so returned to their guns and opened fire again. With time, the French became less fearful, because some of the veterans had seen it all before. As Lieutenant Gillmor wrote in 1810:

> At 7 o'clock Lieutenant Lindsay of the Artillery began to throw Congreve's rockets into Santarem; forty-two let off, about four fell in the town; four burst among ourselves; the French seemed to treat us with great contempt . . . I have a very poor opinion of Congreve's rockets; they can't be thrown with the precision of shells.
>
> Lieutenant C. Gillmor, RN, *Diary*

In 1814, however, the American troops had yet to develop this contempt for the new weapons, although it would not be long coming. The good folk of Baltimore, on the other hand, feared dreadfully the use of rockets against their town, and in the sort of economic warfare then being waged they may well have been right to do so. The Baltimore *Telegraph* advised its readers; 'Should Congreve rockets be thrown into the city, we should recommend to every householder to have a servant ready with buckets of water to extinguish the flames', by then knowing from eye-witnesses how rockets could be used in a town. Michael Shiner, being black, had been left alone by the British in Washington, and he reported how the troops fired their Congreve rockets into the houses: beams and rafters went flying in all directions, he said. Then came the attempt to fire that symbol of rebellion, the Capitol building, which began badly when the British fired rockets into the roof, which was covered with sheet iron. Next, they made a high pile of the mahogany chairs, desks and tables, added some rocket powder, and fired more rockets into the heap, and did this also in the Senate wing. They left, satisfied that the rebellious Congress would not be sitting here again.

A building, especially one packed with piled furniture and incendiaries, is an easy target for Congreve rockets, but a well-constructed fort is another matter. Good forts have only one large collection of flammable material, the magazine where gunpowder is stored, and Baltimore's Fort McHenry remains, even today, an excellent example of an early nineteenth-century defensive structure. There was no way that rockets or cannonballs could be a great threat to the fort, but the fort was a threat to the British land attack on Baltimore, and it had to be taken.

Captain Lord Cochrane had tried rockets against the French fleet in the Basque Roads, a sheltered space east of the Ile d'Oléron, in 1809. On that occasion, he found the rockets almost as dangerous to his own shipping as to the enemy. Now, as Vice-Admiral Lord Cochrane, he had access to bomb vessels that could

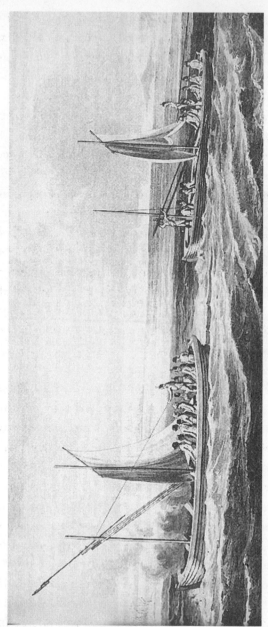

*Rockets could be launched with ease from surprisingly small boats and proved effective in coastal assaults.*

sit at long range and rain down punishment on the fort. If damage was to be done to the fort, it was mortar bombs from those vessels that would do it. If the fort could be taken, Baltimore would fall, and with it, perhaps, the United States of America.

'Bombs', as these special ships were called, were short, stubby and ungainly, but immensely strong. They typically had two main 'guns', a 10-inch and a 13-inch mortar, and they lobbed a bombshell that weighed as much as 200 pounds in a high arc over a range of 4200 yards, some two and a half miles. The ship had a system of beams and springs to absorb some of the tremendous recoil, but still the whole vessel would buck and plunge when one of the guns was fired from the special mount in the bows.

As the mortar fired, a fuse was lit by the flame of the explosion that launched it: trimmed to a suitable length, the fuse would set off the bomb just as it landed. Their main advantage was that they delivered a plunging shot that could get over walls and wreak havoc behind otherwise impregnable defences. The mortar bombs could also pierce a roof that a cannonball would just bounce off.

The bomb vessels were also designed for the safe launching of rockets that could light fires if they hit flammable material, or kill soldiers if they scattered grapeshot, although this would be a matter of luck, not of good aim. In a battle, luck was always worth looking for with grapeshot rockets; in an attack on a fort, the main effect was to unnerve the defenders. Today, we only hear about the rockets used in the 1814 campaign because they are mentioned in the first verse of the American national anthem. In spite of that fame, their military impact was almost non-existent.

The real risk at Fort McHenry was the magazine where the powder was stored. The roof was weak, too weak to withstand the blow of 200 pounds of iron and powder plummeting down from a great height. In time, the inevitable happened and a shell crashed through the roof to lie, its fuse sputtering towards a greater glory, until somebody dowsed it and saved the day. Major Armistead, the commanding officer, ordered the magazine to be cleared, with the powder barrels dispersed about the courtyard under the rear walls, arguing that it was better to have one or two barrels of powder go up than lose the whole lot. The rockets might now have come into their own, if they had made a lucky hit, but it was not to be.

According to Commodore Rodgers, an American naval officer and one of the heroes of the action in the area, some 1800 or 2000 bombshells (Major Armistead put the number a bit lower) were thrown at Fort McHenry, along with some 700 or 800 rockets, but the fort survived. The point of the poem that Francis Scott Key scribbled so soon afterward is that during the night, he and several other Americans, isolated on a truce ship, knew the fort was still holding out, because the attackers kept firing. They were too far away to see the action, but the glare of the rockets and the bursting bombs told them the truth.

Then, by the dawn's early light, they could see that the flag was still there—and even for a non-American, there is something special about the way the National Parks Service reveals this to visitors. You sit through a neat little exposition on screen, presented by an actor in costume, and then a curtain pulls back, and you see the modern flag that still flies over the fort. It is a cleverly contrived piece of emotional play.

The flag would have been taken down at night, but on the morning of 14 September the American troops hoisted their somewhat tattered flag, fired off a morning gun, and the band played 'Yankee Doodle'. The British army and navy withdrew, sailed to Jamaica to gather reinforcements to attack New Orleans, and were finally defeated.

Fort McHenry was almost the rocket's last gasp in the War of 1812. By the time of the battle of New Orleans, Andrew Jackson knew how to draw their teeth. 'Don't mind those rockets, they're mere toys to amuse children,' the general told his men. More dangerous, in fact, were the signal rockets used to coordinate the British attacks. The end had come for war rockets on the American mainland for some years. Skyrockets flew in Washington to celebrate ratification of the Treaty of Ghent that ended the War of 1812, and Americans would use rockets to celebrate their nation's birthday, but war rockets would be few and far between.

Even if the Duke was not celebrating rockets very much in 1814, everybody else was, and before long Napoleon escaped from Elba and had to be beaten all over again. This time, rockets were set to be part of the fray, come what may, but still Wellington tried to avoid using them. Rockets, he said, were still unreliable and skittish, prone to dash off in all directions at once, and even to turn and fly back at those launching them. Tradition has it that the officer who commanded the Rocket troop in Belgium was ordered by Wellington to equip his troop with 6-pounder cannon to replace the rockets.

When Lieutenant-Colonel George Wood, of the Royal Artillery in Belgium, said to Wellington, 'It will break Whinyates' heart to lose his rockets,' Wellington answered, 'Damn his heart; let my order be obeyed.' In the end, though, Wellington allowed Whinyates to take 800 rounds of 12-pounder rockets as well as the guns, and they seem to have had some useful effect. Sir Edward Whinyates, KCB, by the way, died a Lieutenant-General in 1866, and his obituary mentions that he served in the Copenhagen campaign, which must be where he was converted to rockets.

One curious point: it rained the night before the battle of Waterloo, and Napoleon waited till close on noon before starting the engagement, so the ground would be drier for the artillery to manoeuvre. In the end he ran out of time, with Blücher's troops arriving on the battlefield, and so he lost. If he had started earlier, he might have defeated the British, and then have been able to defeat the weary and footsore Prussians—and he could have started earlier if his heavy artillery had been replaced by rocket brigades, and rockets could have sought out the British troops, sheltering behind a convenient rise.

Napoleon, an artillery officer by training, would probably not have accepted rockets in any case, but that probably did not matter too much. Even if he had won the battle, he was still in no position to win a war. All we can say is that neither commander saw much value in rockets on the battlefield.

In the end, the Iron Duke appears to have been done a favour by a rocket, though this particular device was George Stephenson's railway locomotive of that name, rather than one of Congreve's artefacts. A prickly member of the Tory party who was withholding support for the Duke, now leader of the Conservative Party and Prime Minister, was persuaded, as locomotives operated for the first time on the Liverpool–Manchester railway in 1830, to seek a rapprochement with the even more prickly Wellington.

The opening was a grand occasion, and all the important people were there, even Charles Babbage, father of Herschel Babbage. The trainload of passengers, drawn by a locomotive called *Northumbrian*, was stopped as *Rocket* came up on the other line, when the recalcitrant member moved towards the Iron Duke's carriage.

This was William Huskisson, whom we met earlier, and he

was what we would now call a 'wet' within the Tories. He had earlier offered his resignation from the ministry over a matter of principle, and the Duke, who saw even reasoned opposition in his Cabinet as overt mutiny, had accepted the resignation, but now, hoped the party power-brokers, peace might break out, strengthening the tottering government. Given the characters of the two men, however, any peace would have been unlikely to last. As Stephenson's *Rocket* approached on the parallel line, Huskisson dithered, and was horribly and, in the end, fatally injured when he fell back in the path of the oncoming locomotive.

While this removal of a difficult rival might be considered to have been to the Duke's advantage, he lost office less than a month later. If Huskisson had survived, he might well have led the Canningite faction back into support of Wellington, and saved the government. The Duke may have had to make some concessions, but he would have held on to power. As it was, he ceased to hold the office of prime minister, and so may well be said to have been unseated by Stephenson's *Rocket*. Not everybody lost out—the new government gave handsome support to Charles Babbage and his difference engine. The following year, rockets were used by the Royal Navy when the port of Algiers was attacked and many ships were destroyed, but thinking in the armed forces was moving towards a greater emphasis on guns.

Alexander Forsyth had invented mercuric fulminate caps for cannon in 1799. Mercuric fulminate is a chemical which can be ignited by a blow, setting off the gunpowder and thus making guns more reliable. Soon the same system was applied to rockets. We first see fulminate caps in rockets when Congreve and Lieutenant James Colquhoun of the Royal Artillery set out a broad claim for the rocket harpoon in Patent 4563, called 'Application of Rockets to the Destruction and Capture of Whales &C',

writing: '. . . We do not limit ourselves to the use of any particular form of rocket, but secure to ourselves the right of using the projectile commonly called the rocket in the destruction and capture of the whale and other animals . . .'

The rocket harpoon was successfully used in 1821, fired from a shoulder-held tube-launcher which used a fulminate charge to light the rocket. The charge flashed flame behind the rocket and ignited it, sending the rocket plunging into the whale. The rocket-launcher had a circular blast shield to protect the operator, and the fulminate ignition meant rockets could be launched even in rain and spray.

Captain Scoresby Senior, as he was called, took Lieutenant Colquhoun and two gunners on a whaling expedition on *Fame*, a Whitby whaler, to train the crew in the use of the rocket harpoon. His son, known unimaginatively but predictably as Captain Scoresby Junior, and later a clergyman-scientist and Fellow of the Royal Society, took out another inventor of a gun harpoon and rocket life-saving apparatus, George Manby, in the Liverpool whaler *Baffin*. It appears that Manby had come up with an explosive device of some sort to use in the harpoon head, but details are not to be had.

*Fame* arrived back in port on 21 September, and reported killing nine whales and a finner with their rocket apparatus. All were dead in less than fifteen minutes, and five of them took out no line at all, indicating an instant kill. The finner, notes that indefatigable naval historian Basil Lubbock, was a species so swift, and with such a poor yield of oil and bone, that it was normally not hunted. Even that, though, did not guarantee rockets a place in the armoury of the whalers. There seems to be no extant record of Manby's successes or otherwise, but the rocket trials were acclaimed by *The Times* in an editorial on 8 October, 1821:

> The peculiar value and importance of the rocket in the fisheries is, that by means of it, all the destructive effects of a six or even a twelve pounder piece of artillery, both as to penetration, explosion, force, and internal fire, calculated to accelerate the death of the animal, may be given with an apparatus not heavier than a musket, and without any shock or re-action on the boat; whereas it is obvious that no boat applicable to the fishery of the whale can ever be made capable of sustaining the shock necessary to produce the same, or anything like the effects of the six or twelve pound shell, by the ordinary means of artillery.

Rockets found one more unexpected use in the peaceful years that followed the Napoleonic Wars. In 1825, Captain Edward Sabine was appointed as a joint commissioner with Sir John Herschel to act with a French government commission to find the precise difference in longitude between the Paris and Greenwich (London) observatories. They effected this by an unspecified method relying on rockets, possibly using rockets to link the triangulation grids of Britain and France across the English Channel, as that was certainly achieved at about this time.

The difference between the two observatories is normally reported, following the *Dictionary of National Biography*, as 9 minutes and 21.6 seconds—in fact, there is a gap of more than two degrees of longitude between the two, which is equivalent to a time difference of 9 minutes and 21.6 seconds between local noon in each place. This remarkably precise result was later amended to 9 minutes and 21 seconds, equal to a shift in the distance of about 30 feet, or ten metres.

Curiously, Charles Babbage attacked Sabine in 1830, making it fairly clear that he regarded some of Sabine's observations in the period around 1827 as more than a little suspect. The results were too good, he said:

> The remarkable agreement with each other, which was found to exist amongst each class of observations, was as unexpected by those most

conversant with the respective processes, as it was creditable to one who had devoted but a few years to the subject, and who, in the course of those voyages, used some of the instruments for the first time in his life.

This accordance amongst the results was such, that naval officers of the greatest experience, confessed themselves unable to take such lunars; whilst other observers, long versed in the use of the transit instrument, avowed their inability to take such transits. Those who were conversant with pendulums, were at a loss how to make, even under more favourable circumstances, similarly concordant observations. The same opinion prevailed on the continent as well as in England. On whatever subject Captain Sabine touched, the observations he published seemed by their accuracy to leave former observers at a distance. The methods of using the instruments scarcely differed in any important point from those before adopted; and, but for a fortunate discovery, which I shall presently relate, the world must have concluded that Captain Sabine possessed some keenness of vision, or acuteness of touch, which it would be hopeless for any to expect to rival.

Charles Babbage, *Reflections on the Decline of Science in England*, 1830

There is more to this story of in-fighting and scientific intrigue, but it has little to do with rockets, so we must leave it for another day. In fairness to Sabine's good name, he ended up knighted, a major-general, and several times president of the Royal Society, not at all what one would expect if he had in fact falsified his data.

In the mean time, rockets had become accepted and well-known items, seen as more injurious to the enemy than not, as Byron showed in *Don Juan* when he contrasted the destructive rockets with gentle, kind vaccination against smallpox in the first canto, verse CXXIX:

What opposite discoveries we have seen!
(Signs of true genius, and of empty pockets.)

One makes new noses, one a guillotine,

One breaks your bones, one sets them in their sockets;

But vaccination certainly has been

A kind antithesis to Congreve's rockets,

With which the Doctor paid off an old pox,

By borrowing a new one from an ox.

# 6
# AFTER WATERLOO

A selection of artificers and persons conversant in the management of the Congreve rockets, took place at the royal arsenal at Woolwich, previous to those formidable weapons being sent to the presidencies in India, and they are now on their voyage thither. The expenses, it is said, will wholly be defrayed by the East India Company.

*The Times*, 24 January 1816

Every Rocket is fitted with a fuze, screwed into the base of the shell. The fuze is as long as the size of the shell will admit of, so as to leave sufficient space between the end of it and the inner surface of the shell, for putting in the bursting powder; and the end of the fuze is cupped, to serve as a guide in the insertion of the boring bit.

James Cockburn, *Memoir on the Preparation and Use of Rockets*, 1844

After Congreve died in 1828, rockets and the rocket system remained a standard part of the British armed forces, as a little pamphlet, carefully bound in board covers and tucked away in Sydney's Mitchell Library, revealed to me one day when minor flooding drove me from my usual haunts in the more modern wing of the State Library. Chance and curiosity led me to the venerable card catalogue, and so I found how in 1844, James

Cockburn, Director of the Royal Laboratory, set out in careful detail the manner of use of the new form of rockets, where rocketeers would work to precise instructions, because warfare was now part of the new Industrial Age.

Annoyingly, Cockburn is writing for an informed audience of military people, so a number of the technical points of rocketry are assumed, but there is enough there to fill us in, as we can see in the passage at the head of this chapter. Just to clarify, though, the 'boring bit' was a drill bit made of spark-free brass, used to bore a hole in the fuse. In the absence of this device, there would have been many boring bits of rocketeer around the scenery as they became, in an instant, men of many parts, but the boring bit was essential if the fuse was to burn out at the right time.

Later information detailing the extent of the boring and the elevation required to achieve bursts at different ranges suggests that: the idea was to bore out the 'fuze', so that it burned quickly up to that point, and then more slowly, so a 24-pounder would burst at 3300 yards if launched at an angle of 47° with an unbored fuse, but at 2000 yards with the whole of the fuse bored out, when launched at an elevation of 27°.

A 12-pounder rocket with a whole fuse would burst at 3000 yards when launched at 40°, while a 6-pounder with a whole fuse would burst at 2300 yards on a 37° elevation, and a whole fuse 3-pounder would burst at 1800 yards from an elevation of 25°. The same rockets, with their fuses fully bored, would burst at shorter ranges on lesser elevations. These are samples of a much larger table, and each rocket kit came with a boring gauge to allow rocketeers to prepare their rockets to burst at the required range. There was one gauge for 24- and 12-pounders, and a second for 6- and 3-pounders, he explained.

Now it might seem that boring into a powder-filled fuse

with a metal bit would be a bit risky, but the last point before Cockburn's signature is the advice: 'N.B. The boring bit should always be greased'. But then, some sage quartermasterly advice is appended in italics: *'Demands for Rockets had best be made by the gross, or by dozens, on account of convenience of packing'*.

The other thing that becomes clear is that rockets were now being used as explosive shells, or as projectiles:

> If the Rocket is to be used as a Shot Rocket, the only thing to be attended to, is to take care that there is no powder in the shell, and that the plug is secured in the plug hole.
>
> If the Rocket is to be used as a Shell Rocket, at the longest range, the plug is to be taken out and the shell filled, the fuze left at its full length, and the plug replaced.
>
> If at the shortest range, the fuze is to be entirely bored through, and the rocket composition bored into . . . The distances from the surface of the shell to the top of the cone, and from the surface of the shell to the end of the fuze, and also the length of the fuze, being fixed and known, the place on the boring bit at which to screw the stopper . . . is easily determined; these distances are marked on the brass scales for each nature of Rocket.

Nothing was left to chance, everything was entirely systematic: 'In Field service, the bursters are to be carried in the limber boxes, in cartouches similar to those in which the Field ammunition is carried . . . In mountain equipments, the bursters and small stores in a box fitted to the pack-saddle'. It is also clear that rockets were supplied by Cockburn's laboratory to the navy: 'For Her Majesty's Ships of War the bursters will be issued in numbers corresponding to the established number of Rockets, in the metal lined cases of the Service, and the small stores in a box made for the purpose'. The small stores included funnels, a boring stock and boring bits to set the fuse, a special brass scale to gauge the depth to be bored, turnscrew bits and a grease box.

In the British Army and Navy, everything was completely planned and perfectly controlled.

Rockets appear to have been part of the normal equipment on HMS *Beagle*. In his *Voyage of the Beagle*, Charles Darwin mentions how he was told in 1833 of rockets having been used on a previous voyage of the ship to discourage people from Tierra del Fuego who threatened the explorers and fired arrows at them.

> During the former voyage the Fuegians were here very troublesome, and to frighten them a rocket was fired at night over their wigwams; it answered effectually, and one of the officers told me that the clamour first raised, and the barking of the dogs, was quite ludicrous in contrast with the profound silence which in a minute or two afterwards prevailed. The next morning not a single Fuegian was in the neighbourhood.
>
> Charles Darwin, *Voyage of the* Beagle, 1845

In 1835, when *Beagle* was visiting Tahiti, rockets were used, but not to frighten the locals, instead, to put on a show for a sophisticated people far more used to what the Europeans could do. After *Beagle* returned Darwin to England, she sailed again in early 1837 for Australian waters, where her crew's task was to map the northern shores of the continent. They were still there in 1838, charting the tropical north of Western Australia and having trouble with the local inhabitants, when, as Marsden Hordern reports, the commander, John Wickham, 'decided that the time had come to get rid of them, and waiting until dark, fired a Congreve rocket over the camp'.

So while rockets remained standard equipment on ships, they had largely disappeared from the battlefield when the British army went to war, but this was not the case in much of the rest of Europe. A Russian officer named Alexander Zasyadko adopted the British model in 1815, and the Russian military formed their first rocket company in 1826, attached to the St Petersburg Rocket Works. In 1828, under Zasyadko's guidance, Russia used warhead rockets with occasional success against the Turks.

Zasyadko, like other officers from continental Europe, seems to have recognised the off-road capabilities of rockets. On broken ground, soggy ground and in mountainous terrain, rockets had a tremendous advantage over heavy guns because they did not require the same haulage. A soldier might carry a single charge of powder and a cannonball, or a single rocket, but a gun required the combined efforts of animals needing feeding to transport it, and quite possibly a whole company of infantry to drag it into firing position. All it took to launch a rocket was a light framework, and even that could be improvised at a pinch.

The Russians took to the rockets happily, and used them for some years in a number of small wars and skirmishes against the Turks until once again, their use began to fade away. Although they left little more behind than a memory, it was later enough to give impetus to a Russian rocket industry in the 1930s and 1940s.

Austria was in the game at an early stage, producing rockets in 1808, but serious Austrian rocketry only began after Baron Vincenz von Augustin saw rockets in action at the Battle of Leipzig. A major of artillery, Augustin advocated pursuing the use of rockets, and this was agreed to. In 1814 he went to Holland and to London on a diplomatic mission, and saw Congreve's rockets demonstrated at Woolwich Arsenal.

The British were keeping their secrets to themselves, and Augustin was only able to gather information by visiting the Danes, then the only other nation making rockets. Allowed to visit under strict secrecy conditions, by March 1815 he was back in Vienna, with a war rocket establishment being created at

Wiener-Neustadt, south of the capital. By the end of May, the first rocket battery joined the military service, just in time to be used at the siege of Huningue, one of the last battles of the Napoleonic wars.

By 1817, Augustin had risen to lieutenant-colonel, and was commandant of what was now the delightfully named *Feuerwerks-Corps*, or Fireworks Corps. Frank Winter, who has researched the period, reports that the Austrians, like the Danes, considered their rockets to be better than the Congreves.

The Austrian Empire was immense, and had regular problems with restless subjects: Italians, Hungarians, Poles, people from the Balkans and more. In 1821, the perfected rockets were used in Naples, a hilly area where they really came into their own. During the 1820s, an Austrian ship used incendiary rockets against a Moroccan city generally referred to as Meknes —but this must be an error unless there was a small port of the same name as the inland city—in order to punish the Rif pirates, Muslim corsairs who preyed on shipping in the western Mediterranean.

By 1831 Augustin was a major-general, and in 1838 he was appointed field-marshal-lieutenant and with each advance he was able to enhance his precious *Kriegs-Raketen-Anstalt*, or War Rocket Establishment. The technology spread, directly or indirectly, to Sweden, Poland, Prussia, Switzerland—and even Hungary, where the Hungarian revolution and war of independence in 1848–49 tapped into the skills of Hungarian craftsmen who had been working in Vienna. While Hungary was no match for the more experienced Austrians, in 1859 the Austrian rockets failed to stem the advances of a combined French and Italian army at Magenta and Solferino. Worse was to come, but Augustin had died by then, and so was spared the pain of seeing his brainchild put down.

*A rocket troop in 1832.*

All the same, he had seen the original pattern vary greatly. In the 1840s, William Hale in England had come up with a stickless rocket. With no stick and no fin, Hale's rocket relied on small sideways jets to give it spin for stability, so his model was shorter and lighter. Hale sold his new style of rocket to the Austrians in 1858, and while they varied the Hale design, his rocket replaced the earlier style. At about the same time, with Augustin out of the way, a new 1.4 kilogram mountain gun was introduced into the rocket batteries in 1863 to supplement the rockets.

By 1864, troops were being transferred out of the rocket force, and by 1866 the mountain-trained Austrian *Raketeurs* proved no match for the Prussians with their new breech-loading needle gun; and this was shown clearly in the flattish lands of Bohemia, where Austria and Prussia again clashed. Two rocket batteries were brought back into action in 1869 to deal with some Dalmatian rebels, but that was just about the last continental gasp of the rockets for two generations. Rifled steel breech-loading guns were what modern armies trained on and used; light, manoeuvrable guns capable of lobbing shells wherever they were needed.

The new guns had a major advantage over rockets: the accuracy provided by an aimed barrel and a carefully measured charge. The Austrian rocket armoury included shrapnel and incendiary, explosive and flare warheads, just as artillery shells would do, but the greater accuracy and comparable rate of firing made guns preferable, at least away from mountains and soft ground. With the armies of Europe testing their weapons on parade-ground-solid fields, rockets were slowly ignored, forgotten, pushed down the order of importance.

But along with their Austrian heyday, rockets still had their uses in the British army, and not only against restless natives. In April 1854, a British-French squadron bombarded Odessa using, among other things, the Royal Navy's 'new rocket-boats' which fired 24-pound missiles from metal pipes. Mrs Fanny Duberly, that tireless recorder of events large and small, makes reference in 1856 to the French having 'rocket-practice', and records that a Captain Keppel believed a two-decker ship had been set on fire in the harbour by a stray French rocket. Contemporary records also indicate that the French took 13 000 rockets to the Crimea, and fired around 5000 of them.

Rockets did not, however, come into the French army without resistance. A 'distinguished artillery officer' had been quoted in *The Times* of 21 October 1816 as having written in *Le Moniteur* that rockets were no great threat: 'Beside, is not the effect of the rocket entirely paralyzed by the separation of the top or chapiter from the body of the rocket; and is not this separation easy with the blow of a sabre?' One might as well ask: cannot bullets be prevented from doing harm by catching them in the teeth? Cannot cannonballs be driven back at the enemy by a skilfully plied five-iron? But our daring and distinguished artillery officer has not finished:

> . . . the Congreve rockets are far from being so dangerous as some affect to say; that they are, on the contrary, much less terrible than bombs, shells and red-hot balls . . . it is with the sole view of enlightening the soldier as to the real effects of the Congreve rockets, and to fortify him against the exaggerated fears with which it may be sought to inspire him in regard to them, that I have thought it right to commit these observations to paper.

Sense prevailed, and the French army acquired rockets. In the Sea of Azov during the Crimean campaign, a French rocket force landed with 600 rockets to cover the landing of the main army, until the combined French, British and Turkish force could get ashore and deploy its conventional artillery. Luck played a part at Sebastopol, when a rocket bounced off a wall, reversed course, and passed through the door of a magazine that contained 32 000 kilograms of powder. The explosion that followed took out a good part of Fort Saint Nicolas.

The Royal Navy appears to have sent boats' crews close inshore with rockets to support landings around the Crimea. This makes sense, because boats under oars are better able than ships under sail to manoeuvre and to avoid reefs and shoals. They can approach the shore more closely, which makes it less likely they will hit the landing craft; in addition, small boats, with their unpredictable movements, make much more difficult targets for any land-based artillery.

There was also the problem that moored ships often could not bring their guns to bear on a target, and, rocked by waves, were profoundly inaccurate. As they were firing roundshot, this could be a problem when the landing craft approached shore, under (and in front of) the guns that were supposed to protect them. Rockets fired from a rocking boat have a good chance of bouncing and ricocheting inland, and will generally be fired from somewhere in front of the advancing forces in any case. After the Crimea, though, this tactic in amphibious attacks was lost from military thinking for three generations.

Somebody (probably junior) in the Royal Navy was thinking, back in 1854, but the British army had a number of forward-thinking officers as well, and when they camped for a while on the territory of their Turkish allies near Gelibolu, or Gallipoli, as they called it, they conceived of a daring plan to be used in time of war against the Turks.

Perhaps Lord Raglan, one of Britain's senior generals, could not remember who was the enemy (he is said to have called a number of times to attack the French), but some of the younger officers were alert to the prospect of a future war in which Britain might change sides and join Russia to fight Turkey. That scenario demanded a 'warm-water port', and that meant sailing up the narrow waters of the Dardanelles and on into the Black Sea.

The classically educated British knew that Xerxes had crossed from Asia into Europe two-and-a-half millennia ago, and a couple of centuries later Alexander the Great had commenced his invasion of Asia by crossing right there, though going the other way. It was an open and shut case, and if it wasn't, then where was the sense in having a classical education?

Strategically, the Dardanelles was the key to taking Istanbul. The key to the Dardanelles was landing troops on the Aegean side of the Gallipoli Peninsula, taking a few casualties, wiping out the Turks while they were reloading, taking the whole width of the Peninsula, and then bringing in some guns and training them on any ship foolish enough to use the waters of the Dardanelles without the conquerors' say-so. At the same time, they would be able to lob shells down on the two Turkish forts that controlled the strait near Canakkale. It all seemed so easy, but just then the Turks were allies, and so the plan was quietly not mentioned to them, but meticulously pigeonholed for later reference. It would keep until it was needed. Regrettably, these forward thinkers failed to pigeonhole the effectiveness of rockets in supporting amphibious landings.

William Hale seems to have hawked his stickless rocket around the world to anybody who would buy it. The US army used Hale rockets in a war with Mexico in 1847, and in 1861 the remainder were taken from storage at the start of the Civil War. The stock was found to have deteriorated, and new ones were made, but there seem to only be two records of rockets being used in that war.

The Battle of Puketutu, in the Bay of Islands in New Zealand's North Island, in May 1845, involved a British expedition of 300 regulars, about 40 European volunteers, and some 120 seamen and marines, against a large Maori force. The British forces had two rocket tubes in the care of eight seamen, but they had little effect, it appears.

All the same, in a history of the Royal Artillery, two major-generals, Callwell and Headlam, tell us that rockets were still seen as having one minor application in dealing with restless natives, of whom the British Empire had an abundance:

> War rockets had for many years, down to 1870, been regarded as part of the material in charge of the Royal Artillery. They were moreover made use of by the Regiment during the Ashanti Campaign of 1874, and also in the course of the Zulu War. But batteries ceased to carry out practice with them in peace time during the period under review [1857–1914], and all idea of employing them—except possibly in small wars—was definitely abandoned before its conclusion. It was nevertheless enacted that stores of war rockets were to be maintained in charge of the Ordnance Department in certain specified stations overseas, so that some should be available on the spot to meet the case of possible hostilities with savages in forest country and jungle-clad regions.
>
> Callwell and Headlam, *The History of the Royal Artillery*, 1931

In a footnote, they add that 'Colonial Courses' at Britain's School of Gunnery continued to offer training in the use of rockets and 7-pounder guns for English officers who were destined to serve in the colonies. Civilisation, however, had come up with far more efficient ways of killing other, less civilised, people. Sadly, it had not yet come up with enough civilisation to stop killing altogether, and worse was to come. As Hilaire Belloc observed, in assessing the risks from 'natives' in Africa:

> Whatever happens, we have got
> The Maxim gun, and they have not.

It was an excellent time to be in a dominant position in a dominant empire, but elsewhere, people were ready to dream of empires far grander, far larger than any backwater operation confined to a single planet. We might have been running out of savages to subdue and bend to our will on Earth, but there were plenty more to be found on other planets, or so the dreamers thought.

A few of the more thoughtful dreamers like H. G. Wells considered that the boot might be on the other foot, that the savages might subdue us instead. He published his *War of the Worlds* in the same year that Belloc penned his insouciant couplet, but most humans still saw space and its alien inhabitants as something humanity was destined to dominate. Come to think of it, most of us still do.

# 7
# THE DREAM
# OF SPACE

Why should I feel lonely? Is not our planet in the Milky Way?

Henry David Thoreau, *Walden*, 1854

The mathematical professor at Padua hath discovered four new planets rolling about the sphere of Jupiter, besides many other unknown fixed stars [and] that the moon is not spherical but endowed with many prominences [he shall either be] exceeding famous or exceeding ridiculous.

Sir Henry Wotton (1568–1639), English ambassador to Venice, letter to England, 1610, in *Reliquiae Wottoniae*

That was how Wotton reported back to England on Galileo's discovery, when he peered at Jupiter through a telescope, of the four largest moons around the giant planet. It seems that while Galileo made some useful discoveries with the telescope, he probably did not invent it, and he did not name it either, though he was associated with the name being bestowed at a banquet in Rome to honour him on 14 April 1611. The instrument was instead named by a Cephalonian poet called Johann Demisiani who happened to be present, and this seems to be the start of the scientific tradition of giving names to new instruments by dredging up suitable Greek roots and combining them.

Still, Galileo made much of his discovery, and it clearly set him thinking. Take this passage, which appeared as part of the third day of his *Dialogue Concerning the Two Chief World Systems*, published in 1632:

> And since only that hemisphere of theirs is illuminated which faces the sun, they always look entirely illuminated to us who are outside their orbits and closer to the sun; but to anyone on Jupiter they would look completely lighted only when they were at the highest points of their circles. In the lowest part—that is, when between Jupiter and the sun—they would appear horned from Jupiter. In a word, they would make for Jovians the same changes of shape which the moon makes for us Terrestrials.

Here, Galileo has Salviati discussing the phases of the moons of Jupiter, and Salviati's casual reference to Jovians comes entirely out of the blue, with no preliminaries at all. There is no need, it seems, to explain why Salviati assumes there are Jovians on Jupiter, and indeed there wasn't, for that was an issue which had been decided long before, and which, in the next few years, would see a mighty flowering.

It all began in China, where a story dated 83 AD tells of a Taoist called Hsiang Man-Tu who spent several years on the moon, and the tradition continued from there. The palace of the moon was common in both prose and poetry as a place of ice crystals, and in one tale, when Taoist master Yeh Ching-Nêng took the Thang emperor, Hsüan Tsung, there in about 718, the emperor could not stand the cold, and Master Yeh agreed to take him home.

As a side issue, the third and fourth Earls of Rosse were both enthusiastic astronomers, the third Earl building a magnificent

72-inch telescope at Birr Castle in Ireland, which has recently been refurbished. The fourth Earl is of more interest to us, because he set out in 1868 to measure the surface temperature of the moon, using a 36-inch telescope linked to a thermocouple. This revealed that the surface temperature fluctuated wildly, confirming the lack of an atmosphere, but showing also that the temperature did indeed exceed the freezing point of water, so the moon was not permanently iced over. (By the way, the third Earl's telescope was built to examine more closely the nebulae that had been discovered by, as you may have guessed, Sir John Herschel.)

Independently of the Chinese tradition, a Greek satirist called Lucian of Samosata, who lived around 120–190 AD, set out to satirise the fearful travellers' tales that the Phoenicians spread, concerning the horrors that lurked in the eastern Atlantic. Like other early exploiters of new territories, the Phoenicians were keen to ensure that others did not dare venture where they ventured, and so began the era of 'Here There Be Dragons', aimed at frightening off the competition.

Well, Lucian was not particularly impressed with these yarns, but in order to go one better than the Phoenicians, his two stories, generally lumped together as *Vera historia* (*True History*) involved travel to the moon. In one case, this was achieved when his hero, Icaromenippus, used the wing of an eagle and the wing of a vulture to fly to the moon, taking off from Mount Olympus. In the second case, a shipload of athletes is carried to the moon by a whirlwind.

Every author of space fiction has needed a gizmo, a device to explain how transport was achieved. From the wings of Icaromenippus to the whirlwind, to space warps and dilithium crystals, the gizmos confer a licence on the reader to ignore the technicalities and move on. Lucian's main aim was to transport his characters to a new environment without too much getting in the way, and then to allow them to have adventures with giant spiders, ants, fleas and more, but he intended to amuse, not to instruct.

For some time afterwards, those who wished to satirise or use parables were able to set their scenes in places so far off that the audience could not test the tale for veracity. William Shakespeare could tell his tales of events in Illyria, Venice or Verona, freed from the need for precision in every detail, and Thomas More was able to place a whole Utopia in the Americas, where entirely different social structures were found. Later, Jonathan Swift wrote in the eighteenth century of the flying island Laputa, where the astronomers had found two moons of Mars, both obeying Kepler's third law, long before Deimos and Phobos were discovered. Swift could still set his action on Earth—and as we have seen, he located Lilliput in far-off, little-known Australia.

But back to Galileo: there is a bit of a mystery about his comments, because even though Kepler had written his *Somnium* (which we will come to in a moment) before Galileo published his *Two Chief World Systems*, the Kepler work was published posthumously, two years after Galileo. So why did Galileo throw his comment about Jovians into the discussion, as some sort of commonplace, before any serious space travel fiction had been published anywhere? The answer, quite simply, is that it *was* a commonplace at the time.

Education back then was at a turning point. Writers would still defer, most of the time, to the wisdom of the ancients, but experimental science and critical thinking were starting to be valued. So most educated people would have been familiar with ancient teachings, and perhaps even with this passage from Plutarch's *Sentiments Concerning Nature*, Book II, Chapter XXX:

The Pythagoreans say, that the moon appears to us terraneous, by reason it is inhabited as our earth is, and in it there are animals of a larger size and plants of a rarer beauty than our globe affords; that the animals in their virtue and energy are fifteen degrees superior to ours; that they emit nothing excrementitious; and that the days are fifteen times longer.

There was no real problem in conceiving that there might be strange creatures and even more unusual humans than those that Europeans were now meeting in the Americas, in Africa, in Asia, and even more in the tales created for home consumption. All the same, Galileo's casually mentioned Jovians were just another element in the bestiary of unknown beings, the space zoo.

To many science fiction enthusiasts, *Somnium* was the first science fiction. In a short piece with very extensive notes, Kepler discussed the science of getting to the moon rather briefly, but the actual method of surviving space got rather more attention. *Somnium* also describes lunar exploration. The hero is pulled along the track of the Earth's shadow during a lunar eclipse (this was Kepler's gizmo), reaching a neutral point where the gravitational effects are equal and opposite—and all before Newton! From that point, Duracotus falls to the Moon under the influence of its gravity. Kepler also discussed the problems of being above the atmosphere, and outlined ways to keep the human alive.

In every instance the take-off hits him as a severe shock, for he is hurled just as though he had been shot aloft by gunpowder to sail over mountains and seas. For this reason at the outset he must be lulled to sleep immediately with narcotics and opiates. His limbs must be arranged in such a way that his torso will not be torn away from his buttocks nor his head from his body, but the shock will be distributed among his individual limbs. Then a new difficulty follows: extreme cold and impeded breathing. The cold is relieved by a power which we are born with; the breathing, by applying damp sponges to the nostrils.

Kepler knew that the moon has captured rotation, with the same side always facing us: 'Levania consists of two hemispheres. One of these, the Subvolva, always enjoys its Volva, which among them takes the place of our moon. The other one, the Privolva, is deprived forever of the sight of Volva'. That is, one side of the moon always sees the earth (Volva), while Privolva is the side of the moon we never see from Earth. But Kepler was not yet finished with educating his readers, even the name Volva reminding us that from the moon, the Earth is seen to revolve, while we always see the same face of the moon, which rotates once in each orbit. Levania, the moon, was to be reached during an eclipse of the moon:

> Fifty thousand German miles [330 000 km] up in the ether lies the island of Levania. The road to it from here or from it to this earth is seldom open . . . Great as the distance is, the entire trip is consummated in four hours at the most. For we are always very busy, and agree not to start until the moon begins to be eclipsed on its eastern side. Should it regain its full light while we are still in transit, our departure becomes futile.

But Kepler was still not finished. Like much of science fiction up until the 1930s, *Somnium* had a strong didactic element, and plot, like character development, took a distinctly minor role:

> All Levania experiences the succession of day and night as we do, but they lack the variation that goes on all year among us. For throughout the whole of Levania the days are almost exactly equal to the nights, except that each day is uniformly shorter than its night for the Privolvans, and for the Subvolvans longer . . . For us in one year there are 365 revolutions of the sun, and 366 of the sphere of fixed stars, or more accurately, in four years, 1461 revolutions of the sun but 1465 of the sphere of fixed stars. Similarly, for them the sun revolves 12 times in one year and the sphere of fixed stars 13 times, or more precisely, in

eight years the sun revolves 99 times and the sphere of fixed stars 107
times. But they are more familiar with the nineteen-year cycle, for in
that interval the sun rises 235 times, but the fixed stars 254 times.

And now for the Levanians themselves: Kepler explained first
that the lunar night was warmed by light from the much larger
Earth, while the day was cooler, the sun being further away from
Subvolva in the middle of the lunar day when Levania is on the
far side of the Earth, while it is closer to the sun in the middle of
the Privolvan day, when the moon is closer to the Sun. All the
same, the Levanians had ways of not overheating.

As well, he pointed out that Levania has a circumference of
1400 German miles, an accurate enough figure, leading him to
conclude that the moon is a quarter of the size of the Earth, and
this, he realised, well before Newton, would lead to a lower gravitational attraction; then he goes to the biological implications:

> Whatever is born on the land or moves about on the land attains a
> monstrous size. Everything has a short life, since it develops such an
> immensely massive body . . . Most of them are divers; all of them, since
> they live naturally, draw their breath very slowly; hence under water
> they stay down on the bottom, helping nature with art. For in those
> very deep layers of the water, they say, the cold persists while the waves
> on top are heated by the sun; whatever clings to the surface is boiled
> out by the sun at noon, and becomes food for the advancing hordes of
> wandering inhabitants.

In 1600, Bruno of Nola was burned for saying pretty much what
Copernicus had said, but Copernicus was clever enough to
publish only as he was dying, and either he or his editor made it
clear that the Copernican model, with the planets orbiting the
sun, was just a convenient way to calculate. In 1632, Galileo was
given 'the treatment', and persuaded to recant. Kepler's work
was published only after his death, which made him fairly safe

from persecution. John Wilkins, an Anglican churchman at a fairly turbulent time in the Church of England, was surprisingly fortunate.

A consistent moderate, Wilkins annoyed the Puritans with his protection of Anglicans, and later upset the Anglican High Churchmen with his gentle treatment of the Dissenters. His position was made sounder when he married Robina French, the widowed sister of Cromwell; and even after the house of Stuart was restored, Wilkins managed to retain favour, being made Bishop of Chester in 1668. Thirty years earlier, aged just 24, Wilkins had written a careful proof that there was no reason, scientific or theological, why there should not be another world, just like ours, on the moon. He began his *The Discovery of a World in the Moone* like this:

> First Proposition: That the strangenesse of this opinion is no sufficient reason why it should be rejected, because other certaine truths have beene formerly esteemed ridiculous, and great absurdities entertayned by common consent.

So he asks people to keep an open mind, and then he goes to the heart of the question as it then had to be—theological matters:

> Proposition 2: That a plurality of worlds doth not contradict any principle of reason or faith . . . The opinion of more worlds has in ancient times been accounted a heresie, and *Baronius* affirmes that for this very reason, *Virgilius* was cast out of his Bishopricke, and excommunicated from the Church.

Then he offers the opinion of Aquinas on the matter:

> A fourth argument there is urged by Aquinas, if there be more wor[l]ds than one, then they must either be of the same, or of a diverse nature, but they are not of the same kinde, for this were needlesse, and would argue an improvidence, since one would have no more imperfection than the other . . .

Perhaps Wilkins was being cunning here, citing the great Catholic scholar arguing against his case, but after this he turns to more scientific arguments. (It is worth noting here that the moderate Wilkins, in the midst of the fury of civil war in Britain, assembled a scientific community at Wadham College in Oxford which would later become the nucleus of the Royal Society.)

> Proposition 7: That those spots and brighter parts which by our sight may be distinguished in the Moone, doe shew the difference betwixt the Sea and Land in that other World.
>
> Proposition 8: The spots represent the Sea, and the brighter parts the Land.

In the pages that follow, Wilkins argues that the seas of the moon will be darker: 'The Orbe of thicke and vaporous aire which encompasses the Moone, makes the brighter parts of that Planet appeare bigger then in themselves they are . . .', that is, he clearly has no doubt that the moon has an atmosphere. From these statements, which are more or less beliefs, Wilkins jumps to something close to real proof—at the very least, it is logical argument based on observations (the 'mountaines', of course, are mostly the edges of craters).

> Proposition 9: That there are high Mountaines, deepe vallies, and spacious plaines in the body of the Moone . . .
>
> But it may bee objected, that 'tis almost impossible, and altogether unlikely that in the Moone there should be any mountaines so high as those observations make them, for doe but suppose, according to the common principles, that the Moones diameter unto the Earths is very neere to the proportion of 2 to 7, suppose withall that the Earths diameter containes about 7000 Italian miles, and the Moones 2000 (as is commonly granted) now *Galilaeus* hath observed that some parts hath been enlightened when they were the twentieth part of the diameter distant from the common terme of illumination, so that hence it must

necessarily follow that there may be some Mountaines in the Moone so high, that they are able to cast a shadow 100 miles off.

This leads him to a series of case studies of the shadows thrown by mountains on Earth that support the idea of such long shadows, and then come the key conclusions:

Proposition 10: That there is an Atmo-sphaera, or an orbe of grosse vaporous aire, immediately encompassing the body of the Moone.

Proposition 11: That as their world is our Moone, so our world is their Moone.

Proposition 13: That 'tis probable there may be inhabitants in this other World, but of what kinde they are is uncertaine.

One thing this uncommon young man is sure of is that the truth is out there, and it will be found in due course. But now it is time for him to retreat slightly, to cite other authorities and make a few dissembling remarks to keep the people-burners at bay:

*Keplar* doubts not, but that as soone as the art of flying is found out, some of their Nation will make one of the first colonies that shall inhabite that other world. But I leave this and like conjectures to the fancie of the reader; Desiring now to finish this Discourse, wherein I have in some measure proved what at the first I promised, a world in the Moone. However, I am not so resolute in this, that I think it is necessary there must be one, but my opinion is that 'tis possible there may be, and 'tis probable there is another habitable world in that Planet. And this was that I undertooke to prove. In the pursuit whereof, if I have shewed much weaknesse or indiscretion; I shall willingly submit my selfe to the reason and censure of the more judicious.

That was how you covered your rear in the ecclesiastically uncertain 1630s, when a moderate Anglican divine was likely to be equally at risk of attack from Puritans on one side or Catholics on the other—and there was a religious war raging across Europe.

In the same year, 1638, Francis Godwin, Bishop of Hereford, published his *The Man in the Moone*, which had the hero towed to the moon by a flock of swans, and the French were soon at it as well, with Cyrano de Bergerac describing a number of unsuccessful methods for getting into space, such as strapping bottles of dew around the waist (dew rises, so it must have lift), a flying chariot, and the attraction of the moon for marrow-bone jelly. In fairness, Cyrano's tongue was firmly in his cheek, unlike Daniel Russen, who proposed in 1703 that a giant leaf-spring might be used to reach up to the moon, where the passenger would simply step off onto the lunar surface. In 1728, Murtagh McDermot had his hero returned from the moon by the force from detonating 7000 barrels of gunpowder.

Unlike Kepler and Wilkins, Bishop Godwin and Cyrano were concerned more with the romance of 'being there' than the technicalities of 'getting there', but even so, their contributions helped to keep alive the notion of strange people on other planets at a time when it was becoming more difficult to sustain the notion of strange races in odd places on Earth, and so built a desire to travel into space. But as yet, nobody was venturing to suggest that rockets might be used.

While Kepler had pointed out the problem, he was a cutting-edge astronomer and knew how far astronauts would have to travel to reach the moon; because his method of travel required the astronauts to stay in the moon's shadow, large accelerations would be involved, so great, in fact, that the astronauts would as like as not be reduced to marrow-bone jelly. This would then see them attracted to the moon, according to one of Cyrano's models, but hardly in any condition to enjoy the visit.

On 3 August 1777, Joseph Haydn saw the first performance of his farcical opera, to a text by Carlo Goldoni, called *Il Mondo della Luna*. The opera features a father who is a keen astronomer, his two daughters, and two young men seeking the hands of the daughters. Buonafede, the astronomer, is convinced by the young men, who have drugged him, that he has travelled to the moon and, as a result, he agrees to provide dowries for his daughters. The occasion for the opera was the marriage of Prince Nicholas Esterhazy to Countess Maria Weissenwolf. Getting inside the assumptions of the past is never easy, but there must have been a reasonable amount of dreaming about going to the moon in the eighteenth century, if such matters were seen as an appropriate source of amusement for a court performance. Sadly, only one or two arias remain in the repertoire, but Haydn managed to save the overture by using it as the first movement of his Symphony No. 63.

Almost a century later, Offenbach would see an *opéra-féerie* (magical opera) in four acts open at the Gaîté in Paris, called *La Voyage dans la lune*; this was a musical version of Verne's book, in which we meet for the first time a fully-fledged dream decked out in full technical rig. No drugs, no swans, no rising dew now, but mechanical means that might (if you suspended disbelief or did not mind them having their buttocks ripped from their torsos) even get the heroes to the moon.

Now the moon-voyagers were no longer fools and the butts of jokes by wicked satirists: they were heroes. But the time of the dreamers was not yet here, and those who dreamed of space were still derided. It was acceptable, though, to seek humanitarian uses for rockets, which were still by no means ready to reach into space.

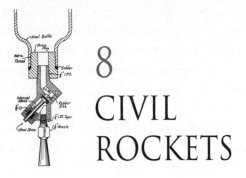

# 8

# CIVIL
# ROCKETS

The maroons were fired a little before 5 o'clock in order to summon the lifeboatmen and the rocket apparatus crews to their stations. When the *Preussen* was first noticed in the afternoon driving inshore it was thought that the tugs would be able to get their hawsers aboard in time and have power enough to haul her off, and thus the launch of the lifeboat was delayed and the rocket was not fired until 4.50 p.m . . .

Basil Lubbock, *The Nitrate Clippers*, pp. 95–6, 1932

As the Industrial Revolution progressed, the nineteenth century saw many changes in the industries of war as well as commerce. In 1801 there were no effective rockets, cannonballs were solid projectiles that only harmed those along their straight line of flight, and firearms from musket to cannon were almost all loaded through the muzzle before a single shot could be fired. Gunpowder was of variable quality, the projectiles were made by hand and equally variable, especially iron cannonballs on a ship, where rust might jam the ball if not chipped off, but if chipped off, made the ball a poor fit in the barrel—quite possibly lop-sided and unable to fly true.

Cannon were made of cast metal, usually iron, laboriously bored-out, monstrously thick cylinders which gained their strength from their thickness, and muskets were fired by lines of infantry, usually standing three deep (in the case of the French; the British tended to use two ranks), and relying on their training to keep reloading and firing under cavalry charge or cannon fire. Any committed enemy, in sufficient numbers, could run down and kill a group of infantry or an artillery position, if they were prepared to take losses along the way.

The charge of the Light Brigade in the Crimean War, in the middle of the nineteenth century, was probably the last time a cavalry commander ever even thought of charging guns with horses. That sort of foolery really only worked in the days when a cannon was fired, then had to be sponged out to get rid of sparks, after which it was loaded with a bag of powder, then packed with wadding, followed by the solid ball and another load of wadding. In those days, cavalry could move a long way while that was being done, and the cannon were too heavy to move around to a new angle as the cavalry wheeled. Even infantry could move a fair way while cannon were reloading, and infantry could also take cover behind embankments on a roadside, or walls, or the crest of a hill.

That was where rockets excelled in the early nineteenth century. They were light enough to move to a new position, they were launched from a light frame that one man could adjust, and as soon as one rocket was gone, the next one could be loaded on the frame and fired in turn. Like shells, rockets could explode in the air, hitting troops who were behind cover. All the same, the rockets were dismissed as less than accurate, so when guns could do the job as well as rockets, the rockets took a back seat; but at other times rockets might well find favour.

By 1901, firearms of all sizes were breech-loaded with ready-made ammunition that combined in a single unit the percussion cap to set off the round of ammunition, the actual charge and the projectile; newer, more powerful and more even-burning explosives replaced black powder; and lighter, thinner steel replaced the heavy old cast barrels, making it easier to manoeuvre and relocate artillery during a battle. Most importantly, the new guns could fire a round every few seconds, if necessary.

By 1901, rifles with aerodynamic bullets and a magazine to reload the breech were standard, machine guns were available that fired more bullets than a whole battalion of 1815 infantry, and the bullets went much further. A committed enemy, charging in sufficient numbers, was now far more likely to fall in the charge on an infantry group than to carry the day, and the infantry was now drilled more in marksmanship than in rapid reloading and firing. The infantry was now more valuable than as mere cannon-fodder, and tended to be dug into trenches and foxholes rather than exposed in squares and thin red lines.

Shrapnel had been developed by Henry Shrapnel around 1793 as a replacement for canister, a tin box of projectiles that burst when the gun was fired, scattering shot in all directions, but the shot immediately began to slow down. In essence, the shrapnel shell was a half-hollow cannonball packed with musketballs and powder that would be fused to explode above enemy troop formations. The single projectile was less slowed by air friction than individual balls, and would explode some 75 metres in front of the enemy, sending faster, closely-packed shot ploughing into them.

While shrapnel was a surprise to the French when it was first used against them, by the end of the nineteenth century, all shells fired by the world's artillery exploded and hurled shrapnel in all directions—and the same principle was used in Congreve's rockets.

A cannon in 1815 could hurl a single solid cannonball or case shot as far as 2000 metres for a 12-pounder, or 1400 metres for a 4-pounder, and the ball might skip on for another 1500 metres on hard, dry ground, but it could only strike those in its line of flight. A musket was inaccurate beyond 80 metres, and a rifle beyond 200 metres. Riflemen were lucky to get off two rounds a minute, and trained infantry could fire four rounds a minute from a musket.

Then there was grapeshot, a cloth bag of musketballs fired from a cannon, and highly effective against close-packed troops up to 300 metres. Warfare under these conditions meant getting up close and personal on your enemy, approaching as he reloaded, standing up to reload, and moving into bayonet range. The same approach was used in attacking a town, as Gleig describes in *The Subaltern* (1821): 'Grape, canister, musketry, shells, grenades and every species of missile were hurled from the ramparts, beneath which our gallant fellows dropped like corn beneath the reaper'.

These are the things to keep in mind while pondering the way in which rockets came and went in the nineteenth-century military mind, at first extending the range of things the artillery could do, only to be overtaken and replaced by the better artillery that the industrial age had produced. Nobody was forging swords into ploughshares. That meant that the slightly less bellicose uses for rockets now coming into play worked against them as serious weapons.

Until 1807, Henry Trengrouse worked as a cabinetmaker in the family business. Then, in his thirty-fifth year, a somewhat ungainly frigate, HMS *Anson*, left Falmouth to support the British fleet off the French coast. Forced to turn back by bad weather, her skipper, Captain Lydiard, mistook the Lizard for Falmouth, and saw his error too late. He dropped anchor, but in the high winds the anchor cables snapped, and *Anson* was forced towards the shore. Early on the morning of 29 December, Lydiard tried to sail her onto the beach at Looe bar. Only a few hundred feet from shore, she hit an uncharted reef and turned over. Of the 330 crew, some 190 died just after 7 am, in full view of the watchers on shore.

Seeing all those men die so close to safety was a heavy shock. Later, when Trengrouse was watching some birthday celebrations for George III, legend has it that he conceived the notion of using rockets to throw lines to a foundering ship. In the *Anson* wreck, the mainmast actually provided a bridge to the beach for the sailors who survived, so this may also have been a part of the idea, but it took him several years and £3,000 of his own money to perfect. The result was a rocket that fitted into a chest, and could carry a line to a ship as far as 1000 feet (300 metres) off shore.

Inventors commonly weave myths around their inventions (or have them woven for them, like James Watt's boiling kettle), and others had certainly thought along the same lines. In 1802,

*A French stand for launching life-saving rockets, c. 1882. Note the box designed to feed the line out behind the rocket.*

Claude Ruggieri claimed that his father, Petroni Ruggieri, had written of such an idea at an even earlier date—and this was five years before *Anson* was wrecked. The British seem to have done the best development work, but it has to be noted that there are other claimants for credit out there.

Later, around 1855, inspired by the two-stage rocket designs published by François Frézier in 1741, Edward Boxer came up with a superior form of rescue rocket; by 1870, they were standard around the coasts of Britain. These devices were certainly in use up to World War I, as the story of the wreck of the nitrate clipper *Preussen* reveals. (The source, by the way, is Basil Lubbock, whom we have already met.)

The clipper was on the Chile saltpetre run, and was sailing through the English Channel. In thick fog, just before midnight on Saturday, 6 November 1910, she ran down a Channel steamer, the SS *Brighton*, bound for Dieppe with 90 passengers. *Brighton* suffered no real damage, but *Preussen* lost her bowsprit and all her head gear, while her foremast was swaying dangerously; as she was also holed forward, *Preussen* was left with about the same sailing qualities as a drowned cow.

The German skipper made a valiant attempt to drop two anchors, but *Preussen* was a large ship, and had too much way on, so both anchor cables parted and the ship had to stand out to sea. The next day, several attempts were made to pass lines from tugboats, but without success, and the ship ended up striking a cliff near Dover at 4.30 pm on the Sunday afternoon. Lubbock's tale, which starts at the head of this chapter, continues:

> Meanwhile two bodies of Coastguards with rocket apparatus, one lot from Dover and the other from St. Margaret's, made their way along the shore and the cliffs, the one party below and the other above. The cliffs here are about 200 feet high, and Coastguard Hughes

volunteered to go down the cliff by means of a rope ladder. This was no pleasant job in the gale that was blowing, and he was about half-way down the cliff when the lower party at the foot of the cliffs fired their rocket. The shot was a good one, and it fell over *Preussen's* main rigging, thus establishing communication between ship and shore . . .

About 11 p.m. the *Preussen* began firing off rockets of distress, whereupon the lifeboat was again manned and towed off to the scene of the wreck.

Basil Lubbock, *The Nitrate Clippers*, 1932

In just about every other way, 1910 was a low time for rockets. Alfred Nobel, Alfred Maul and others had experimented with rocket-raised cameras, but rockets only took one shot, and might take it when clouds were in the way, or when the camera was pointing in the wrong direction. After the first aeroplanes flew, it was possible to take multiple pictures under human control, and get all the most exciting detail. It was rather like the difference between sending a clockwork rock-shoveller to Mars, and sending a trained geologist to choose the samples.

New technology was besetting rockets on all sides. Signal rockets were replaced by radio, and nobody could see the need for light, transportable artillery, but a few rocket developments continued. In 1890, Wilhelm Unge asked the wealthy Swedish inventor Alfred Nobel to provide funds for work on an 'aerial torpedo', a rocket for military use; as Nobel had experimented with rockets himself, he agreed. The result was a rocket 75 centimetres long and 11 centimetres across, weighing 35 kilograms with a 2-kilogram warhead. It used solid fuel and could fly 5 kilometres at 300 metres/second (and it was made by a company called Mars!). The von Unge patents were bought by Friedrich Krupp in 1909, but the Germans seem to have made little use of them.

Nobody else seemed that interested in rockets either, aside

from the dreamers who wanted to get into space and were now beginning to dream of doing so in rockets. No longer would the rocket be merely a firework or a weapon; it might also be a vehicle. Military minds were still expressing their doubts about rockets as weapons. In 1911, H.A. Bethell commented, in *Modern Artillery in the Field*: 'a dirigible armed with rockets would be at a disadvantage compared to one armed with a gun. But until the question has been settled either by ordeal of combat or at least by practical experiment, it would be rash to dogmatize as to the outcome'.

The start of the twentieth century can be seen in retrospect as a time spoiling for war. On every side, bigger and better warships were being built, superintended by nineteenth-century men of action transformed into early twentieth-century officials adequately over-filling the chairs behind their desks. If some of them had had their superior buttocks ripped from their torsos, this might have left them so brain-damaged that the war might have been over sooner. As it was, what passed for their wisdom prevailed for far too long.

Bethell was probably a good example of military thinking in his day. Forward-looking, he wrote in 1911:

> The rocket has often been proposed for the armament of airships, on account of the lightness of the discharging apparatus or rocket tube. The objection to it has been, and is still, the want of accuracy. However, recent improvement in rockets, specially designed for aero-naval purposes, have mitigated this defect. The Unge balloon rocket, which has been taken up by Messrs. Krupp, is a good example of modern type . . .

The idea of sending a fiery rocket off from a light fabric balloon filled with hydrogen seems not to have alarmed the nonchalant

*Alfred Maul's camera rocket, mounted in its launcher, taken in about 1912.*

Bethell. Still, in 1851, a Sydney doctor, William Bland, had proposed sending steam-powered hydrogen balloon freighters between Australia and England, and even earlier in 1821, whalers had relied successfully on a blast shield while rocketing whales to death. (Bland was not alone; an article by C. P. Lent in *Astronautics* as late as 1943 advocated the use of helium-filled dirigibles powered by a rocket engine, crossing oceans far more efficiently than flying boats. Each airship would lift 15 tons, have a crew of 40 and a power of just 5000 horsepower, but they could fly for days, if necessary.)

Colonel Bethell, however, was far from finished with his vision of the future, and he *was* aware of the problems rockets might cause balloons:

> The inventor proposes a 40 lb rocket, fired from a rifled tube or light gun weighing 140 lb., and carrying a small high-explosive shell, with sensitive fuze, in its head. It is stated that good accuracy has been obtained with this rocket, but no exact data are available. Neither is it known whether the flame from the rocket will set fire to the balloon.

So far, so good, but Bethell goes on to show that it would be better to mount a gun firing a 5-pound shell, rather than a rocket, seemingly oblivious to the problems that would follow from the recoil of such a gun, ripping apart the flimsy framework of the balloon. It might have been better if he had tried the armaments he proposed for aircraft:

> The present type of military aeroplane is a light craft which can be packed in a wagon and taken into the field with the troops. It is only constructed to carry two men; if made larger it would become unwieldy and difficult to start without special launching ways, and would require a shed for its protection. It is clear, therefore, that the present type cannot carry a gun weighing 3 cwt. with an extra man to

work it. Moreover, the vibration of the framework would render it necessary to stop the engine in order to fire; this is easy in a dirigible, but is risky in an aeroplane. It would appear therefore that a repeating rifle is the only weapon which an aviator can carry. It has been proposed to carry grenades or high explosive shell for fighting dirigibles, the idea being to rise above a dirigible and drop the shell on her . . . But probably a star-shaped arrangement of scythe blades would be as effective as a shell if dropped on top of the gas bag, and would be safer to handle.

Perhaps Bethell realised that an aircraft would have time to get away before the incendiary grenade ignited the hydrogen below, unlike the higher of two balloons, which would almost certainly perish along with the enemy, enveloped in the rising flames.

Incidentally, there is a delicious parallel here between Bethell's wagonable 'military aeroplane' and the wagon-borne light guns of the Turks before the gates of Vienna in 1559, which we encountered earlier. It is little wonder that Britain's Royal Air Force (among others) calls the rank equivalent to an army major a 'squadron leader', since this is what the Armoured Corps also calls its majors. Each service acquired the term from the cavalry, seen by senior commanders as the logical predecessors of those who 'rode' tanks and aircraft. The air force ranks of Wing Commander and Group Captain have similar cavalry origins.

In short, the first World War was planned by men who saw the pilots of aircraft as latter-day knights, jousting in the lists (even if they were to use Lee-Enfield .303 rifles rather than lances), dreamers who should not have been in charge of anything with more feeling than a side of beef. Still, they were not completely unaware; later in his work Bethell returns to the matter of military aircraft, and shows that in some circumstances, he could see the problem of recoil:

It would no doubt be possible to make an aeroplane large enough to carry a gun, and strong enough to stand its recoil. But this would be an enormous machine, too large to carry with an army in the field, and too clumsy to rise except from a large expanse of open ground.

That option soundly smashed, the colonel turns his agile and analytic mind to a careful contemplation of the damage that an aeroplane might do:

When hostile aeroplanes meet, they will fight as certainly as hostile dirigibles. Their weapons of offence are more limited, being restricted to rifles, hand-grenades and the scythe-blade arrangement referred to above . . . If this grenade, or the scythe-blade star, were dropped on to the wing of an aeroplane, it would certainly do some damage and might very possibly disable her. If neither can rise above the other, the more active plane will try to circle and come up behind the other within a range at which there is a prospect of hitting with the rifle. There is also a possibility of one aeroplane 'sinking' another with its down-draught by flying close over it.

In fact, rockets were sometimes used against balloons in World War I, at least until incendiary bullets were developed. These were rockets with long sticks, mounted on the struts of biplanes, and fired from a dangerously close range, about 125 yards, giving the pilot limited room to pull up and avoid a collision or becoming involved in the ball of flame that the balloon was hopefully about to become.

Remember the gallant British officers who dreamed of one day taking action to control the strait of the Dardanelles? In 1915, the plans might have been two generations old, but what was good for 1854 was good for now, surely? Old methods had worked in the Seven Years' War, they worked against Boney, so why not here? Just send in a few chaps from the Aegean shore, take some casualties, charge up the slope while the enemy are reloading, over-run them, bring in some guns and site them on top of the hill, and there you are—you've taken Gallipoli, and the Dardanelles.

There you would be indeed, but for the invention of breech-loading rifles, machine guns, barbed wire, searchlights, aeroplanes that could drop bombs and photograph positions, and a few other trappings of civilisation. The standard bolt-action rifle could fire 20 or 30 rounds a minute in good hands, and one Turk, who had very large hands, was said to be able to fire off 60 rounds a minute, operating bolt and trigger in a continuous one-handed motion. Compare that with the two rounds a minute from a trained muzzle-loader rifleman, allow for the fact that the muzzle-loader rifle was accurate to about 200 yards (while the early twentieth-century rifle required no adjustment to the sights unless the range was more than 200 yards), and you have a world in which a slow steady advance across the field of honour by an infantry square was butchery. In fact, it had been butchery for quite a long while before that, but up until then it had been successful.

The first thing that strikes you as you look up from the beach where the troops landed is the appalling slope the invaders had to climb. The raw colonial troops from Australia and New Zealand, lumped together as the Australia and New Zealand Army Corps, or ANZACs, were dropped at what is now, as a courtesy from the Turkish people, Anzac Cove. They faced a determined and prepared enemy, well-equipped and dug in, and they spent eight months fighting over every inch of the slopes.

They came ashore first on 25 April 1915, a day that is still marked in their home nations as Anzac Day, and over the next eight months some 9000 of them died. Each year now, more than twice that number of Australians and New Zealanders, young and old, flock to Gallipoli as Anzac Day comes around.

They walk the battlefields, riding between them on coaches, they visit the graves—at least the graves of one or two special heroes like Simpson who, with his donkey, carried the wounded down off the hills until he too was killed. Some of them look up at the slopes, and wonder what sort of men chose to attack this coast, and many more wonder at the stupidity of the men who sent them there.

Few know that the invasion plan was 61 years old, and even fewer realise that this hill, this climb to the ridge, might have been taken if the men on the ground had been able to use rockets as local and independent artillery, rather than relying on naval guns, firing from far out in the Aegean Sea. Even mountain guns had no place in the war on the Gallipoli Peninsula, but Hale rockets, locally directed by infantry who knew what was happening, might have made all the difference.

Half the army commanders at Gallipoli were competent, which was probably about average. The Antipodean myth of all of them being blundering British Colonel Blimps does not stand up, because there were some good men there along with the idiots. But there can be no doubt that a sufficiently aware administration, back at Woolwich Arsenal, might have given the ANZACs a better range of materials to use—especially rockets.

It is also worth noting that, as in other instances in that long and bloody war, they were inclined to send infantry, without tanks, to charge on foot across 'No Man's Land', through shell holes, under, over or through barbed wire, in the face of rapid rifle fire and machine gun fire, in the best traditions of Waterloo. Here also, rockets would have made a considerable difference.

Not that it really mattered if the Gallipoli invasion succeeded or not: delivering guns and ammunition to the Russians through the ports on the Black Sea was always just a pipe dream.

On the other hand, the Dardanelles campaign weakened the Turks to an extent that they could not hold on to their empire, and the Arabic-speaking people of the area gained their independence—or that was how T. E. Lawrence, 'Lawrence of Arabia' saw it. It is interesting to speculate what might have happened in the Middle East if tactical rockets had allowed a quick Allied victory and a Turkish capitulation with an empire and army that remained intact as Turkey changed sides.

When the next World War came around, the rocket advocates were better placed, as we shall see in Chapter 11, but as long as the decisions about rockets lay in the lap of the military, particularly the elderly senior surviving military, rockets would not go far. Whenever rockets made an advance, it was because mere youngsters, or people with no military training and traditions, stepped in, youngsters or those who got their inspirations about the use of science and technology from reading fiction. Even there, some people thought guns were the answer to everything. Thanks to the science fiction writers who followed Verne and Wells, the dream of space travel was spreading and, with time, rockets would be seen as the only way to get into space— but first, the space dream had to mature.

# 9
# THE UNIVERSAL TOURING GENE

'It is perhaps reserved for us to become the Columbuses of this unknown world. Only enter into my plans, and second me with all your power, and I will lead you to its conquest, and its name shall be added to those of the thirty-six states which compose this Great Union.'

So spoke Impey Barbicane, President of the Gun Club in Jules Verne's *From the Earth to the Moon* (1868). Perhaps, if we are to understand humanity's hunger to get out into space, we have to consider the urge to find new worlds, to conquer new worlds, and to wonder if this nomadic urge is somehow hard-wired into our genes.

Depending on how you see humanity, either *Homo erectus* emerged from Africa and evolved into modern humans, or *Homo sapiens* evolved in Africa and spread out across the world, replacing *Homo erectus*. Or maybe *H. erectus* and *H. sapiens* interbred. In any of these scenarios, we remain the descendants of hominid ancestors who had an urge to wander, to spread to new places, to be like Columbus. Certainly some sort of human wish to spread outward can be read into the conclusion of Konstantin Tsiolkovsky's 1911–12 masterpiece, *Investigation of World Spaces by Reactive Vehicles*:

> In all likelihood, the better part of humanity will never perish but will move from sun to sun as each one dies out in succession. Many decillion years hence we may be living near a sun which today has not even flared up but exists only in the embryo, in the form of nebulous matter designed for eternity and high purposes.

There is the yearning, the outward urge, but there is more where that came from:

> Thus, there is no end to life, to reason and to perfection of mankind. Its progress is eternal. And if that is so, one cannot doubt the attainment of immortality.
>
> Advance boldly, great and small workers of the human race, and you may be assured that not a single bit of your labours will vanish without a trace but will bring you great fruit in infinity.

The dream of distant realms to conquer is a key ingredient in large slabs of science fiction, but not all people want to conquer and rule; some of them would just like to visit, while others merely wish to hear tales of far-off places. But whether we make a big deal of the urge or play it down, it is undoubtedly there. Once people realised that rockets might be used to get into space, their enthusiasm for rockets increased greatly, even when they were supposedly pursuing military goals. When an A-4 rocket, the model we now know as the V-2, flew 190 kilometres on 3 October 1942, Wernher von Braun is reported to have said, 'What a pity it landed on the wrong planet!' This may have been part of the process of post-war laundering of von Braun, a bit of PR spin doctoring, but it rings true and it appeals to our humanity.

The human wish to believe in beings on other worlds can be seen as the sustaining factor behind a hoax pulled in 1835. The *New York Sun* reported that astronomer Sir John Herschel (yes, the same one), using a 7-ton telescope lens with a magnification of 42 000 set up in South Africa, had been able to see rocks, trees, flowers and intelligent winged beings of both sexes on the moon, though there were a number of factors that came into play here.

The hoax worked, because the Herschel name was well known (both Sir John's father, William, and his aunt, Caroline, had been famous for their astronomy), and also because Sir John Herschel really *was* in South Africa, though not quite that well equipped. Before the days of the telegraph, other New York newspapers could not check the story, and so they joined in, running their own versions rather than be left behind. Most importantly, the hoax worked because people wanted to believe it, and they still do.

But while people might have a yen to travel to faraway places and distant worlds, they lacked any way of getting there. Slowly they inched their way closer to a feasible mode of travel. Wings and dew, like exploiting the shadow of the moon, might be out, but there was still some distance to go, and humanity still believed, enthusiastically, that people could live on the moon.

There was a small step taken in the right direction in 1881 when a condemned prisoner in his cell in St Petersburg scribbled down some last ideas. He proposed a piloted rocket-powered air-vehicle, an unstable platform where the pilot apparently played the role of a stoker in a steamship, feeding gunpowder to a combustion chamber, where the burning powder would provide lift.

Nikolai Kibalchich was under sentence of death and, in due course, the sentence was carried out, but in bureaucratic Tsarist Russia the papers he left, including one called *A Draft of a Flying*

*Device*, were preserved, to be found after the Revolution in state security archives. Kibalchich was part of a group called Narodnaya Volya ('the People's Will'), and it appears that he was either the bomb maker or designer for a successful suicide-assassination attempt on Tsar Alexander II in 1881. He died, and no more was heard of him until his paper was revealed in a magazine called *Byloye (The Past)*.

Keen to be remembered, Kibalchich asked, just before his execution, that his paper be passed to an expert committee for evaluation. Almost a year after his death, the request was passed on, but politics came into play. The paper was judged untimely, and a note was appended which said that any examination of it might evoke inappropriate comments. So Kibalchich went into the deep freeze, but matters changed when the paper was found in 1917.

The new order needed revolutionary heroes of vision, and here was one who had the good fortune also to have been martyred, more or less. It was a good time to be discovered, because if you had died for disposing of a Tsar, you were now, posthumously, on the winning side. And N. I. Kibalchich, revolutionary and perceived visionary, entered the new Russian Pantheon when the paper was revealed in April 1918 by one Nikolai Rynin.

Kibalchich rejected steam and electricity as unwieldy and proposed a remarkably crude rocket engine. One Russian website has a short translation of his paper that quotes him as saying:

> Imagine a hollow vertical cylinder with no orifice in it except in the centre of its lower bottom. Install a narrower cylinder of compressed gunpowder for an axis and ignite this latter cylinder from the lower end. Given sufficient gas pressure inside, the whole big cylinder has to move up.

It is easy to read too much into something like this, and while Kibalchich did seem to have some ideas of including wings for stability, and some sort of steering system, this was a long way from a workable rocket. Nonetheless, the Soviet régime would later claim that a young rocket-maker called Sergei Korolev was influenced by Kibalchich to go further down the same road. It seems now that this was just propaganda, that the nineteenth-century Russian tradition of rocket artillery had more to do with it. We need also to recall that Kibalchich was proposing a flying platform, not a spacecraft, even if it *was* rocket powered. This was no craft headed for space, but by 1917 that was where the serious thinkers were looking.

The modern space era began with Jules Verne, who proposed using a gun to launch his heroes into space, and it continued with Hermann Ganswindt in Germany, who was thinking along the same lines as Kibalchich. Ganswindt seems to have had a fairly loose grasp of Newtonian mechanics, and since he is some-times credited with doing first what Newton had done, two centuries earlier, perhaps we need to stop and look at the practicalities of getting away from the Earth. But before we do, we might give those ultra-modernists at the *New York Times* another small outing from their 1920 opinion piece on why rockets are foolish, because it reminds us that even Verne was not completely safe from their criticism.

> . . . there are such things as intentional mistakes or oversights, and, as it happens, Jules Verne, who also knew a thing or two in assorted sciences—and had, besides, a surprising amount of prophetic power —deliberately seemed to make the same mistake that Professor GODDARD seems to make. For the Frenchman, having got his travelers to or toward the moon into riding a tiny satellite of the satellite, saved them from circling it forever by means of an explosion, rocket fashion,

where an explosion would not have had in the slightest degree the effect of releasing them from their dreadful slavery. That was one of VERNE's few scientific slips, or else it was a deliberate step aside from scientific accuracy, pardonable enough in him as a romancer, but its like is not so easily explained when made by a savant who isn't writing a novel of adventure.

All the same, if Professor GODDARD's rocket attains sufficient speed before it passes out of our atmosphere—which is a thinkable possibility—and if its aiming takes into account all of the many deflective forces that will affect its flight, it may reach the moon. That the rocket may carry enough explosive to make on impact a flash large and bright enough to be seen from the earth by the biggest of our telescopes—that will be believed when it is done.

*New York Times*, 13 January, 1920

The reason Verne succeeded in impressing people with his science was that he knew the art of the con man, the snake-oil salesman the world over. This involves providing a few testable pieces of data, and quickly glossing over the rest. Just as the magician's quickness of the hand deceives the eye, so the glibness of the con man's patter deceives the ear. It is used by circle-squarers, perpetual-motion peddlers, a certain class of preacher and those who claim to use a pinch of science to prove evolution impossible.

In each case, we are so busy admiring their knowledge of the shape of the orbit or some other detail that we fail to note that the gun would burst under the pressure, or collapse under its own weight, or some other minor impediment that makes the whole idea ridiculous. We are so busy watching the ace up the sleeve that we fail to notice that our pocket is being picked.

Verne's trick was to present the escape velocity that would be required to leave our planet. Gravity is a peculiar thing, pulling with less force as you move away from a planet or other large piece of mass, but still exerting a force on things on the other side of the universe. The force of gravity of two masses is proportional to the product of their two masses, divided by the square of the distance between them. To get this value in the standard physicist's unit of newtons, that value has to be multiplied by G, the universal gravitational constant.

That is, $F = G(M_1M_2/R^2)$, where $M_1$ and $M_2$ are the two masses, and R is the distance between their centres of gravity. On the surface of the Earth, we are at a distance of some 6400 kilometres from the centre of the planet; if we lift something to 6400 kilometres above the surface, the gravitational force is a quarter of what it is here where we feel most comfortable. The scramjet rocket that I watched rose to 314 kilometres, where the gravitational force is about 9 per cent less than on the ground.

Newton knew that the force changed like that, though he had no way of calculating the value of G because he had no idea of the mass of the Earth, so he had two missing values in the equation. Today, we have the value of G, so we can calculate that an average golfer, striking a ball on the asteroid Eros, would never see the ball again, because an average golfer can propel a golfball faster than the escape velocity of Eros.

At the end of the eighteenth century, John Michell worked out how to find the value of G, and when he died Henry Cavendish actually did the work, using Michell's apparatus. The problem is that the force of gravity, for all that it ties us to our planet, is incredibly weak (despite how it feels to us), and measuring small forces brought special challenges. The answer, Michell realised, was to make a torsion pendulum, a large beam suspended on a very fine thread and allowed to settle down in a draught-proof container. When it is turned to one side, it will swing slowly back, pass the rest point, swing to the other side, and so on.

Now every pendulum has a period, the time it takes to make one complete cycle, and this depends on the restoring force. So an ordinary mass-on-a-string pendulum can be used to measure the force of gravity in different parts of the world (Edward Sabine had done some of that, in the work that Babbage queried), but you can do even cleverer things with a torsion pendulum. If you know the period of the pendulum, you can calculate the restoring force for each degree of turn away from the rest point. So if you move a mass near the pendulum, and the pendulum moves, ever so slightly, and then settles down, you know from the change in angle just what the force is. Here is how Cavendish describes it (the 'wooden arm', by the way, was a truss structure):

> The apparatus is very simple; it consists of a wooden arm, 6 feet long, made so as to unite great strength with little weight. This arm is suspended in an horizontal position, by a slender wire 40 inches long, and to each extremity is hung a leaden ball, about 2 inches in diameter; and the whole is inclosed in a narrow wooden case, to defend it from the wind.
>
> As no more force is required to make this arm turn round on its centre than what is necessary to twist the suspending wire, it is plain, that if the wire is sufficiently slender, the most minute force, such as the attraction of a leaden weight a few inches in diameter, will be sufficient to draw the arm sensibly aside. The weights which Mr. Michell intended to use were 8 inches in diameter. One of these was to be placed on one side of the case, opposite to one of the balls, and as near as it could conveniently be done, and the other on the other side, opposite to the other ball, so that the attraction of both these weights would conspire in drawing the arm aside; and, when its position, as affected by the weights, was ascertained, the weights were to be removed to the other side of the case, so as to draw the arm the contrary way, and the position of the arm was to be again determined; and, consequently,

half the difference of these positions would show how much the arm was drawn aside by the attraction of the weights.

In order to determine from hence the density of the earth, it is necessary to ascertain what force is required to draw the arm aside through a given space. This Mr. Michell intended to do, by putting the arm in motion, and observing the time of its vibrations, from which it may easily be computed.

*Scientific Papers of Henry Cavendish*, published 1921
(Cavendish probably wrote this around 1800)

Yet more than a century before G was measured, Newton had worked out the escape velocity for Earth, the speed you would need to be travelling at on the Earth's surface, in order to fly away from the planet and never fall back, and it was Newton's calculation that Verne would have had in mind at the end of Chapter 2 of *From the Earth to the Moon*; when the President of the Gun Club is speaking:

'Suffer me to finish,' he calmly continued. 'I have looked at the question in all its bearings, I have resolutely attacked it, and by incontrovertible calculations I find that a projectile endowed with an initial velocity of 12,000 yards per second, and aimed at the moon, must necessarily reach it. I have the honour, my brave colleagues, to propose a trial of this little experiment.'

So how could Newton know this value? Well, if you know the acceleration due to gravity, and you imagine something falling under just the gravitational pull of the Earth from a few hundred million kilometres away, and if you ignore atmospheric friction, then the object will be travelling at something very close to the escape velocity when it hits. That is one way to do it, and probably Newton did it that way first, but there are other ways, all brutally mathematical.

So we will just accept that the escape velocity at the surface of the Earth is about 11.18 kilometres per second, some 25 000 miles per hour. The important thing to keep in mind is that the force of gravity diminishes as you move away from ground level, even though it keeps on pulling. When Jupiter is closest to the Earth, it exerts a force on you equal to what you would feel in the void of space when you were sitting on a stony asteroid 3.5 metres across. When Jupiter is at its furthest, the force is that exerted by a sat-upon asteroid just 1.5 metres across.

A spacecraft at the surface of Jupiter would need to reach a speed of some 59.6 kilometres per second in order to leave Jupiter forever. If you can travel slowly and steadily, you need never reach that speed, and that is the point where a rocket has it all over a gun. With a gun, all of the acceleration has to happen while the projectile is inside the barrel of the gun, but a rocket can keep on accelerating. A rocket with liquid fuel can also be turned on and off, and that gives a great deal more control.

The other argument for liquid fuels came from Tsiolkovsky, after he had shown in 1903 that only rockets would work in the vacuum of space: 'Gunpowder will not work as a fuel because it simply does not have enough energy . . . Some liquids do have enough energy to power a space rocket . . . Liquid oxygen and liquid hydrogen would make an excellent oxidiser and fuel.' This was rather perceptive of Tsiolkovsky, as hydrogen had only been available as a liquid for eight years, and only in reasonable amounts for about two years. By 1914, Robert Goddard had been dreaming of going into space for a decade and a half, but although he had a patent for liquid-fuelled rockets, he only launched his first liquid-fuel (gasoline and oxygen) rocket in 1926. The question of liquid fuels is one we will pursue more closely in Chapter 10.

Just as we can see a continual jostling between the rocket and the gun for military attention, so it was with those writing of early space flight. Science fiction writers of a certain sort will take refuge in a mumbled reference to Bloggsite, dilithium crystals, abaric fields or some other way of defeating gravity or shaping it, rough-hewn, to meet the needs of spacefarers. To rise above the level of the pulps, it is necessary to develop a bit more science, based on known technology.

In Chapter 13, we will see how Edward Everett Hale solved his dream of a space station with an astronaut-pulping flywheel launch system, but it was clear to any real scientist that only a rocket would do to launch humans into space. Only a rocket has the slow and steady acceleration over long periods which is all that our bodies can stand, and it took Tsiolkovsky to point it out.

Tsiolkovsky's 1883 description of a gas-filled barrel fitted with stopcocks, quoted in Chapter 2, is commonly misconstrued to suggest that he had actually tried 'flying' such a machine, but this is not only patently absurd, it is also entirely unsupported by reading the actual notebook. All the same, Tsiolkovsky was a most unusual person, and while he supposedly never did any serious experimental work, he most probably dabbled and tried a variety of effects, given that he wrote in 1929: 'I am already 72 years of age. I have long given up working with my hands and do not perform any experiments'.

At about the age of ten, Tsiolkovsky became deaf in one ear, apparently from scarlet fever, the same disease that affected Thomas Alva Edison's hearing, but it had no effect on either man's intellect. In those days, the loss of hearing meant being withdrawn from school, but Tsiolkovsky set out to educate himself, and in the end, his family sent him from Kaluga, 150 kilometres west of Moscow, to study in the capital. He later returned to teach at Kaluga.

Apparently inspired by Jules Verne, the young schoolteacher began writing what we would now call science fiction, tales of travel between the stars, but he rapidly changed to deal with the practicalities of it all, at a time when the first heavier-than-air flight was still twenty years away.

He was the first to realise that a rocket, a craft relying on Newtonian action and reaction, was the only sort of craft that could fly through empty space. At first, this reaction machine was no more than his barrel with six stop-cocks, but by 1903 Tsiolkovsky had thought matters through, and without a doubt was as completely caught up in the dream of space as any other human ever had been, or would be. Here, he talks of how a rocket can be made to orbit the planet, but notice the last sentence, written in 1911–12:

> It is possible, by restricting the explosion, to rise only to a desired altitude; then, having lost all speed, and so as not to allow ourselves to drop back to the planet, we turn the vehicle with the aid of bodies rotating inside the rocket and produce a new explosion in a direction perpendicular to the original direction . . . all the now familiar phenomena of a medium with gravity are repeated; they will again vanish; and silence and peace will set in, but the rocket will now already be secure from falling; it will . . . like the moon . . . continue eternally to revolve about the earth . . .
>
> Now we can calm down completely because the rocket has acquired a 'firm' position: it has become a satellite of the earth . . . The distance may be so small that one circuit round the earth will last two hours, and in the course of several minutes we will view different points on the earth from various angles and at a close distance. This picture is so magnificent, alluring and infinitely diversified that I heartily wish you and I could see it.
>
> Konstantin Tsiolkovsky, *Investigation of World Spaces*, 1911

Today, as we pull satellite images of our world off the Internet, we can all see the vision that Tsiolkovsky could only dream of, but some of his other dreams are still to reach fruition:

The plan for further exploitation of solar energy will probably be as follows.

Man will launch his vehicles to one of the asteroids and will make it a base for the initial work. He will use the material of the tiny planetoid (decomposing it and carrying the material away, down to the very centre) for building structures that will make up the first ring around the sun. This ring will be inhabited by intelligent beings and will consist of mobile parts like the ring of Saturn.

After taking apart and utilizing the other minute asteroids, intelligent beings will form another series of rings somewhere between the orbits of Mars and Jupiter in the space cleared of all asteroids.

By then Tsiolkovsky was in his mid-fifties, but he had a clear picture of what was needed to get into space, effortlessly flinging in ideas like heat shields when writing of a rocket glowing white-hot, protected by its 'protective refractory and non-oxidizable shell'. He also had a very clear picture of what it would be like getting there:

The signal is given, the explosion is set off and is attended by a deafening noise. The rocket shakes and takes off. We have the sensation of terrible heaviness. Four poods of my weight have turned into 40 poods.* I am knocked to the floor, severely injured and perhaps even have been killed; can there be any talk of observations? There are ways of standing up to this terrible weight, but in a, so to speak, packed up form or in a liquid . . .

So what would the acceleration force be like, before weightlessness set in? He had the answer there as well:

If the density of the earth were increased 10 times or if we found ourselves on a planet where the attraction is 10 times greater than on the earth, we would find no difference between the phenomena in the rocket and those on the planet with enhanced gravity . . .

* A Russian weight measure: one pood is 40 Russian pounds, or about 36 lbs avoirdupois or 16 kilograms.

The awful gravity that we experience will last 113 seconds, or about 2 minutes, until the explosion and the noise come to an end. Then, as dead silence sets in, the gravity will vanish instantaneously, just as it appeared. We are now out beyond the limits of the atmosphere at an altitude of 575 km . . . The distance of 575 km is very little, it is almost at the surface of the earth and the gravity should have diminished ever so slightly. And that actually is the case. But we have to do with relative phenomena, and for them there is no gravity.

The force of terrestrial gravitation acts on the rocket and on the bodies in it in the same way. For this reason there is no difference in the motion of the rocket and the bodies in it. They are carried along by the same stream, the same force, and as far as the rocket is concerned, there is no gravity.

A quick back-of-the-envelope scribble reveals that he is considering an average acceleration of about seven times that due to gravity, with an implied maximum of 10g. Kepler had suggested that the force of acceleration might tear a torso away from the buttocks, and he saw curling up as the way around this problem. Tsiolkovsky was going to surround people with liquid for support. In other words, we would go into space in some sort of water-bath, cushioned from the worst of the acceleration:

Now that the explosion in the rocket is over and the terrible gravity is no more, we can safely climb out of our casing, wipe away the remaining liquid and put on some clothes. As if by way of reward for the multifold gravity that we have just withstood, we are now completely free of all gravity.

Immediately the question comes to mind, will not this absence of gravity adversely affect our health? Should we not take some protective measures here too?

Then Tsiolkovsky argues that we experience freedom from gravity when we jump or fall, and when we are in water, with no ill effects, so we hardly need 'special experiments to prove that a medium devoid of gravity is harmless'. Today, of course, we know that a prolonged absence of gravity can cause severe problems of wasting, but that was a long way ahead. All the same, Tsiolkovsky had an answer:

> But even if it were found that people cannot live without gravity, it would be easy to create artificial gravity in a medium where it is absent. For this purpose, man's dwelling, say a rocket, would have to be set into rotational motion; then, through the centrifugal force, an apparent gravity would be established . . .

Today this is a familiar concept, for we have all seen footage of people floating gravity-free, either in reality, or in the fictional worlds of space. That knowledge was not common in 1911, so it had to be explained:

> The force of terrestrial gravitation acts on the rocket and on the bodies in it in the same way. For this reason there is no difference in the motion of the rocket and the bodies in it. They are carried along by the same stream, the same force, and as far as the rocket is concerned there is no gravity.
>
> There are many things that convince us of this. All objects in the rocket that are not attached have left their places and are hanging in the air, out of contact with anything; and if they are touching something, they do not exert any pressure on each other or on the support. We ourselves can have any position and be in any direction: we can stand on the floor, on the ceiling or on the wall; we can stand perpendicularly or have an inclined attitude; we float in the middle of the rocket like fish, without any effort whatsoever, and we do not come in contact with anything; no object exerts pressure on any other one if they are not pressed together.
>
> Water does not pour out of a carafe, a pendulum does not oscillate and hangs to the side. An enormous mass hung from the hook of a spring balance does not make the spring taut—it always indicates zero . . .

The mercury barometer has risen upwards and the mercury has filled the entire tube.

A double-knee syphon does not convey water.

An object that is dropped does not fall; one that is pushed moves in a straight line and uniformly until it strikes the wall or some object, and again comes into motion, though with a smaller velocity. Generally it is also in rotation like a toy top. It is even difficult to push a body without imparting some rotation to it.

And how will it feel to the people inside the rocket? He has an answer there as well:

There is, properly speaking, no up and down in the rocket, for there is no relative gravity and a body left without support does not tend towards any wall of the rocket, but there do remain the subjective sensations of up and down . . . We recognize 'up' in the direction of our head and 'down' where our feet are located.

However you look at it, Tsiolkovsky could see it all. Perhaps he is best summed up by these prophetic words over his grave in Kaluga: 'Man will not stay on Earth forever, but in the pursuit of light and space will first emerge timidly beyond the bounds of the atmosphere and then advance until he has conquered the whole of circumsolar space'.

In so many ways, 1912 was a key year for the future of rockets. It was the year in which Konstantin Eduardovich Tsiolkovsky completed and published his second version of *Investigation of World Spaces by Reactive Vehicles*, and the year in which Robert Hutchings Goddard was just beginning to explore mathematically the practicality of using rockets to reach high altitudes or even the moon, although neither Tsiolkovsky or Goddard knew of each other at this stage. And neither of them could have had any possible interest, at that stage, in the birth in Pomerania of Wernher von Braun, but he comes later.

But was Verne right, claiming through Barbicane that an 'initial velocity of 12,000 yards per second' was needed? I leave this analysis to the reader, but Kepler knew at least part of the answer.

# 10

# A QUESTION OF FUELS

In liquid rockets, the principal propellants used in the early days at Aerojet were red fuming nitric acid (RFNA) as the oxidizer, and aniline, a synthetic hydrocarbon, as the fuel. Neither of these liquids was near ideal for the intended purpose, yielding a specific impulse ($I_{sp}$) of only about 220 lbf sec/ lbm (at 300 to 14.7 psi expansion). Nitric acid is extremely corrosive and, when exposed to air, gives off dangerously toxic fumes, which are equally corrosive. Aniline, the fuel, is not corrosive but causes extreme irritation on contact with the human skin. (Other fuels such as furfural alcohol, xylidine, and mixtures with aniline were tried, but improvements were minor.) It was soon found that all metal parts used for the containment of the fuel were required to be corrosion resistant to the same degree as the oxidizer parts, because of the exposure to the nitric oxide fumes which were ever present.

Chan Ross, in charge of liquid rocket engineering at Aerojet, 1940s to 1960s,
*Aerojet: The Creative Company*, 1995

The twentieth century saw hectic research aimed at finding the best fuel to use. Congreve's simple rockets might fly with no more than gunpowder, but as soon as they left the launcher there was no control. Vanes and fins might steady the rocket in its direction, or impart a spin to it, but the solid fuel rocket typically goes at full blast until the fuel is all used. Liquid fuels, on the other hand, are delivered to a combustion chamber by a pump that may be turned on and off, as determined by the pilot or a control mechanism.

The switch from solid fuel to liquid fuel would allow astronauts to control their flights, and allow missiles to become guided, but the liquids involved bring their own special problems. For example, hydrogen 'wants to leak through metal'—the metal of the tank embrittles and turns into something rather like a pretzel. Many of the liquids require immense cold, and many are intensely corrosive. And because they are rocket fuels, they tend to be both unstable and packed with energy—and looking for something to react with. A solid fuel, of course, is just there, where it needs to be, but a liquid fuel has to come from a tank, controlled by valves and pumps that can stand up to all this chemical unpleasantness.

Even the pumps are a challenge. The liquid fuel rockets need pumps that deliver the fuel and the oxidiser at appropriate rates. Goddard's first liquid fuel rocket used pressure from the oxygen tank to force both oxygen and gasoline into the combustion chamber, with a comparatively crude valve to control the mix, but all later rockets used pumps. The Germans used hydrogen peroxide to power the pumps, but since then, blast turbines taking power from the rocket itself, compressed air drawn from turbojet compression fans, and systems using the expanding fuel itself have all been tried. No single system is perfect.

Erasmus Darwin (Charles Darwin's grandfather) is said to have invented a hydrogen-oxygen rocket motor in the 1770s, but compressed gas takes up too much space, so serious use of gases had to wait until they were available in liquid form. This

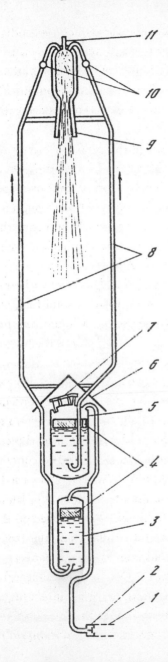

The design of Goddard's first rocket, taken from a Russian diagram. The upper tank (5) contained oxygen and the lower tank (3) gasoline. The pressure from the oxygen is used to feed gasoline into the combustion chamber (9), with the flow rate being managed by two cocks (10). (11) is the igniter and the protective cap to keep the rocket exhaust away from the tanks is (6).

came first in Cracow, in what was then Austrian Poland, when Z. F. Wroblewski and K. S. Olszewski first reported achieving the production of liquid oxygen, and oddly enough, they used an effect that Erasmus Darwin had discovered to achieve it.

Trying to explain why clouds form in the sky, Darwin discovered adiabatic cooling. This is the effect that causes an expanding gas to get cooler. If the gas is air, and the air is moist, fog may form in the cool air, so when air rises it cools, and clouds form. If the gas is highly compressed oxygen which has just been cooled, then as some escapes, the remainder may be chilled enough to form a liquid. This is the basic principle behind the refrigerator, tricked out so the main concern is what would otherwise be the refrigerant.

In simple terms, you compress some cold gas, and it gets hot. You let it cool off, then let some of it expand, carrying energy away, so that the remainder is even colder, and you keep doing this until you extract some liquefied gas. But while the two Poles had shown that oxygen could be liquefied in 1883, it was only in 1895 that Carl von Linde found a means to provide significant amounts of liquid oxygen.

Hydrogen was more of a challenge, because it has a much lower boiling and condensation temperature, and James Dewar produced the first liquid hydrogen in 1895, using the famous flask that we know best as the commercial 'Thermos' flask. After just six years, Dewar was able to transport five litres, about a gallon, of the strange liquid from the Royal Society to the Royal Institution in London. And in Russia, Konstantin Tsiolkovsky was reading and watching. Here, he saw, was a solution for a serious spacefaring rocket.

For most purposes, a liquid fuel rocket has two tanks: one containing the energy-rich fuel, the other containing a powerful oxidiser to 'burn' the fuel. Liquid hydrogen and liquid oxygen fit this description, and this is what Tsiolkovsky realised. Just two years after Dewar's triumphant ride across London, the Russian was looking to take a journey across the skies. What was more, he realised that the intensely cold liquids could help stop a rocket overheating:

> At the present time, it is not particularly difficult to convert hydrogen and oxygen into liquids. These liquids must be separated by a partition. Their temperatures are extremely low; it is therefore practicable to use them to surround either jackets with circulating metal or the cannons [combustion chambers] themselves directly.

In the same 1903 work, *Exploration of Space with Reactive Devices*, Tsiolkovsky also made the first explicit suggestion for using a rocket. A rocket, he said, was the only known device that will work in a vacuum, and he could even see how it would operate:

> The chamber has a large supply of substances which, upon being mixed, straightway form an explosive mass. These substances, which explode properly and rather uniformly in a definite place, will flow in the form of hot gases through pipes that flare out at the ends like a megaphone or a musical instrument. These pipes are situated lengthwise along the walls of the chamber. At one end ( the narrow one) of the pipe the explosives are mixed together: here condensed, flaming gases are formed. At the other, broader, end the gases expand and cool and then race out through the flared pipes with a tremendous relative velocity.

By 1909, Robert Goddard had come up independently with the same combination, but when he began serious experimental work in 1922, he used gasoline as the fuel because it was easier to obtain, along with liquid oxygen. It was this combination that he used in his first successful flight in 1926.

According to John Clark, whose *Ignition! An Informal History of Liquid Rocket Propellants* is essential reading in such matters, in

1927 one Pedro Paulet wrote to the newspaper *Il Commercio* of Lima, Peru, claiming that he had experimented with a gasoline-nitrogen tetroxide rocket in Paris in 1895–97. Clark shows this to be unlikely—it would have sounded like a machine gun, and would undoubtedly have caused considerable anguish among the Parisians, enough to be recorded and recalled—but even so, Paulet was one of the first to mention the use of nitrogen tetroxide as an oxidiser.

By 1929, Luigi Crocco was using nitrogen tetroxide in Italy, but while his group knew the great advantage of $N_2O_4$ was that it would keep indefinitely at room temperature, others did not realise this until 1954. Meanwhile, in France, Robert Esnault-Pelterie used gasoline and oxygen, then benzene and nitrogen tetroxide, and finally tetranitromethane—otherwise known as TNM or $C(NO_2)_4$—and blew off four fingers. According to Clark, 'this event was to prove typical of TNM work'.

In the mid-1930s, Crocco used methyl nitrate ($CH_3NO_3$) as a monopropellant—both fuel and oxidiser. A solution of benzene in $N_2O_4$ is another example of a monopropellant, but as John Clark happily pointed out:

> Any intimate mixture of a fuel and an oxidizer is a potential explosive, and a molecule with one reducing [fuel] end and one oxidizing end, separated by a pair of firmly crossed fingers, is an invitation to disaster. All of which Crocco knew. But with a species of courage which can only with difficulty be distinguished from certifiable lunacy, he started in 1932 on a long series of test firings with nitroglycerine (no less!) only slightly tranquilized by the addition of 30 percent of methyl alcohol. By some miracle he managed to avoid killing himself, and he extended the work to the somewhat less sensitive nitromethane, $CH_3NO_2$. His results were promising, but the money ran out in 1935, and nothing much came of the investigation.

> John Clark, *Ignition!*, 1972

(Aside from Crocco's heart-stopping use of it, nitroglycerine has some less alarming uses, as a medical treatment for respiratory and circulatory problems. In mid-2001, the *European Journal of Obstetrics Gynecology and Reproductive Biology* carried a report about the use of nitroglycerine ointment to treat a case of vaginismus, a condition which causes extremely painful intercourse. The patient, a young Bedouin woman, was unwilling to undergo the embarrassment of counselling, and this was tried, successfully, as an alternative.)

Perhaps he would have had his doubts about the nitro-glycerine, but none of the other fuels would have surprised Tsiolkovsky, who had described any number of other potential fuels—methane, ethylene, benzene, methanol and ethanol, tur-pentine, gasoline and even kerosene, but always with liquid oxygen. By the early 1930s, though, liquid fuels were seen as the way to go, and engineers and physicists around the world were tackling the challenges of pumping dreadfully cold fluids through pumps under fearful acceleration, and stopping the pumps from freezing solid.

As rocket building became an exact science in the 1930s, and people began to test rockets and rocket propellants on the ground, it became necessary to come up with a measure of their strength, a combination of the force they exerted, and how long they kept it up for. If the force and duration were the same, then the rocket that produced the result with the smallest mass of fuel (take this to mean both the oxidiser and the fuel that was burnt in it) was the better. That gives us three variables: the mass of propellant chemicals, how long they burn, and the force exerted.

Force is probably the hardest concept for non-physicists to deal with. A force is that which makes a mass accelerate, or change its velocity, but here lies the first trap: velocity involves both a speed and a direction. Isaac Newton pinned it down when he said a moving body will keep on going in a straight line unless a force acts on it. If a force is acting on something, it will either slow down or change direction; these days, physicists measure force in newtons, where a force of 1 newton will produce an acceleration of 1 metre per second per second.

That is the second trap—what is this metres per second per second (or worse, $ms^{-2}$) stuff all about? Let's imagine we are in a small spacecraft, attached to a giant reflective sail, something that Arthur C. Clarke called a sunjammer. Just as a windjammer speeds along under the force of the wind, so the solar wind accelerates a sunjammer, as photons and other bits thrown out by the sun bounce off the sail. Sunjammers would be slow but, given time, they could pick up speed. At the end of the tenth hour from launch, a sunjammer might be doing 3600 metres per hour, a mere 3.6 kilometres (or a bit over 2 miles) an hour. But the sun keeps pushing, and after 20 hours it may be doing 7200 metres per hour.

The average rate of increase in velocity from hour to hour is 360 metres per hour—that is, the acceleration is 360 metres per hour per hour. If we did the sums again, but talked about metres per second, that acceleration is 0.1 metres per second per second. In other words, if we know the acceleration rate, we know how much faster the object will be going in the next time interval. From one second to the next, the sunjammer increases its velocity by 10 centimetres/second. After 10 seconds, it will be travelling 1 metre per second faster than it was at the start of that time. Its acceleration is $0.1 ms^{-2}$.

Of course, if you think of a car that accelerates to 100 miles per hour in 10 seconds, that is an acceleration of 10 miles per hour per second, which may be a convenient way of thinking of things; however, to keep things tidy, physicists don't like to mix units. So they convert the 100 miles per hour to (100 ×

5280)/3600, or 146.67 feet per second, so the acceleration is 14.67 feet per second per second (or about 4.5 ms$^{-2}$).

(While we are looking at physicist-speak, *weight* is the force that an object exerts, due to the attractive force of gravity, as it is perceived. In a spacecraft in free fall, everything is moving along together, so there is no weight, but objects still have *mass*, and you need to use force to make them move. So if you are hauling a 10-tonne pallet of dog food around, and you keep pushing, it will very slowly accelerate, and probably crush whoever is on the other side when they try to stop it—but it will crush them very slowly. Even though everything seems weightless, it is wrong to say 'there is no gravity in space'. There *is* gravity in space, and it acts on you all the time, but you are only able to observe it by the way your course describes an interesting curve. There is gravity there, and mass, but you have the feeling of weightlessness.)

A stationary mass of 1 kilogram exerts a force of 9.8 newtons at the surface of our planet, because the rate of acceleration due to gravity is 9.8 ms$^{-2}$, and if the units are defined the right way, $F = ma$; that is, the force (F) is the product of the mass (m) and the acceleration (a).

Even in clumsy old Imperial units, this sort of relationship holds, but we tend to say that a mass of 1 pound exerts a 1-pound force, this being the force that will accelerate a 1-pound mass from zero to 32 feet per second in one second. As much of the work was done by Americans, these units were the preferred ones—though this tenacious use of the old and clumsy was to lead, eventually, to the loss of a spacecraft around Mars, because one team had used Imperial, and one had used metric—and when this translated to the force to be applied, bang went one Mars lander, but we won't mention that here. Nor will we consider poundals.

The effectiveness of a rocket propellant is measured in a practical unit called the specific impulse ($I_{sp}$ or ISP), which is defined as the amount of thrust produced from each pound of propellant per second. Most of the $I_{sp}$ figures for practical propellants come in the range 200 to 400. A propellant with an $I_{sp}$ of 200 is one where a pound of the fuel/oxidiser combination can deliver 1 pound of thrust for 200 seconds, while an $I_{sp}$ of 400 would deliver the same thrust for 400 seconds; in the rocket business, the bigger the better—although at the top end, the combinations are so energetic as to be rather risky.

The quotation at the head of this chapter gives a more complex unit for $I_{sp}$, but seconds are sufficient—just don't worry about the rest of it. One interesting side-issue, presented as an end-result: multiplying the $I_{sp}$ by the acceleration due to gravity delivers the exhaust velocity in metres per second, so a rocket motor with a specific impulse of 250 delivers an exhaust velocity of $250 \times 9.8 = 2450$ metres per second (or $250 \times 32 = 8000$ feet per second). A rocket with a specific impulse of 250 will deliver a thrust of 2450 newtons for one second, or one newton for 2450 seconds, and so on.

There are a few other caveats: specific impulse is measured under specified conditions, usually a pressure of 1000 psi in the chamber and 14.7 psi (sea level pressure) outside. That is, from 6.8 megapascals to 100 kilopascals—and then we need only nominate the temperature to be used, and we have turned a trick of trial-and-error alchemy into a more-or-less exact science.

There was a need, though, for considerable exactitude in some cases. Around 1950, William Doyle had some problems with liquid fluorine as the oxidiser; his 18 per cent discrepancy between theory and measured results was explained when workers at Aerojet found that liquid fluorine had a density of about 1.55 rather than the reference-book value of 1.13. As we have already seen, Pierre Dulong came in for some trouble when he shied away from tellurium, and it seems that people preferred reference works to lab work when it came to measuring such things. The new value made theory and reality come into line.

We can gain an understanding of the new sorts of problems cryogenic fuels bring if we consider hydrogen. This element comes as $H_2$, molecules with two atoms, and atoms have a property called spin. If the two atoms in a molecule have the same direction of spin, this is called the ortho form, but if the spins are opposite, the molecule is in the para form. Now quantum theory tells us that when they are at room temperature, three-quarters of all molecules will be ortho, but boiling liquid hydrogen at 21 kelvin should be entirely in the para state.

The two forms have different thermal conductivity, and it should have been possible to observe the change, but nobody could see it happening, apparently because it was slow. All the same, it happened, and theory said that as 2 grams of hydrogen changed from the ortho to para form, heat was released, 337 calories of it, but vaporising the same mass of hydrogen takes only 219 calories! This was disaster territory, and it was necessary to find a 'catalyst' that would help the transition, so that the liquid hydrogen condensed already converted into the para form. Hydrated ferric oxide was found to do the trick, and other 'catalysts' were found later, but the main thing was that the problem had been solved.

There were other problems, of course. A Saturn V rocket engine delivers a thrust of 7.5 million pounds, around $33.36 \times 10^6$ newtons, and the exhaust velocity is around 2500 metres per second, which means about 56 million horsepower, if you prefer a unit like that. Or you can have it as about 42 gigawatts—it means the same thing. All well and good, but how do you calculate this?

In the classroom, we would write an equation for burning hydrogen and oxygen like this: $2H_2 + O_2 \rightarrow 2H_2O$. That may do for school chemistry theory, but rocket science is big and hairy, and even if you have just the right stoichiometric mix (which means the correct proportions of hydrogen and oxygen), things come apart at high temperatures, and so it is necessary to assume that the products boiling out include $H_2O$, O, $O_2$, H, $H_2$ and OH, but in proportions that can only be guessed at. Luckily, the 'rocket scientists' learned to guess fairly accurately, to make assumptions that could be tested, but the last 1 per cent was always measured best by actual trials.

People developed their own rules of thumb (especially Esnault-Pelterie), and during World War II, German rocket people even used a weird reciprocal of specific impulse which translated as 'specific propellant consumption' and delivered values like 0.00314, where smaller was better than larger. In the end, though, specific impulse became the standard.

There was, however, one other problem with fuels like liquid hydrogen, and that was that they were continually being depleted, boiling away, and having to be topped up, while the less volatile fuels were typically hideously nasty things like aniline and RFNA, or butyl mercaptan, of which John Clark comments:

> Well it had two virtues, or maybe three. It was hypergolic with mixed acid, and it had a rather high density for a fuel. And it wasn't corrosive. But its performance was below that of a straight hydrocarbon, and its odor—! Well its odor was something to consider. Intense, pervasive and penetrating, and resembling the stink of an enraged skunk, but surpassing by far, the best efforts of *Mephitis mephitis*. It also clings to the clothes and the skin. But rocketeers are a hardy breed, and the stuff was duly and successfully fired, although it is rumored that certain rocket mechanics were excluded from their car pools and had to run

behind. Ten years after it was fired at the Naval Air Rocket Test Station—NARTS—the odor was still noticeable around the test areas.

As I burrowed in museums, libraries, archives and reminiscences, it became clear that I needed to look closely at Robert Goddard, who is acclaimed by NASA as 'the father of modern rocket propulsion'. Born in 1882, Goddard died in August 1945, at the end of World War II, knowing that there was a family resemblance between his designs and those of the V-2 rocket, and that these rockets had indeed gone into space, and knowing, too, that the smaller solid fuel rockets that developed from his work and that of his disciples, had saved many, many lives on his side of a long and bloody war. Blessed are the weapons makers, who break a stalemate and stop a war from being prolonged, and those who followed Goddard certainly did that, as we will see later.

# 11

# CHASING GODDARD

The main problem with passages like that sneering piece against Goddard in the *New York Times* in 1920 is that they are rarely, if ever, taken back to their original source. They are passed from hand to hand, travelling from book to magazine article to website and back again, gathering small additions, errors and deletions as they go. It is not a new problem: by the time printing was ready to take on Chaucer's *Canterbury Tales*, there were more than 50 manuscript copies available, and scholars are only now working out the family tree of these copies in an attempt to identify the most faithful version.

A secondary problem is that such passages are often taken out of context. Take this passage from the *Quarterly Review*, as it is usually delivered at nth-hand, presented as a critique of the practicality of steam locomotives. Here is one standard version, commonly found on the Web, where it is usually presented as the writer's own grim forebodings:

> We would as soon expect the people of Woolwich to suffer themselves
> to ride one of Congreve's ricochet rockets as to trust themselves to the
> mercy of such a machine going at such a rate.

Here it is as it appears in the actual journal, published in March 1825, on page 362—notice the subtle changes:

> It is certainly some consolation to those who are to be whirled at a rate of eighteen or twenty miles an hour, by means of a high pressure engine, to be told that they are in no danger of being seasick while on shore; that they are not to be scalded to death nor drowned by the bursting of the boiler; and that they need not mind being shot by the scattered fragments, or dashed in pieces by the flying off, or the breaking of a wheel. But with all these assurances, we should as soon expect the people of Woolwich to suffer themselves to be fired off upon one of Congreve's *ricochet* rockets, as trust themselves to the mercy of such a machine, going at such a rate . . .

While the intention of the writer is clearly to prove that a 'general railway' will not replace coaches, canals or wagons, the actual concern is with the perceptions of potential users of the system, and whether they will use it, and not about how the writer sees railways. It is interesting, though, to note that even in 1825, well after Waterloo, 'Congreve's *ricochet* rockets' held the public's attention. We may also have a suspicion of where Stephenson's *Rocket* acquired its name.

But turning back to our space sceptics, we find a favourite recycled quotation on Web pages that set out to show how blind scientists can be, attributed to one A. W. Bickerton, listed as Professor of Physics and Chemistry, Canterbury College, New Zealand, and said to be writing in 1926:

> This foolish idea of shooting at the moon is an example of the absurd lengths to which vicious specialization will carry scientist working in thought-tight compartments. Let us critically examine the proposal. For a projectile entirely to escape the gravitation of earth, it needs a velocity of 7 miles a second. The thermal energy of a gramme at this speed is 15,180 calories . . . The energy of our most violent explosive—

nitroglycerine—is less than 1,500 calories per gramme. Consequently, even had the explosive nothing to carry, it has only one-tenth of the energy necessary to escape the earth . . . Hence the proposition appears to be basically impossible . . .

No source is given for this passage, which makes it questionable as evidence. Bickerton was 84 in 1926; he retired from his chair in 1902 and left New Zealand in 1914, so the quote appears to be a little bit suspect. Bickerton was well known as an eccentric, but if he did in fact make a statement like this, it would only have helped the less qualified nay-sayers and pooh-poohers. It also occurred to me that 1926 was the year in which Robert Hutchings Goddard gained a certain notoriety over one of his rocket tests.

That made me wonder even more about Goddard, and what was said about him, so I went in search of him in Worcester, Massachusetts, about 40 miles by commuter train from Boston; even today, it takes an hour and a half by slow train to get there. That allows enough time for some fairly competent thinking, especially if you travel it often, as Robert Goddard must have done. Satisfyingly for a physicist, the train passes through Newtonville and West Newton before reaching the stations named Wellesley Farms, Wellesley Hills and Wellesley Square (yes, there's that name again!). But for all that there is a railway station called Wellesley Hills, the terrain is amazingly flat, with barely a rise worthy of the name. The greatest prominences as you cross the floodplain are the woodpiles at the backs of the houses along the line.

The train rattles along beside bodies of water, some looking like rivers, others like lakes, others mere swamps with dead trees standing in them. In the distance, it is a moot point whether the horizon is provided by a slight elevation on the far side of the water, or merely by the tree tops. From time to time, the ground rises slightly as the train passes through a miserable cutting, barely more than waist-high, in what appears to be material dumped at some past time by a glacier. This is the sort of territory that an ambitious tunnel engineer, wanting to develop a reputation, would avoid like the plague, for it is almost two-dimensional.

Then finally, as Worcester comes into view, there are some hills large enough to cause the occasional cutting, and even to offer the chance of hidden cliffs among the trees, or at least a falling-down place. Coming into Worcester, the line begins to rise, high enough that we can look down on the roofs of the two-storey clapboard houses so typical of this area. Then the train pulls into a real cutting though bedrock, high enough that the windows get no sunlight. At long last, we have reached a place where cyclists might begin to appreciate gears on their bicycles.

Perhaps it was this flatness that Goddard would have seen as he journeyed to Boston, that made him think and express his ideas in terms of *Methods of Reaching Extreme Altitudes*, as he described it in his base paper on rocketry. It was in this flat country that young Goddard grew up, and you might imagine it was his surroundings that made him dream of rising to at least considerable height, but it seems that behind it all there was a steely determination to aim a rocket, not at the moon, but at Mars, and that determination came to him before he moved to Worcester.

Two stories, both published in the *Boston Post* in 1898, entranced him. One was H. G. Wells' *War of the Worlds*, and the second was Garrett P. Serviss' work, *Edison's Conquest of Mars*. The Wells story, of course, is famous and still in print, but the Serviss work seems not to have been published in book form until 1947, and when I was there, the Library of Congress copy had gone missing. Nonetheless, Goddard recognised both writers as formative influences, and his papers from later years include correspondence with both of them.

Goddard spent almost his entire working life associated with Clark College and Clark University in Worcester. He had studied there, and after only a brief period away, followed by a bout of tuberculosis that was expected to kill him, he was on the faculty of Clark for the rest of his life, and his papers remain there to this day—carbon copies of his letters, and originals from the many luminaries of science and rocketry who wrote to him. One fascinating sideline emerged in the manuscripts collection at the Library of Congress, in the form of two letters from Goddard to one Edwin E. Aldrin, then an army lieutenant. It appears that Aldrin's papers have gone to the Library of Congress, and the two letters constitute the entirety of the library's Goddard holdings, aside from many rolls of microfilm. In the Goddard papers, there are carbon copies of these letters, and many other exchanges over the years with Aldrin.

The name E. E. Aldrin may ring a slight bell—this correspondent and friend was, in fact, the father of 'Buzz' Aldrin, otherwise Edwin Eugene Aldrin junior, astronaut on the Apollo 11 mission. Aldrin senior had been a student at Clark (he graduated in 1915), where he knew Goddard well, and he clearly shared Goddard's enthusiasm for rockets, as we can see from their correspondence over the years. Where Goddard barely lived long enough to see the V-2 rockets and know that his dreams had some sort of basis in reality, Aldrin lived long enough to see his son walk on the moon.

The point where Clark University meets Main Street, Worcester is marked by an iron railing with stone spheres, just like Turkish cannonballs, on the major posts, and smaller iron spheres, just like British cannonballs, on the smaller iron posts. Main Street is a busy road in small-town USA where cars thunder rap music through the open windows of summer, and screech to a halt to allow squirrels to cross in safety. Just after the end of spring term, the Clark University bookstore on Main Street had all sorts of memorabilia for new graduates to celebrate their alumnification, but Goddard was nowhere to be seen. The clerk in the store did not even recognise the name. The manager did know the name, and promised to 'look into it', but I went away empty-handed.

No matter, though, for just around the corner Goddard's papers are stored in a purpose-built structure, the Robert H. Goddard Library. This is in the New Brutalist style, with the main library perching on concrete pillars that offer just a hint of the fins of a 1930s rocket, and not a cannonball, faux or otherwise, in sight. Most of the ground floor area is clear and, in the centre, a 500-year time capsule sits. Put in place by then Vice-President Hubert H. Humphrey, it is due to be opened in 2466 when, with any sort of luck, the seekers will find intact a model of a 1940 Goddard rocket, complete with tail fins.

Overhead, the New Brutalist concrete is already beginning to fret, but I have to suspect that if it collapses, even if the fine conceit of the time capsule is lost, Goddard's name will live on, even if, like Roger Bacon, he is sometimes confused with other later owners of the same surname. It seems an appropriate place for a phallic rocket to be represented, for the library stands on the site where the American Psychological Association was founded, and Clark is where Freud and Jung were first listened to attentively by an audience.

Carl Sagan mentions these lectures, and wonders whether Goddard might have ever listened to one of Freud's lectures, but it is unlikely, for he would have had his own full program that

*The Robert H. Goddard Library in Worcester, with its concrete representations of rocket fins.*

week, all devoted to physics, and his inspiration came not from psychologists' theories. As a matter of fact, while Goddard said later that he first caught the bug of space travel in 1898 when he read the stories in the *Boston Post*, his notes and diaries identify 19 October 1899 as the date on which he decided to devote the rest of his life to space travel by rockets.

First, though, he needed to get some qualifications, and while he would later advise young rocket enthusiasts to study mechanical engineering, he trained as a physicist. By June 1907 he was 25, and had his first publication (on balancing an aircraft with a gyroscope) in *Scientific American*, although in October 1907 the journal rejected his proposal for a paper on the 'Possibility of investigating interplanetary space'. Thereafter, mentions of jets and rockets may be found scattered through his papers. By July 1913, Goddard sent his first patent application for rockets to his patent attorneys, the first of 214 that he was to obtain.

Goddard the physicist looked at both guncotton and hydrogen/oxygen as propellants in 1914, but this was not really novel, given that Tsiolkovsky had already been down this path. One of his other comments, a year earlier, has a startling modernity. After ruling out guns and waves as methods of launching a mass to the moon, he continues: 'The storing of kinetic energy by rapidly moving charged particles, and the utilization of intra-atomic energy, are not so self-evidently impossible'.

Then again, perhaps it is not that startling. The same year, in *The World Set Free*, H. G. Wells actually prophesied atomic bombs. First he describes something remarkably like a chain reaction:

> Why is the change gradual? Why does only a minute fraction of the radium disintegrate in any particular second? Why does it dole itself out so slowly and so exactly? Why does not all the uranium change to radium and all the radium change to the next lowest thing at once?

Why this decay by driblets; why not a decay *en masse*? Suppose presently we find it possible to quicken that decay?

H.G. Wells, *The World Set Free*, 1913

Later in the book, Wells describes the use of the bomb, which he sees as being used against Berlin in 1956:

> The gaunt face hardened to grimness, and with both hands the bomb-thrower lifted the big atomic bomb from the box and steadied it against the side. It was a black sphere two feet in diameter. Between its handles was a little celluloid stud, and to this he bent his head until his lips touched it. Then he had to bite in order to let the air in upon the inducive. Sure of its accessibility, he craned his neck over the side of the aeroplane and judged his pace and distance. Then very quickly he bent forward, bit the stud, and hoisted the bomb over the side.

While there is no evidence that Goddard ever read the book, it is likely he did, as he read most of Wells' other works, but he had his own ideas on nuclear power even earlier. Wells may have suggested an atomic bomb in 1913, but as far back as 1907 Goddard was speculating about the use of atomic power in a rocket, noting that the energy emitted by one gram of radium was 790 000 times that of a gram of cordite, 'enough to lift 5000 tons a height somewhat over 100 yards'. In 1915, he records how he had read Wells' *The First Men in the Moon*, and a few days later dreamed of going to the moon and setting off a 'red fire' to indicate his arrival, a theme that would recur some years later.

While Goddard could see the value of liquid fuels, he began working on solid fuels first, since these can at least be used to establish some of the principles of rocketry. The main problem with liquid fuels lies with their delivery to the combustion chamber, and most of the obvious methods like gas pressure drives and gravity do not work all that well in reality, since such systems do not offer the constant conditions required. It comes down to using some sort of pump, but what sort of pump do you use to deliver ultracold liquids? And what lubricants can you use that will not freeze up?

In the end, liquids would offer one major advantage, in that they can be turned on and off at will, whereas a solid fuel rocket is just a very large tube of high explosive, burning with enormous fury until it is snuffed out. Tsiolkovsky recognised the advantage of liquid fuel, and so did Goddard, but he needed money to develop his ideas, and that generated his major problem.

On 6 April 1917, the United States entered the war against Germany, and by 11 April Goddard had made his first approach to the government, urging the use of his rocket. Being restricted to rockets based on solid fuel meant limited control, aside from what the launching tube could offer in the way of a starting direction, but all the same, a light and recoil-free weapon that could be used at a range of 50 or 100 yards to hurl grenade-sized explosives was going to be a definite start in the right direction.

One of Goddard's supporters at this time was Charles Abbot, director of the Smithsonian Astrophysical Observatory, who would have dearly loved to get his hands on a high-flying rocket able to take measurements beyond the atmosphere; within a few days, he wrote to C. D. Walcott, Secretary at the Smithsonian, suggesting that a budget of $50 000 would allow Goddard to produce bombs that might travel 100 miles. With war-fever morality, he wrote:

> The lateral aim I should think would be good, but the under- or over-shooting of the target quite probable. However if it were desired to destroy the Krupp works at Essen a large number of trials with different probable ranges might probably accomplish it from the French

lines by means of Goddard's invention, provided the Allies were as
willing to disregard the rights of noncombatants in Germany as are the
Germans to murder noncombatants everywhere.

C.G. Abbot, letter to C.D. Walcott, 14 April 1917

In other words, he was urging a course of action rather like that
of the German use of the V-2 a generation later—except that the
German were not aiming the V-2 for anything more precise than
cities and ports, given their limited accuracy. The Germans
themselves had no such qualms, and on 23 March 1918 they
brought in what they called either *Lange Max* or *Wilhelm
Geschutz* ('William's Gun'), but generally known as the 'Paris
Gun' or, confusingly, 'Big Bertha', a name that really belongs to
a different gun.

The true 'Paris Gun' was 34 metres long and had a range of
about 130 kilometres—big enough to fire from behind the
German lines into Paris, though with absolutely no accuracy.
Not that this mattered, because, like the later V-2, it was
intended to destroy morale. Between March and August, 351
shells were launched, killing 256 people and wounding 620,
enough to make people angry, but probably not enough to sap
morale.

In fairness, both sides were losing huge numbers of men, and
so could not really be blamed for casting around for ways out of
the stalemate that was trench warfare. Goddard may or may not
have known of Walcott's war-mongering speculations, but he
never got close to the sort of range that would be needed. He did
get some money to work on a demonstration rocket, but even
then still had his eye on the peaceful uses that his rockets could
later be applied to, as this letter reveals:

The finished article should be referred to as the 'Goddard Rocket,' or
something of that sort. This is because, as I told you, I wish eventually

to use the thing for scientific work, and inasmuch as this promises
to be expensive, I shall probably have to call for grants or subscrip-
tions . . .

Robert H. Goddard, letter to George Rockwood, 26 December, 1916

Rockwood was a local manufacturer of sprinkler fittings, who
later tried his hardest to steal Goddard's work, hiring away his
foreman and trying to arrange contracts with other parts of the
US Army, saying that he could produce rockets of the Goddard
design. Ever after, Goddard would require confidentiality agree-
ments of his staff, and the upshot was that he moved to
Pasadena, California, for the rest of the war.

In hindsight, this was an excellent move, as it led directly to
Goddard's acquiring the services of Clarence Hickman, who
remained his loyal supporter even after mangling both hands in
an accident that Goddard reported to the Smithsonian:

> This morning, while Mr. Hickman was removing the paper cap from
> the blasting cap on a 10-gram cartridge, the cartridge exploded, and
> necessitated the amputation, on the left hand, of the thumb to the first
> joint, and the first two fingers to the second joint; and on the right
> hand, of the first finger to the first joint. There were also numerous
> cuts on the face and the chest, but these were of minor consequence.
> Fortunately, his eyes escaped any injury.

Robert H. Goddard, letter to secretary, Smithsonian Institution,<br>8 August, 1918

Later, Hickman would say how fortunate he was that the normal
surgeon was unavailable, and a railroad surgeon was called in, a
man who knew that every joint lost meant more cost to the railroad in compensation, and who saved far more than Hickman
could otherwise have hoped for. Hickman was back at work
almost immediately, and stayed with Goddard as his right-hand
man to the end of World War I, before joining Bell Telephone

Laboratories, from which he will re-emerge, a little later in this story, to sponsor wholesale rocket work as World War II loomed.

One of Goddard's problems was that by the time he and Hickman set up their demonstration of the 'recoilless gun' at the Aberdeen Proving Ground, up the coast from Fort McHenry, it was November 1918, and while the trials went off superbly, with a rocket being launched from a flimsy music stand which remained upright, the war was over and the need for rockets had died away. Nobody wanted to know about armaments any more.

There is a curious parallel here: Ralph Wedgwood, a member of the famous potting family, proposed an electric telegraph to the Royal Navy in 1814, just as peace broke out all over war-weary Europe. Lord Castlereagh at the Admiralty replied that the existing system of shutter semaphores on hilltops was enough, since the war was at an end, and money was scarce. Maybe if Napoleon had kept going for a bit longer in 1815, Wedgwood might have stood a chance, but as it was, no more came of his ideas either, and the electric telegraph had to wait another twenty years, by which time the electric relay had been invented, making electric telegraphy feasible.

With no military support, Goddard went back to civil sources for finance. In 1919, he wrote his famous report for the Smithsonian, 'A Method of Reaching Extreme Altitudes', in which he spoke of using rockets to go higher than a sounding balloon, then and now limited to around 20 miles or 30 kilometres.

At one point, the report mentions heights as great as 232 miles (some 370 km) above ground, citing Alfred Wegener (better recalled these days for his notions on continental drift) as an expert on what might be found there. Wegener apparently suggested in 1911 that a new element, 'geocoronium', with a mass 0.4 times that of hydrogen, surrounded the earth. In fact, his geocoronium was atomic nitrogen in the upper atmosphere.

Talking to the press, the usually cautious Goddard put his foot in it somewhat. He speculated about sending a rocket to the moon, laden with eight or ten tons of flash powder, where an explosion would be set off, signalling that the rocket had landed. Once this got out, of course, the press were agog over 'Goddard's moon rocket'. The strange mail began to arrive, and some of it is to be found in the published papers of Goddard, though his editors (one of whom was Mrs Goddard) seem to have left out some of the most outrageous, perhaps out of a sense of respect. Nonetheless, some of the wilder material is still to be found in the collection. For example, film star Mary Pickford's publicity agent wired Goddard in January 1920:

> WOULD BE GRATEFUL FOR OPPORTUNITY TO SEND MESSAGE TO MOON
> FROM MARY PICKFORD ON YOUR TORPEDO ROCKET WHEN IT STARTS.

There appears to be no record of what Goddard said to this, or to a proposal from Hurd and Reidy, an outdoor advertising firm from Elgin, Illinois, hoping 'to secure space for a suitable ad'.

More numerous were the volunteers for passengers on the 'moon rocket'; we will sample just one, emanating from Khartoum in 1922. While the overtypings and hand-made amendments are left out, the original spelling is retained.

> I have the honour to lay the following for your information and views in the matter.
>
> I am a Mwalad 19 years of age and a translator at Khartoum Province. During my youth I thought many times to discover a new thing in this World, but no pecuniary help to encourage me to go into the matter. It appears to me that ther are some mountains in the moon and such news in the Sudan care no body.
>
> Lately I thought to go to America to study there to exceed my knowledges and perhaps I may find an assistant to give me a hand to

help make a journey round the World, but I found that the entrance conditions are very difficult for me.

A week ago I read in the (Rewayat el Mossara) that you have already invented a rocket which fly to the moon in a few hours and I understand that two fellows and a Miss offerre themselves to fly up but you have postponed their long journey.

Now I write you this OFFERING myself to be added to the society going to the moon and if not possible now I wish to come and remain with you under your service as a voltuneer pupil to try me in your own dangerous inventions.

It came to my knowledge that many of the mindless people mock at your HIGH INVENTION, which I consider very excellent.

I am a poor one and possess nothing else my pay, which is 7 Pounds monthly, any how I am hoping to receive your favourable reply by the first possible chance, to come to you.

Yours most obediently,

Ahmed Hassan

Translator, Khartoum Province

Most of the volunteers came from America, others from Europe and Britain. Letters of protest seemed to have no particular centre, though there was a common theme: the risk of disturbing or harming or provoking the people in the moon—there was no lack of certainty that there were people in the moon.

In fact, Goddard's mind was more set on going to Mars, and had been since 1898, and he felt later that if he had referred to that aim there might have been less excitement from the general public, back in the days before Orson Welles terrified America with his radio production of H. G. Wells' *War of the Worlds*. It was too late: the die was cast, and his rockets would be moon rockets, no matter what he ever said. Goddard had now been burned twice: once by the foreman who deserted him for Rockwood, the rival would-be rocket maker in Worcester, and once

*Goddard used a simple, and pretty flimsy-looking, frame to stabilise his earliest rockets.*

by the public outcry. He was still to learn what a hindrance the public gaze and press interest could be.

Goddard's science was impeccable, however, so he got the money he sought from the Smithsonian, and in 1926 achieved a milestone, the first launch of a liquid fuel rocket. This start of an era was seen by four people: Goddard, his wife, Henry Sachs, the machinist who lit the rocket with a blowtorch, and Dr Percy Roope, who tracked its course with a theodolite. Fuelled by liquid oxygen and gasoline, the rocket flew for only 2.5 seconds, climbed 41 feet, and landed 184 feet away in a cabbage patch. When the rocket was lit, Esther Goddard started a movie camera, but the film ran out after seven seconds. Too heavy to lift off immediately, the rocket burned for another thirteen seconds before the thrust was greater than the mass, and it flew. Goddard described it in his diary:

> It looked almost magical as it rose, without any appreciably greater noise or flame, as if it said, 'I've been here long enough; I think I'll be going somewhere else, if you don't mind' . . . Some of the surprising things were the absence of smoke, the lack of a very loud roar, and the smallness of the flame.

The lack of smoke would indeed be a surprise. Goddard used a rich fuel mix, with only 1.3 to 1.4 pounds of oxygen for each pound of gasoline, where about 3.5 pounds would have been needed for complete combustion. This rich mix still gave him a specific impulse of around 170 seconds, and he probably used it to keep the temperature down and prolong his rockets' lives.

The lack of a roar was certainly not a problem with the next milestone launch in 1929. Goddard's notebooks tell the story:

> Owing to the flight being the highest so far attained, and the flame, using an excess of gasoline, producing a loud noise and a bright white flare, neighbors sent in calls for ambulances, thinking that an airplane

had caught fire and crashed. Unknown to me, two police ambulances searched through Auburn for 'victims', and an airplane was sent from the Grafton airport for the same purpose.

Goddard issued a soothing statement, pointing out that this was not a moon shot, that all had gone to plan, and so on and so forth, and that nothing had exploded, but to no avail. The press had descended, seen blackened spots near the test stand, charred vegetation and twisted pipes, and that was enough. They thought (and wrote) the worst:

TERRIFIC EXPLOSION AS PROF. GODDARD OF CLARK SHOOTS HIS MOON ROCKET

*Worcester Evening Post*

'MOON ROCKET' MAN'S TEST ALARMS WHOLE COUNTRYSIDE

*Boston Globe*

GODDARD EXPERIMENTAL ROCKET EXPLODES IN AIR

*Worcester Evening Gazette*

Professor Goddard had been burned for the third and last time. With the locals carrying on about explosions, and the risk of excitable accounts appearing at any time, he felt it was time to move on. Abbot, the secretary of the Smithsonian Institution, firmly admonished the press, stating that the Smithsonian had no part in wild schemes to go to the moon, that the Goddard rocket was merely a way of getting scientific packages to a great height—but the comparative privacy of New Mexico was beckoning.

There was a good side to all the publicity, because aviator Charles Lindbergh read one of the stories that followed, in *Popular Science Monthly*. In his autobiography, Lindbergh said he sought to know if man could conquer space, and so asked for and obtained a meeting with Goddard (and in his account reveals

what Goddard was privately saying, no matter what the Smithsonian secretary denied):

> Goddard said a rocket could be built that would reach the moon, and
> that jet propulsion could be used advantageously to power airplanes.
> The thought of sending a rocket to the moon set my mind spinning. If
> man could reach the moon, then why not thence to the planets, even to
> the stars? My interest in Goddard's accomplishments and ideas began a
> collaboration and friendship that continued until his death. Through-
> out, I was able to help him obtain essential funds for his experiments.

More importantly, Lindbergh had been at the home of Harry and
Carol Guggenheim when Carol Guggenheim showed him the
story. The end result was that for most of the 1930s, Goddard
was given financial support by Daniel Guggenheim, the father
of Lindbergh's friend Harry, as well as by the Smithsonian.

It did no harm that a stunt had taken place in Germany the
previous year, when Fritz von Opel and Max Valier had demonstrated a rocket car. This merely used gunpowder, but to a lay
audience a rocket was a rocket, and people believed that the
Germans were getting the upper hand. Goddard got his money.

Working slowly, with scientific aims, Goddard never
pursued distance records, as it was enough to have a rocket fly
under control—if a new method worked on a short flight, there
was no reason to expect that it would fail on a longer one, but it
was essential to get the elements of the method just right. These
included vanes that dipped into the rocket exhaust, guided by
gyroscopes, to bring the rocket under control and keep it stable.

Throughout the 1930s there was a steady stream of requests
for information from military attachés around the world, all
neatly avoided with careful inscrutability. A few of these letters
surface in the published papers, but many more lie in the
archives held at the Goddard Library, and all were fended off in

Robert Goddard and his crew prepare to launch test no. 74, in October 1931.

the same bland and genial way, with Goddard saying that he was not yet ready to publish, but that the enquirer would hear all about it when there was something to report. Two letters seem to indicate that Goddard was aware of the problem of releasing any kind of information as far back as 1926 (perhaps after his experiences with Rockwood and the US military). The first is from Robert Lademann, who was engaged in translating Goddard's 1919 paper into German:

> I am writing this letter in a great hurry to you because I have just found out that a Russian with name: Mr. Alexander Boris Scherschevsky, who as a matter of fact is not known as a gentleman here and from whom I have the pretty sure feeling that he is working in some capacity for the Russian Government has the intention to write to you in order to get some information to build a rocket . . .

The second is a reply to Goddard from Abbot at the Smithsonian Institution, which is perhaps as interesting for its use of what seems a modern word, 'leaks', in 1927: 'We have your letter of a few weeks ago, cautioning us to avoid leaks in regard to your work, and are duly attending to it'.

It is also clear that Goddard had in the back of his mind that his own nation might one day use rockets, and regular approaches to the military are apparent in his papers. After Lindbergh wrote to Goddard in some alarm in 1937 about German rocket developments, there are hints in the published papers that more military interest might have been developing. In May 1938, Goddard felt his liquid fuel rockets were far enough advanced to ask Clarence Hickman to return to work with him for a while, and while Hickman's response was enthusiastic he entered a plea of other commitments.

By this time, Germany had annexed Austria, and nobody doubted that war was on the way. The Goddards had been planning a trip to Hawaii, but when accommodation fell through, Goddard suggested seeing Europe 'before it blew up'.

By now there were parallel rocket strands beginning to appear in the USA. Frank Malina was at work in Caltech, and in 1937 made himself infamous when he tried nitrogen tetroxide and methanol inside a building, garnering a reputation as 'head of the suicide squad'. A year earlier, in 1936, another new face appeared on the scene when Midshipman Robert Truax wrote to Goddard asking for some basic information. Later generations seem only to refer to him as Bob Truax, and most who have heard of him know him best as the maker of Evil Knievel's rocket bike, but there was much more to Truax than that. There was rocket work going on in Britain under Alwyn (later, Sir Alwyn) Crow, mainly directed at anti-aircraft uses and depth-charge launchers, but at least it was rocket work; in Russia, work was also progressing. In fact, when war came, the Russians would be the first to make large-scale use of rockets.

And as the United States began to prepare for war, one man was well placed to promote the use of rockets. Dr C. N. Hickman of Bell Telephone Laboratories, Goddard's friend Clarence, proposed that the National Defense Research Committee use rockets in many ways. Among the uses he listed in 1940 were recoilless guns, jet-propelled armour-piercing bombs, rockets on tanks and other vehicles, for infantry, for submarines and small boats, rockets to deliver chemicals, and even aircraft rockets. The problem was that the services were sceptical about the inaccurate and unreliable rockets. The younger men, and those young in their minds, could see the way to go, but senior officers who had entered their careers on horseback still had some problems.

One blow for Goddard was that he was pulled into developing JATO units, rocket boosters to get aircraft into the air, and while he explored 'gasoline-lox' systems for JATO during the war, his liquid-fuelled rocket work came to a halt. It is perhaps symptomatic of the way rockets were regarded even then that the word 'rocket' was avoided in favour of 'jet' when the acronym JATO (jet-assisted take-off) was coined. Most of the other work before the war was on short-range tactical weapons using solid propellants that would require no special containers or treatment, that would deliver high explosive rather further than it could be thrown, without recoil.

The main problem with JATOs was that the early models were filled with black powder, and they tended to explode after they had been left a few days. The powder mix dried and cracked, and flame penetrated those cracks, producing uncontrolled burning that generated too much gas. A proper burn was

*An Ercoupe aircraft, taking off during the early JATO tests, August 1942.*

only on the face of the hollow drilled into the mass of powder, and it proceeded smoothly along, eating away at a regular pace, keeping the thrust constant.

The simple solution was to heat roofing tar, asphalt, to around 350°F, and then add potassium perchlorate. The procedure may sound risky, but that was a temperature of 175°C, and potassium perchlorate only decomposes at 400°C. This was added to the casings, and it turned out to last—and to burn more slowly, giving better performance.

There seems to have been a remarkable degree of high-up commitment to simple rockets, however, and when war came Bob Truax was allowed to have whoever he liked for his research program, according to the people who worked with him at Aerojet. 'He just looked at the cards, and said which ones he wanted,' they told me. Truax himself had qualified as a 'rocket scientist' only by experimenting with rockets in his spare time, using scrounged parts, but now it began to pay off.

Robert Goddard died of cancer at the age of 62, in early August 1945, not long after Clark University gave him an honorary Doctorate of Science. He never got back to New Mexico to launch any more rockets, he never saw the captured V-2s fly in the year that followed, though he had seen some of the parts and recognised that the principles behind them were all familiar. He never saw, as he deserved to, satellites launched, or humans in space. Unjustly, he was deprived of the triumph he might have had through things he might have seen.

Even seeing landings on the moon would not have been out of the realms of possibility for him, for he would only have been 86 at the time. Even so, he died knowing that his vision was sound, he could be sure that there would be a future and he probably had the confidence in his work to know that his name would be recalled.

Goddard undoubtedly had the vision, but was he the real pioneer that he is often seen as? Two of the early hands from Aerojet, Bill Zisch and Robert Gordon, objected to a comment in *Aerojet: The Creative Company*, an unofficial history of the company, that referred to Goddard as the 'unquestioned inventive genius of modern liquid propellant rockets', arguing that Theodore von Kármán and Frank Malina and their associates deserved that recognition. Goddard, they said, was too secretive and failed to cooperate. Of course, both von Kármán and Malina were associated with Aerojet, so they might be expected to say that. It is true, however, that while Goddard had led by example, and was responsible for there being people ready to think in terms of rockets, it was other workers who, inspired by Goddard, came through and actually produced successful rockets.

And in Germany, of course, it did no harm at all for the rocket workers there to know that rocket flight using liquid fuels was indeed possible, even if they lacked the fine detail on Goddard's work. If they had access to the *Neues Wiener Journal* for 23 July 1929, they knew all about Goddard, and were not going to be fooled by yarns about going to the moon:

> Professor Goddard is only incidentally a physicist at the Worcester University. In his chief profession he is the most important expert in America for the building of long-range heavy guns. His real field is ballistics, a branch of knowledge which has little to do with a trip to the moon, but on the contrary has much to do with the business of war. Ballistics is the science of building guns and Professor Goddard is the most important theoretician in the manufacture of cannons and munitions in America. His so-frequently announced and much-discussed moon rocket and the numerous experiments for its achievement are nothing more than a screen for the building and testing of new kinds of long-range guns, whose shells will not hit the moon, but instead the terrestrial fortifications or tanks of the enemies of America in a future world war.

# 12

# ROCKETS
# IN WORLD
# WAR II

... by applying itself to an improper object science may eventually fall by its own hand. In reference to this subject we must also deplore the prostitution of science for the aggrandisement of individuals and nations, the result being that the weaker is destroyed and the stronger is established on its ruins.

James Prescott Joule, speech written but never delivered as
President of the British Association

Let those who find themselves fascinated by this idea go quietly about the business of improving rocket design, rather than drum up publicity and complain of neglect. Mr. Cleator thinks it a pity that the Air Ministry evinced not the slightest interest in his ideas; provided that an equal indifference is shown by other Ministries elsewhere, we all ought to be profoundly thankful.

Professor Richard Woolley, *Nature*, 14 March 1936, p. 442

How those Nazi rockets reminded me of Professor Goddard's, blown up in size, and how deadly efficient they had grown! The Professor's record altitude was between eight and nine thousand feet, but he never tried for distance across ground. At the top of its trajectory a V-2 hurtled about sixty miles above the earth, and it carried a one-ton warhead from the Continent to England. How could the Germans have jumped so quickly and so far ahead of Goddard's pioneering work? Partly because America built rockets for scientific knowledge, at a tempo set for peace, while Germany developed them for war.

Charles Lindbergh, *Autobiography of Values*, 1945

It all began, probably, with the terms of the Treaty of Versailles in 1918, which limited any future German rearmament, but failed to mention rockets while barring large-calibre artillery. By the time Woolley made his comment in 1936, the German drive to develop what would become the V-2 was well on the way to what Lindbergh would see in May 1945. Anybody looking unkindly at Goddard's slow progress would need to look then at the similarly slow process, with a much larger team and a steady budget, made by the German rocket team as they worked on the development of what they called at that time the A-4.

The *Neues Wiener Journal* knew who would win the race into space. The 1929 article cited at the end of the last chapter, having outed Goddard as a gun maker, went on in rather chilling terms:

And what will happen to the moon rocket? It was born as the daughter of the American war technique, but it will not remain so. The Saxon Oberth and his young men have long since taken over leadership in this area . . . [a]nd this moon rocket, the real one, will rise to its cosmic goal, not from America, but from old Europe.

*Neues Wiener Journal*, 23 July, 1929

Germany was on the way back, and the *Neues Wiener Journal* was talking to German speakers, wherever they were. Hermann Oberth is an example: born in 1894 in the Austro-Hungarian Transylvania that later became Rumania, he studied first at the University of Cluj (Klausenburg) in Romania, then went on to Munich, Göttingen and Heidelberg. He missed out on a doctorate because his dissertation related to practical problems of space flight rather than to astronomy.

But if the new Germany saw Goddard as one of those 'everybody's-doing-it' secret armaments makers, Oberth was pursuing a dream of space travel at that stage—at least in public. In 1917, he had proposed a monster missile-rocket to the German War Department. This would have used watered alcohol, derived from sugar beet, and liquid oxygen, but the idea was turned down—by then, the War Department was on the way to using the 'Paris Gun'.

So Oberth turned to peaceful space rockets, proposing an alcohol-powered first stage and a hydrogen-powered second stage, and raising a number of other issues in public for the first time. For example, he proposed that the rocket nozzle conform to the shape designed by Carl Gustaf De Laval, a Swedish turbine engineer, and known as the convergent-divergent De Laval nozzle. Both Goddard and Tsiolkovsky had considered this design and approved it, but Oberth was the first to name it in public.

He did this in 1923 in a popular book based on his doctoral work, *Die Rakete zu den Planetenraümen* (*The Rocket into Interplanetary Space*), otherwise *Die Rakete*. In just 87 pages, Oberth managed to thoroughly ruffle Goddard's feathers, because many of the things Goddard had thought of, Oberth published first.

Oberth proposed a hydrogen-lox engine that could be stopped and started in space, a space telescope, space suits, a space station and much more, and it was *Die Rakete* that inspired the German interest at this time. By 1929, Oberth had published a second edition of more than 400 pages, *Wege zur Raumschiffahrt* (*The Road to Space Travel*), which drew also on the burgeoning space-flight literature of the 1920s. In Germany at least, the space dreamers were wide awake, even if their ideas would be borrowed in a few years to further the war effort.

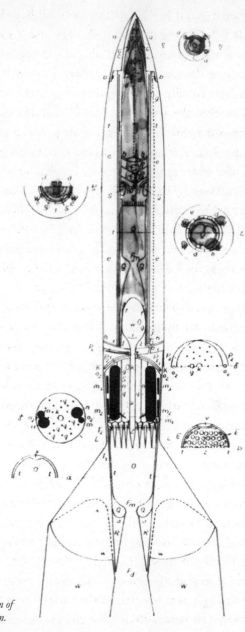

*A schematic diagram of
Oberth's rocket design.*

Oberth found himself championed by Max Valier, who contemplated something rather like the space shuttle, and who believed that the moon and all the planets are coated in ice (something that had long since been disproven at Birr Castle); others were equally enthusiastic in their own strange ways.

Whatever the truth of some of the claims, we know that Walter Hohmann was looking at the peaceful uses of rockets in space by 1925, and some of his calculations are still in use, in particular where space probes use a 'slingshot' or 'gravity assist' like those used by the Galileo and Cassini missions. The German Rocket Society was formed in June 1927 (known in German as the VfR or Verein fur Raumschiffart); in 1928, rocket societies were formed in Leningrad and Moscow. The same year, Opel and Valier showed off a 'rocket car' in public, but Goddard dismissed this as a mere 'black powder rocket', a stunt.

The year 1930 was an interesting time: Otto Ruff discovered a substance far more lively than nitrogen triiodide: chlorine trifluoride, which was magnificently hypergolic with almost anything, exploding in contact with water, ice, cloth, wood, flesh, and even silica-containing items like sand, glass and asbestos. This hideously dangerous material had a short experimental life, but even conventional fuels carried risks—Max Valier was killed in May when a rocket exploded, and his aorta was cut by flying debris.

The dream of a space-going rocket plane did not die with Valier, though. Eugen Sänger worked in Austria for many years on his idea for the 'Silver Bird', although during the war he changed it to the 'Antipodal Bomber' to keep his funding. It was to be a 100-ton rocket plane that would climb into space, and then skip around the world, bouncing off the atmosphere like a stone skipping across water. In the end the project was cancelled, and Sänger died in 1964 before the plans for the space shuttle were formed—although his collaborator, Irene Bredt (later his wife, Irene Sänger) did see the shuttle fly.

In 1933, Reinhold Tiling had his laboratory blow up. Fatally burned, he crawled to a nearby pond and died, but by then, he had a 2-metre rocket said to be capable of crossing the English Channel. In 1934, Karl Wahmke was also killed, and several of his assistants were injured. Experimenters in other nations were being injured as well, like Robert Esnault-Pelterie in France, but over time the more exotic fuels were passed up in favour of safer formulations.

The major problem with fuelling military rockets, at least, was that they either needed to be ready to fly at all times, or had to be topped up with fuel and oxidiser, possibly under battle conditions. In most situations, defensive weapons such as anti-tank and anti-aircraft missiles were far more effective with their always-ready solid fuels, but the V-2, which was to be set up and used to rain terror on static targets at the convenience of the attacker, could use a liquid fuel and a liquid oxidiser.

Germany started exploring the power of liquid fuel rockets in an official way in about 1930, when Walter Dornberger was supposedly working on liquid fuel rockets under Karl Emil Becker, though he really concentrated mainly on small battlefield solid-fuel rockets. By 1932, Wernher von Braun was on the scene, holding a civilian position in the army's rocket program. When most of the VfR followed von Braun, it was disbanded, possibly with Gestapo encouragement.

While von Braun was undertaking a PhD program, he also managed to get his first rocket in the air in 1934, the A-2, which used ethanol and liquid oxygen. Soon after, the whole operation got too large, and it was moved to Peenemünde, on the Baltic coast.

By 1937, work was under way on the A-4, the rocket that

would later be used as the V-2 (and I will use this better-known name hereafter, to avoid confusion). This used a mix of ethanol and water as fuel, with liquid oxygen, although the fuel pumps were driven by 80 per cent hydrogen peroxide, a system that had been developed by Helmuth Walter to use directly as a rocket. At first kept under wraps by the Luftwaffe, the Walter system was used in early 1937 to help launch a Heinkel Kadett off the ground, making it the first successful JATO unit. Later that year, the first rocket-plane, also using $H_2O_2$ was flown, and the later Messerschmitt 163-A also used hydrogen peroxide, which operates as a monopropellant.

Just as Goddard's work took time and many trials, so the V-2 went through many troubles. The first trial launch in March 1942 flew less than a kilometre before crashing. In August 1942, the second trial rocket rose to a height of seven miles before it exploded. After Lübeck was bombed in the spring of 1942, Hitler wanted revenge and called for 3000 V-2 rockets a month, a quota later raised to 5000 a month. This would have consumed an annual 75 000 tons of liquid oxygen when German production was just 26 000 tons/year.

The third try was perfect. On 3 October 1942, another A-4 roared aloft from Peenemünde, followed its programmed trajectory perfectly, and landed on target 120 miles (almost 200 kilometres) away. This launch can fairly be said to mark the beginning of the space age.

Within two months, the first successful V-1 flight also occurred. Far from being a rocket, however, this was a pilotless plane or flying bomb. It was driven by a pulse-jet engine that gave 200–300 pulses per minute, making the characteristic buzzing noise that gave it the British name of 'buzz-bomb'. It used 1 gallon per mile of 80 octane petrol, carried in a 150 gallon tank, and it was guided by three gyroscopes for direction and altitude. (The V in the V weapons, incidentally, stands for *Vergeltungswaffe*, or revenge.)

About the same time, an unnamed Danish chemist got word through to the British of a German rocket able to fly 300 kilometres; a second report said it could carry a 5-ton warhead, while another informant raised that to 10 tons, which scientists said translated into a rocket 120 feet tall. That was enough to worry about.

The Germans also had something to worry about, and that was a V-2 that had gone missing when it was test-fired into Poland. One of the problems with marching into another country and trashing the place is that the residents don't like you. They get surly and uncooperative, and when the Polish resistance saw the missing V-2 rocket in May 1944, they decided the Germans would probably want it back. So they sank it in a bog near the River Bug.

The Poles retrieved some corrosive fluid that turned out to be hydrogen peroxide, used to drive the pumps and other parts, and prepared a report on what they had found. The next problem was to get this information to London. A New Zealander, Stanley Culliford, flew in a Dakota (DC-3) from Brindisi with a British crew and a Polish co-pilot interpreter. They collected the courier with the report and a bag of parts.

The plane got stuck at take-off, and in attempting to get it free the crew deliberately cut the hydraulic cables on the undercarriage; it had to land back in Brindisi without brakes, but the DC-3 is a robust craft, and after some quick mechanical work it was off again, first to Rabat in Morocco, and then to London. Then followed some elaborate farce as the Polish courier declared that he would only hand the material to a Polish officer, drawing a knife when British officers tried to separate him from the bag. In the end it was delivered, and another piece of the jigsaw fell into place at the end of July 1944.

Production of the V-2s had started in 1943, and they were launched against London in September 1944. The offensive came too late to affect the course of the war, but the V-2s did considerable damage to Antwerp (which was hit by twice as many of the rockets as London), and they demonstrated that rockets could indeed fly into space and return again.

One odd effect of the V-2 program was the triggering of the Arnhem offensive in 1944. The V-2 had a range of just 320 kilometres, so if the Allies advanced far enough into the Netherlands to push back the German lines, the rockets would not be able to reach London. The bridge over the Rhine near Arnhem was the key to a successful push, and so a British Division and the Polish Independent Parachute Brigade were detailed to capture it.

Unfortunately the troops were dropped 13 kilometres from the bridge, for fear of stronger anti-aircraft defences in its vicinity. Unbeknown to the Allies, there were two Panzer divisions in the area, and there was just too much ground to be covered. While the pressure was briefly taken off London as the remainder of the V-2s were withdrawn to the north and east, it was at severe cost. With only trench mortars (some of them 'sawn-offs' that would fit in a greatcoat pocket), the British and Polish infantry were no match for German heavy armour and artillery.

Perhaps if they had been equipped with bazookas to use on the tanks, they might have stood a chance, but a lesson learned 130 years earlier by Beresford outside Toulouse at the end of the Napoleonic wars had still not been learned by all. Troops equipped with rockets can carry far more sting across bad ground than any group equipped with more normal artillery—and almost all of the load can be expended against the enemy.

The result at Arnhem was that 1200 soldiers pitted against the tanks died, and another 3000, mostly those who had been wounded, were captured. Compared with the final London death toll from the V-2 of 2511, there might have been better ways of dealing with the problem, but it was not purely a military problem. The rockets had a mystique about them, because they came by stealth. The V-2 killed less than half the 5864 Londoners killed by the V-1 buzz-bomb, but did much more damage to civilian morale at a time when the people of Britain had seen the D-day landings and the liberation of Paris in August 1944, and thought the war was going rather well.

To make the Allies' job more difficult, the Germans now set up V-2 launch sites in populated parts of The Hague. The Allies then concentrated on bombing rocket depots pinpointed by the Dutch resistance and on the roads, bridges and rail lines used to transport the V-2s and, bit by bit, the damage was limited and then stopped.

When the Americans reached the Nordhausen assembly area in April 1945, they collected 100 V-2 missiles before handing over the machine tools and some parts to the Russians. Some of the V-2s went to the British and French, but most went to the United States.

When General Eisenhower approved Operation Backfire, the launch of three V-2s in Europe in June 1945, one of those present was Sergei Korolev. The Russian colonel watched the three missiles rise from Cuxhaven, and ten years later was the master rocket designer of the USSR, credited with inspiring Vostok, Voshkod and Soyuz.

By then, the USA and the USSR had gone far beyond the V-2, and probably could have done so even without the captured V-2s to start from, but the knowledge that such a rocket could be made had to help in the dark days when so many launches ended in failure, when the catch-phrase 'back to the drawing board' was on people's lips.

Looking back, the V-2 was a failure as a weapon. It was a useful basis to begin a full-scale rocket development, and it inspired an age of nuclear missiles that is still not past, but it was nowhere near as dreadful as people thought. What were they worried about, both before and after the missiles started to land?

The logic of the V-2 is hard to work out for either side. It is hard to understand why the Germans relied on either the V-1 or the V-2 as weapons, but it is particularly difficult to explain why they thought the V-2 was a good choice. There is also a secondary mystery in explaining why the British government went into such a panic over its existence.

The first hints that the Germans might have a rocket weapon like the V-2 came from the 'Oslo report' that reached London in 1939, but the first V-2 did not actually fly until October 1942, in a test flight covering 290 kilometres. It was almost two years later, on 6 September 1944, that the first two rockets were launched against Paris, with the first two launched against London two days later.

By that time, the Allies knew a great deal about the V-2, and had downgraded their estimate of the warhead's mass, originally set at 10 tons, to 1 ton, the same as the warhead of the V-1. They did not know the exact difference in production costs for the two weapons, but they could still tell that the V-2 was far more expensive than the V-1, and no more dangerous. Why then, did it cause so much fear?

Part of the problem was that the V-2 could be launched anywhere, unlike the V-1 that could be seen and bombed on or near its launching ramps. The V-1 was vulnerable because it flew low, at about 2000 metres, it showed up on radar by day and its exhaust showed up at night. Once in sight, it could be shot down from the air or the ground, or it could be diverted by bringing a fighter plane's wing tip up under its stubby wing—as it banked, so it turned, away from its path towards a city or town.

In sum, the weakness of the V-1 was that it could be beaten. In the last four weeks of its use, the proportion destroyed rose from 24 per cent to 46 per cent to 67 per cent, and in the last week, 79 per cent were downed. Against that, the V-2 gave no chance for defence, so that it was rapidly becoming more cost-effective. Even if it could be detected by radar as it came in, it travelled too fast to be shot down or diverted, and it came without warning. The pulse-jet of the V-1, on the other hand, emitted the distinctive buzz-bomb noise that allowed people to take cover when they heard it stop—once that happened, the plane was about to go into a diving glide to destruction, both of itself, and whatever lay in its path.

Warfare is about the will to win, and the will to survive. When there is a chance of fighting back at the enemy, a sense of empowerment, a civilian population will take a great deal more punishment than when faced with an attack which offers no defence. The German Stuka dive-bombers destroyed the wills of their victims through their apparent invulnerability, and the potential was there for the V-2 weapons to sap the political will of Londoners in the same way.

Albert Speer, Germany's director of weapons production during the war, could not see the V-2 working as a serious mili- tary weapon: 'Even 5,000 long-range rockets, that is more than five months' production, would have delivered only 3,750 tons of explosives; a single attack by the combined British and Amer- ican air forces delivered a good 8,000 tons'. Speer would have been well aware that a single V-2 rocket cost as much as a hundred of the V-1 pilotless planes.

It seems likely that dreams of the 'Paris Gun' were still around. Veteran artilleryman Walter Dornberger's stated aim was to produce a rocket with 'double the range of the Paris Gun', though some of the constraints were challenging: the fin size of the V-2 was dictated by the rocket having to be transported by train, and so having to fit through railway tunnels.

There is a probably apocryphal tale that claims the standard rail gauge went far back past Stephenson's *Rocket* to the wheel ruts in ancient Roman roads, determined by the width of a wagon, itself dependent on the width of two horses' hindquarters. Moving forward, the tale asserts that the rail gauge determined the size of rail tunnels, and thus limited the size of today's booster rockets—so Space Age scales are based on two horses' arses (or asses, if an American tells it). The story probably has its genesis in the true limitation placed on the V-2 rockets.

Horses' rears and other extraneous matters seem to be common when we try to work out what was going on around the V-2, and why people reacted as they did. Britain's chief scientific intelligence expert in World War II, R.V. Jones, proposed an explanation in an official report (which was withdrawn just after it was distributed). Luckily for us, he later reproduced the key passage in his *Most Secret War*. The problem, he said, was to explain the German decision to develop the weapon in the first place. Hitler, he suggested, had been carried away by the romance of the rocket, just as British politicians were carried away by the threat of the rocket:

> A rational approach brought us nearest the truth regarding the technique of the Rocket. When, however, we try to understand the policy behind it, we are forced to abandon rationality, and instead to enter a fantasy where romance has replaced economy.
>
> The Germans have produced a weapon which, at the cost of years of intense research, throws perhaps a one or two ton warhead into the London area for the expenditure of an elaborate radio controlled carcase consuming eight or so tons of fuel. Their own Flying Bomb

achieves the same order of result far more cheaply. Why, then have they made the Rocket?

The answer is simple: no weapon yet produced has a comparable appeal. Here is a 13 ton missile which traces out a flaming ascent to heights hitherto beyond the reach of man, and hurls itself 200 miles across the stratosphere at unparallelled speed to descend—with luck— on a defenceless target. One of the greatest realizations of human power is the ability to destroy at a distance, and the *Nazeus* would call down his thunderbolts on all who displeased him. Perhaps we may be permitted to express a slight envy of his ability, if not to destroy his victims, at least to raise one of the biggest scares in history by virtue of the inverted romance with which those victims regard the Rocket.

R.V. Jones, *Most Secret War*, 1978

In early 2002, the world learned for the first time of a letter, written between 1957 and 1962, in which Niels Bohr rejected Werner Heisenberg's claim, made at Copenhagen in 1941, that he was doing all in his power to sabotage any German nuclear weaponry. This is in line with what R. V. Jones says Bohr believed in 1943, after he travelled from Copenhagen to Sweden and then on to Britain in October of that year. That being so, the British government almost certainly believed that Heisenberg was involved in developing an 'atomic bomb'. In November 1944, British Intelligence detected evidence of activity near Hechingen, where Heisenberg was located, but this turned out to be an operation to obtain oil from shale in the area.

Still, could a (hypothetical) German A-bomb have been delivered by a V-2? The uranium-235 'Little Boy', dropped on Hiroshima, weighed 4.5 tons, while the Nagasaki bomb, the plutonium 'Fat Man', weighed 5 tons. Towards the end of 1943, there would probably have been a fair idea of the size of a nuclear warhead. Until August 1944, Jones was rather an outsider in suggesting that the V-2 had a payload of only one ton. Other estimates ranged much higher, up to 10 tons—and that would have made it distinctly possible the rocket could deliver a small nuclear warhead.

As well, there were two other German rockets in planning: the A-9, a winged version, and the A-10, a two-stage rocket that might reach America from Europe, but in the balance, it seems that the main concern in the Arnhem campaign was with civilian morale—and to keep civilian morale high, it was worth sacrificing a few troops. It was just a pity that this essentially anti-rocket military action was not supported by tactical rocket weapons.

There were, after all, enough of them, and by 1944 they were proven on the battlefield, because the American army had recognised just how useful they might be in amphibious landings. Three generations earlier, rockets were fired from the craft landing troops in the Crimea, and that had now become a standard method for keeping the defenders' heads down without taking the attackers' heads off.

In 1919, at the very end of World War I, Goddard had demonstrated how a rocket could be launched from a music stand without knocking it over, so minimal was the recoil. In the ensuing 20 years, some of the people Goddard had convinced had moved into positions of influence and power. They might be ready-to-go solid fuel rockets, but now rockets came into their own.

Depending on who you ask, the very first bazooka seems to have been either a comedy musical instrument invented by Bob Burns or a jazz instrument played by Sanford Kendrick of a band called Bob Skyles Skyrockets, and featured in such hits as 'The Arkansas Bazooka Swing', 'Blue Bazooka Blues', and 'Mr Bazooka and Miss Clarinet'. The odds seem to favour Bob Burns, who was quite a lot older than Kendrick, but it is possible that the Burns instrument was in the public mind because of Kendrick's use of it—as I say, it depends on who is explaining it. Either way, it was a long tubular object, and when somebody saw one of the first rocket launching tubes they were reminded of the musical bazooka.

The first military bazooka fired a rifle-propelled grenade mounted on a rocket motor and launched from a tube that was knocked up from the casings of fire extinguishers. Like the origins of the name, the origins of the bits mattered little—it worked, and it was pressed into production. While a device to fire grenades was not that much of an advance, the charges used were shaped charges, using something called the Munroe effect—and that counted for quite a lot.

*The American troops were much taken with the bazooka, as were the makers.*
*This illustration is taken from a Philco advertisement.*

This effect was discovered in America in the 1880s, when Charles Munroe noticed that when a block of guncotton was detonated with its lettered surface against a steel surface, a mirror image of the letters was impressed into the steel. This led, over time, to a shaped charge warhead, where a suitable explosive is formed around a hollow metal liner, usually copper or aluminium. Suitable explosives have a high speed detonation wave, and when the explosive ignites from the back, a wave passes through the explosive to a conical or paraboloid hollow at the front, sending a narrow jet of molten, high-temperature microscopic particles and plasma at the target.

The wave arrives at a pressure in the hundreds of kilobars range (where normal air pressure around us is one bar, and car tyres are inflated to about two bars), and it is now travelling at about 30 times the speed of sound—this is a very serious, knock-'em-down explosion. Ordinary matter is just not made to take that sort of strain, and shaped charges will blast holes in almost anything, including the apparently invincible German tanks. The trick was to get the shaped charge up against the tank, and rifle-propelled grenades seemed the answer. There was just one small problem: recoil. Enter the bazooka, which could send the shaped charge to the right place, where the Munroe effect could do its work.

The trench warfare of 1914–18 used artillery well back behind immense fortifications and left almost no way for the stalemate to be broken, save by massive carnage. By the end of the war, tanks were just beginning to make a difference, and by 1939, trench warfare could not be established in the face of air power and tanks. The tank brought the artillery up close and personal, and provided shelter for advancing infantry, and the armour they carried could withstand any shell or bullet—until the shaped charges came along.

In the Pacific, the Japanese were able to fortify islands rather more easily, and they established concrete fortresses with vast walls, able to withstand anything that could be thrown at them—until the shaped charges came along. All of a sudden, the strong points were strong no more.

Reading through Goddard's papers, and works like Baxter's *Scientists Against Time*, there is one very clear message, and that is that the American military fully expected to enter the war at some stage. They were not only exchanging information and materials across the Atlantic with Britain, they were in full flight with weapons development: new radars, new rocket weapons, and much more, most of it developed after 1938.

Almost as soon as America entered the European theatre of war, bazookas were used during the north African landings of November 1942, and they were an immediate success. They may only have had an effective range of 200 metres, but that was enough to put infantry on a more equal footing with the German Mark VI tanks. Baxter quotes one GI as follows:

> This Mark VI tank was really giving us a going over, and something had to be done about it. Although I had never used a bazooka before, I knew how to handle it. So one of my buddies loaded the weapon for me, and I crawled up a ditch until I was close to the German tank [he was within 40 yards]. I couldn't miss, and let them have it. That one round really did the trick.
>
> James Phinney Baxter, *Scientists Against Time*, 1946

Baxter also quotes what he calls 'a restrained report' on ground-fired barrage rockets: 'The rockets are very popular with the various combat units because of the effective support they provide.'

A number of things had changed, among them, a more democratic environment allowing the users to feed back to the developers, but more importantly, much of this work was happening in an America that was imbued with a can-do spirit open to new ideas. Far away in the USSR, other military scientists were also developing effective rocket weapons, though whether the spur was Marxist and proletarian pride, Stalinist fear or something else, we probably could not now judge, but the Russians were certainly the first to make truly effective use of rockets in World War II.

Perhaps there is something to be said for periodic purges of the top brass, either to clear the way for new ideas or, as Dr Pangloss observed in regard to the shooting of admirals, in order to encourage the others.

Yet it was the Americans, without purges, who moved into new applications for rockets most effectively. A single fighter plane loaded with 5-inch 'Holy Moses' rockets had the same firepower as a destroyer salvo, and the planes were much faster-moving as targets. A squadron of Grumman Hellcats with 'Tiny Tim' rockets was considered equal to a broadside from a division of heavy cruisers.

It was clear from the start that air power added a new element to war. Command of the sea was essential if you were to deny an enemy needed resources in a world war, and the only way to command the sea for any length of time was to command the air above it. Torpedo bombs by themselves, however, did not have much effect on battleships and their defences: The German ships *Scharnhorst*, *Gneisenau* and *Prinz Eugen* shot down all six Fairey Swordfish biplanes of a British torpedo squadron in February 1942, and in June, all six Grumman Avengers of Torpedo Squadron Eight, flown by inexperienced pilots, were shot down in the Battle of Midway.

What was needed was a torpedo that could be launched from a greater height and a greater range. That meant a torpedo with rocket assistance, and 'Tiny Tim' was not long in coming. More importantly, the same weapon proved useful against submarines, pillboxes and other land facilities, as well as against shipping. By 1944, the US Navy was ordering more than $100 million worth of rockets every month.

Rockets were used in many other forms as well, such as bombs that were launched backwards at the same speed as the forward speed of the plane so they fell straight down, all forward momentum cancelled. Then there were the so-called JATO units, jet-assisted take-off units that were in fact rockets, used to accelerate aircraft to get them airborne with a heavy load of bombs and fuel on short airstrips, depth-charge throwers, systems for clearing a path over a minefield by firing a line across, and more.

By the end of the war, the US military was in love with rockets, and so was the general populace, entranced by the image of rockets rising into space, and falling to smite an enemy, raining down a righteous wrath. The operation to gather up German rocket scientists, known as Project Paperclip, could not have come at a better time, and where Goddard had struggled to raise the money to develop new technology, the American government was now racing to defeat the perceived threat of communism, just as Russia was racing to defeat capitalism.

Curiously, if rockets ever managed to win a war outright, it was a small undeclared war, and one that relied on tiny rockets, so small that people were largely unaware of them. At 6 am on 24 June 1948, the Soviet Military Administration closed all rail, road and canal links to West Berlin, cutting off 2.5 million Berliners.

Stalin's USSR was concerned that West Germany was being rebuilt, and wanted to absorb the whole of Germany into the communist bloc. There were no written provisions about land links, so they were within their rights in closing the land access,

*The B47 looked barnacle-encrusted when fitted with solid propellant JATO units.*

but there were guaranteed rights to three air corridors from the West.

The Allied response was to fill these corridors with aircraft, lifted with JATOs, to deliver 5000 tons of supplies a day to West Berlin: coal, food, even cars were carried in this way. There was a plane landing every 90 seconds at times during the Berlin airlift. Other planes, like the Sunderland flying boats, landed on the River Havel, laden with salt that would have corroded other aircraft. In the end, the Soviets lifted the blockade in May 1949. Without the little JATO rockets, this war-that-never-was might have been lost—or it might have escalated into World War III. The end result was a more rapid creation of the NATO alliance.

# 13
# THE SPACE
# AGE

It may interest you to know that we always regarded von Braun as more of a visionary and front man than a scientist and technician. This may have been unfair because obviously he had great scientific and technical flair. I have in my notebook an extract from an intelligence report which was made in the very early days of the war, which reads as follows: 'this gentleman, despite his Nazi convictions and the fact that he often appeared in a uniform suggesting that he held some form of honorary SS rank, was not greatly enamoured of the operational possibilities of the A4 (i.e., the V2). He regarded it more as a medium for stratospheric and meteorological research and as a necessary stepping stone to bigger things.'

Colonel W. J. S. Carter, former assistant chief,
SHAEF Air Defence Division (1973)

At the end of the war, the German rocket scientists were nothing if not realistic. As the leading Nazis were planning to slip off to South America, most of the top rocketeers (there were many thousands of workers, but fewer genuine rocket experts) seem to have had their hearts set on North America.

A few chose (or were chosen by) the USSR, but most ended up in American hands, as did most of the surviving V-2 rockets. They were collected under the code name Paperclip, and spirited off to the USA.

As the European campaign closed down, Goddard was able to examine pieces of the V-2, and recognise similar design features. Sorting the information from the Cold War disinformation and the public relations misinformation will always be hard, and the American media tended to assert that the Germans had done little more than filch American patents, while stressing that with no close neighbours who were enemies, the USA had held aloof from developing rockets like the V-2, even though they knew all about how to do it. It seems more likely, however, that the very large German workforce would have had more than enough time to rediscover all of Goddard's developments—there were only so many ways of solving the problems, after all.

In the same vein, but probably an invention of wartime or postwar German or American propaganda, there is a cheerful tale of a 13-year-old Wernher von Braun first getting interested in explosives and fireworks. In this yarn, his father could not understand his son's consuming interest in so dangerous a hobby, and feared he might become a safecracker. Tales like this always continue, and some of them, perhaps, are the work of official propagandists.

This one is fun, too: one day, we are told, the young teenager obtained six skyrockets, strapped them to a toy wagon and set them off. Streaming flames and a long trail of smoke, the wagon roared five blocks through the streets of his town, and finally exploded, as skyrockets do. The toy wagon is said to have emerged as a charred wreck, young von Braun to have found himself the centre of police attention and his rocket studies to have been curtailed for a while.

What we do know for certain is that the German V-2 scientists were regarded as a fine catch, and as many as possible were carried across the Atlantic. Significantly, it was about this time that the story emerged of von Braun regretting that the first successful V-2 (in October, 1942) had landed on the wrong planet, and once again, the fine hand of the propagandist must be suspected. Then again, maybe Colonel Carter's assessment was correct.

Later, it was claimed that the entire V-2 team had been ordered killed by Hitler, but Wernher's brother, Magnus, had managed to contact American forces before they could be wiped out. On 2 May, as Berlin was falling to the Soviet Army, von Braun and much of his rocket team entered the American lines and safety. Later still, it has become more fashionable to claim that the Germans contributed little, that America already had all the expertise it needed to build rockets and launch them, but one assumes it looked like a good deal at the time, and probably was.

Even if the Germans did give America a starting point, perhaps the most amazing thing about the space race is the speed with which it developed. As Boris Rauschenbach observed in a 1993 paper: 'Only three-and-a-half years had passed since the first launching of the Sputnik (which was actually only a small-size sphere with the simplest equipment aboard) to the flight of Yuri Gagarin into space . . .'. Rauschenbach goes on to argue that a *Sputnik* might have been created in the 1930s, and perhaps even a spacecraft, given the technology that was available for making airtight, watertight submarines, for example, so that all that was missing was the carrier rocket to launch it. I took up this matter with the retired Aerojet chemists and engineers whom I interviewed. They were inclined to think that there was very little change in the technology between 1936, when Robert Goddard was getting close to success with his gasoline and liquid oxygen rockets, and 1956, when the *Sputnik* era was close.

The changes, they suggested, were more incremental than crucial, a matter of experience, so that if the US military had begun to capitalise on Goddard's expertise in 1936, they could have been a lot further ahead.

As it was, Goddard was largely secretive about his progress, and seems never to have approached the military with suggestions for a long-range liquid fuel rocket. It is just feasible that a determined USA, knowing of Goddard's progress, could have started building rockets 20 years earlier, and instead of launching humans into space in 1961 might have been raining missiles down on Japan at the end of 1941—but luckily for us, they did not, because no long-distance missile packed with explosives was ever going to win wars. Bazookas, JATO units and rocket-propelled bombs and torpedoes were much more important.

Once you can combine a nuclear warhead with a reliable missile, you are looking at a very different situation. With Russia trampling on American heels in the nuclear race of the Cold War, and perhaps even leading in rocketry and missiles, people found their attention remarkably focused. Other changes that happened during that time made a difference, too. Computers and even desk calculators became more available as time went by, and there were huge advances in electronics that made telemetry and guidance easier.

As far as manufacturing rockets was concerned, however, there were very few engineering advances between 1936 and 1956. The real change was that people knew rockets could fly long distances, and there was now a new competition between the USA and the USSR, even more so after the Berlin Blockade, which Stalin was persuaded to lift in part by the stationing of nuclear-capable American B-29 bombers in Britain.

This international competition is often overstated, with changes in the American science curriculum, the 'alphabet soup' of new teaching materials in chemistry, physics and biology, all being attributed to the shock of *Sputnik*'s launch. The reality is that the planning of these materials was already well under way when *Sputnik* flew. After *Sputnik*, it was just easier to get funding to do what people already knew needed to be done.

The principles were all in place by the end of the war, and changes in rocket production, such as they were, came largely in the form of refinements—attempts to find better fuels, more efficient pumps (where needed) and better controls. Once again, the tension between immediately ready solid fuel rockets and more effective but slow-to-prepare liquid fuel rockets was apparent. In a scenario where there might only be a few minutes in which to prepare a counter-launch, there simply would not be time to open the silos, top up the tanks and launch, and if liquid fuels were to be used, hydrogen was out of the question, even if liquid oxygen (lox) was perhaps feasible. Either solid fuels or stable, storable, hypergolic liquid fuels were needed.

Where rockets were being prepared for civil purposes, to launch satellites, scientific payloads and humans into orbit, there was not the same desperate urgency. In that sense, the whole rhetoric of rocket-brandishing as a form of mid-twentieth-century sabre-rattling was rather hollow, and we have to wonder about the extent to which the space dreamers had hijacked the military-industrial complex, rather than the other way around. As time went on, smaller nuclear missiles that could be launched from a submarine with solid fuels became a far greater threat to peace than the intercontinental ballistic missile-based rockets that powered the space flights with liquid fuels.

In the end, it seems to have been the space dreamers who got their way, and it was rockets as satellite launchers that really changed our society. Small tactical missiles grew ever more complex, and were used in warfare more often, but the big birds rarely flew except in tests, or to launch people and satellites, usually for non-military purposes; it was through satellites that rockets had their major social impact.

Most people who claim a passing acquaintance with technology would say that Arthur C. Clarke was the first person to propose satellites, and indeed he does seem to have been the first to talk about a communications satellite, in particular, the geosynchronous sort that appears to stay in one place over the equator as the planet rotates:

> One orbit, with a radius of twenty-six thousand miles, has a period of exactly twenty-four hours. A body in such an orbit, if its plane coincided with that of the Earth's equator, would revolve with the Earth and would thus be stationary about the same spot above the planet. It would remain fixed in the sky of a whole hemisphere . . .
>
> Let us now suppose that such a station were built in this orbit. It could be provided with receiving and transmitting equipment . . . and could act as a repeater to relay transmissions between any two points in the hemisphere beneath, using any frequency that will penetrate the ionosphere.
>
> Arthur C. Clarke, 'Can rocket stations give world coverage', 1945

Clarke even knew how to power such a station: a solar engine was to capture sunlight with mirrors to drive a steam-powered generator, but while he points out that this could be done efficiently, he also recognises that thermoelectric and photoelectric effects might be able to make better use of solar power. So where did the idea of a satellite first come from?

In 1992 Clarke credited the invention of the concept of a manned space station to unnamed Russians and Germans, encountered by him at second-hand in David Lasser's 1931 volume *The Conquest of Space*, and P. E. Cleator's 1936 book

*Rockets Through Space*. These visionaries would have included Tsiolkovsky, von Pirquet and Noordung, but however you look at it, the first in the field to discuss artificial satellites was an American clergyman, Edward Everett Hale.

Sadly for my love of resonances, the reverend was no relation to William Hale, the inventor of the Hale rocket, nor of astronomer George E. Hale, who was Goddard's friend. Still, he knew something of the skies, and dreamed of them—and shared his dreams in 'The Brick Moon', a story published in the *Atlantic Monthly* in 1870–71. Hale told of assembling a satellite made of bricks, launched using energy stored in water-powered flywheels.

Why bricks? Well, the craft would have to be launched through the air, and would get very hot from the friction as it rushed through the atmosphere. Iron would not do: only brick would withstand the furious heat. In a sense, Hale anticipated the ablation tiles used on spacecraft, but in this case, the ablation tiles *were* the spacecraft. After that, though, his scientific awareness began to falter.

Hale's moon was to travel in a polar orbit, 4000 miles above the planet, and was to act as a navigational aid for mariners trying to detect their longitude. It was to be 200 feet (about 60 metres) across. For some odd reason, Hale assumed that a brick moon launched northward would continue to travel along that meridian and its opposite meridian forever, providing a convenient navigational reference. Later, he suggested there might be as many as four of the brick moons, the same number of moons that Jupiter was then known to have.

Even the launching method was interesting in its scientific nonsense, for there were no guns and no rockets here. Not one, but two flywheels of slightly differing sizes were to be powered up by waterfalls, then the brick moon was to be rolled onto them:

Of course it would not rest there, not the ten-thousandth part of a second. It would be snapped upward, as a drop of water from a grindstone. Upward and upward; but the heavier wheel would have deflected it a little from the vertical. Upward and northward it would rise, therefore, till it had passed the axis of the world. It would, of course, feel the world's attraction all the time, which would bend its flight gently, but still it would leave the world more and more behind. Upward still, but now southward, till it had traversed more than one hundred and eighty degrees of a circle. Little resistance, indeed, after it had cleared the forty or fifty miles of visible atmosphere. 'Now let it fall,' said Q., inspired with the vision. 'Let it fall, and the sooner the better! The curve it is now on will forever clear the world; and over the meridian of that lonely waterfall,—if only we have rightly adjusted the gigantic flies,—will forever revolve, in its obedient orbit . . .

Edward Everett Hale, *The Brick Moon*, 1870

In fact, any brick moon launched like this would travel in an approximate ellipse, and necessarily pass through its launching point, even if we ignore the friction of the atmosphere. Once we take that into account, it would inevitably crash into the ground, if it did not break up or burn up first. Of course, no mere bricks and mortar could withstand the acceleration that took the structure to a speed sufficient to reach space, especially when that was applied in Hale's tenth of a millisecond.

As a rule of thumb, imparting a velocity of one kilometre per second would require an acceleration a million times greater than the gravity on the surface of our planet, and the brick moon needed to travel at more than 10 kilometres a second. Think of hitting a brick wall at a speed that is a multiple of 3600 kilometres an hour, and you are getting a feel for the problem faced by Hale's passengers.

Hale offered the notion of a brick moon, complete with an atmosphere and a human community living on the produce that they were able to grow in a mysterious soil that formed, using seed that just happened to be on board when the satellite was accidentally launched. In all probability, the space warps, dilithium crystals and other ploys used by today's science fiction writers will seem equally silly in the twenty-second century, but they are mere props, required to make the yarn *seem* plausible to contemporary eyes. All the same, there are some amusing features to consider as Hale sorts the various problems.

The cost would amaze today's aerospace industry: it was less than a quarter of a million dollars. The satellite was launched by accident when it rolled without warning onto the flywheels and flew into space, carrying with it a convenient supply of food, animals, families, and even some snow which had drifted in during construction, and which provided water 'quite sufficient for all purposes of thirst and of ablution'. But how, before radio, before the first electric lamps were patented, could the brick moon people communicate with the earth?

They could have used mirrors and sunlight to communicate by Morse code; instead, Hale had his spacefarers signal the Earth by making group long and short leaps (200 feet and 20 feet) to form Morse code signals on the outer surface of the brick moon. They were able to perform this feat entirely without the benefit of spacesuits, because, as Hale explains, their atmosphere had stuck to them. On the Earth, people signalled back with Morse code with black cambric ('enough for the funerals of two Presidents') laid out on flat snow-covered ground. The earth communicators, of course, had powerful telescopes, but those on the brick moon needed to be able to read the messages by the naked eye.

Later in Hale's story, there were largely unsuccessful attempts to use the flywheels to launch needed items into space, surrounded by protective wet sandbags, and so the tale ended with the families still in space, saving Hale from the problem of explaining how they might be rescued—but the notion of humans in space, circling the globe, had been planted.

In a collection of his stories published in 1899, Hale tells us in the preface of events in 1877, when Asaph Hall found the moons of Mars:

> In sending me the ephemeris of the two moons of Mars, which he revealed to this world of ours, he wrote, 'The smaller of these moons is the veritable Brick Moon.' That, in the moment of triumph for the greatest astronomical discovery of a generation, Dr. Hall should have time or thought to give to my little parable,—this was praise indeed.
>
> Edward Everett Hale, Preface to *The Brick Moon and Other Stories*, 1899

However you look at it, Arthur C. Clarke has to be the chief prophet of satellites, however, especially when we consider what he said in 1957, just before the first *Sputnik* flew:

> It may seem premature, if not ludicrous, to talk about the commercial possibilities of satellites. Yet the aeroplane became of commercial importance within 30 years of its birth, and there are good reasons for thinking that this time may be shortened in the case of the satellite, because of its immense value in the field of communications.
>
> Arthur C. Clarke, *Making the Moon*, 1957

So the idea of satellites for communications was alive and well, even before *Sputnik*, and the commercial possibilities arrived within about seven years. There were even grandiose schemes for high-flying aircraft to beam televised lessons to large parts of India—different technology, but the same principle, although the technology was less than fully worked out. From 1958 to 1964, researchers around the world experimented with communications satellites, identifying the frequencies that worked, ground stations and launch systems.

*Telstar* was launched on 10 July 1962, with a perigee of 950 kilometres, an apogee of 5600 kilometres, and a period of 158 minutes, which meant that it was far from ideal as a communications device. *Telstar II* was launched in May 1963; it had a higher orbit, around 10 800 kilometres, and a period of 225 minutes, leaving it in view for longer periods, but it was still not geosynchronous, and the phrase 'we are losing the satellite' came into the language.

The *Syncom* models, on the other hand, were spin-stabilised and geosynchronous. *Syncom* I went up in February 1963 but failed; *Syncom* II and III, launched in July 1963 and August 1964, made it into orbit and worked beautifully. After that, the model was in place, and communications satellites became a part of life. Along the way, they changed the way sporting events like the World Cup and the Olympics were seen, and they brought us instant footage of missiles falling on Baghdad. We don't 'lose the satellite' any more, and the world is permanently linked—for better or worse. Like the telegraph in the Crimea, satellite links told and tell stories the military and politicians do not want told, but the satellite also brings a veneer of common culture.

In June 2002, with the first draft of this book half-complete, I sat in a press conference in Washington DC, and listened as NASA scientists outlined why it is important to go to Mars, to gather material and to bring it back. It occurred to me then that these media-savvy individuals were working in an entirely different way from Goddard, but that in a real sense they were after the same dream, human landings on the planet most likely to have life. It is by no means a new dream.

The Mars exploration story really begins with Giovanni Schiaparelli, who proposed in 1877 that there were markings on Mars, lines that he called *canali* in Italian. While this could have been translated as a life-neutral 'channels', it was taken instead to mean 'canals', and where there are canals, in an age when the Suez Canal was brand-new and the plans for the Panama Canal were being argued over, there will be canal-diggers. And just as Thomas More used Utopia to show how our world might be, so the Utopians of the nineteenth century used Mars.

In 1880, Percy Greg published his two-volume *Across the Zodiac*, describing a voyage to Mars in a craft relying on a substance called 'apergy' that negated gravity. There, the skies were green and the vegetation orange, and the people were scientifically advanced.

In 1891, Robert Cromie described how a steel globe constructed in the Alaskan wilderness was sent to Mars by controlling the law of gravity, which 'may be diverted, directed or destroyed'. The natives were friendly and lived an idyllic life, thanks to advanced science and technology.

The next year Camille Flammarion, a French populariser of astronomy, offered us an explanation of the reasoning that allowed people to deduce peaceful Martians—it all stemmed from the nineteenth-century view that the outer planets formed first, with planet formation working its way inwards, so Mars had to be older than Earth. This is why we find Flammarion assuring us in his *La planète Mars et ses conditions d'habitabilité* that 'we may hope that, because the world of Mars is older than ours, mankind there will be more advanced and wiser'.

In 1897, Kurt Lasswitz had his *Auf Zwei Planeten* (*Two Planets*) published. This depicts distinctly non-monstrous Martians who establish a station over the North Pole to allow contact between Earth and Mars, a station kept in place by a form of antigravity device. So far, so good, but the monsters were about to erupt: in the same year, H. G. Wells had his *War of the Worlds* serialised in *Cosmopolitan* magazine—and now the

*Two very different views of space travel. Percy Greg's 1880* Across the Zodiac *took a more literal interpretation of a voyage to Mars, while Robert Cromie's 1891 Mars-bound spaceship* Steel Globe *was powered by the 'law of gravitation'.*

THE LAST MAN ENTERS THE STEEL GLOBE

Martians were depicted as ravening monsters intent on destroying us and our planet.

The following year, Wells had his story, now published as a book, reviewed in *The Academy Review*, with the following comments:

> According to Mr. Percival Lowell, who made an extensive study of Mars in 1894, these canals are really belts of fertilised land, and are the only habitable tracts on Mars, the remainder of the land surface being desert. The view that the Martians—it is less unreasonable to think that Mars is inhabited than that it is not—would look towards our Earth with longing eyes is thus quite within the bounds of legitimate speculation . . .

The early 1900s saw a number others (Garrett P. Serviss, Ellsworth Douglass, Edwin L. Arnold, Fenton Ash and Mark Wicks among them) writing of life on Mars, with semi-Utopian descriptions of life there, but waiting in the wings was a former member of the US cavalry, an ex-miner and one-time salesman called Edgar Rice Burroughs.

His first Martian adventure began to appear in serial form in 1912. All of a sudden Mars was the place to set new stories to fill the pulp magazines, and writers rushed to join the bandwagon. Between them, Schiaparelli, Lowell, Wells and Burroughs had set in the human mind the belief that there was life on Mars. The canals, it turned out later, had never been there in the first place, but that mattered little. The mistake had performed its allotted task, and people were free now to dream of travel to Mars, of finding other intelligent races.

Sadly, the alien-as-monster notion is never far from the surface, as shown by the public reaction to Orson Welles' radio adaptation of *War of the Worlds* on 30 October 1938, and by the many claims of alien abductions in the second half of the twentieth century—

although the sympathy filmgoers feel for ET shows that it is a view that could be changed.

To many of us, though, humanity has a manifest destiny, and that is to land on the surface of another planet. Of course, that will not be enough: after that comes a trip to Europa, one of Jupiter's moons, where there is some chance of finding life beneath the ice, in an ocean that may perhaps lie 100 kilometres down. Right now, that may sound like science fiction, but a lot can change in 50 years.

The early twenty-first century sees the rocket as a potent force for good and for ill. Satellite communications, put in place by rockets, help to unify our world, but at the same time rockets offer the risk that they will be used to deliver chemical, biological and nuclear weapons over long distances. Other smaller weapons, shoulder-fired missiles, have the potential to make a single infantry soldier the destroyer of a tank, a gunship or a fully loaded bomber—or a civilian airliner in flight.

When the British made their first attempt at setting fire to Washington DC, Walter Lord tells us the the flames were put out by 'one of Washington's patented thunderstorms'. I landed at Dulles airport in the middle of one of those patented thunderstorms, some months after September 11 when the World Trade Center towers were destroyed, and when my co-passengers saw a column of steam in the clouds to port, they could only think of one thing. 'Somebody's fired off a missile,' they told each other. In fact it was a condensation track where a lightning bolt had passed, but that is the power of the rocket in the popular mind.

Rockets are not good weapons of stealth, so if chemical or biological warfare is to set off a blanket of illness or death before counter-measures can be taken, rockets are poor vehicles of delivery. On the other hand, if the aim is to interdict an area, to make it off-limits because of a chemical, biological or nuclear hazard, then a visible and public delivery is no problem at all, and may even be more effective. Quite clearly, nobody is ever likely to rule out using rockets to deliver nuclear weapons because there is no need, or chance, for secrecy after the event.

The Falklands War of the 1980s was between Britain and Argentina, but the only real winner was the French manufacturer of the Exocet missiles that allowed a single aircraft to destroy a warship. As this book was being written, thousands of rockets were being fired, mainly in the area of the Middle East. Rockets are the perfect weapons for helicopter gunships because there is no recoil, and they are excellent for skirmishers on foot, because the launcher is light enough to carry away to use again, unlike an artillery piece—and cheap enough to be discarded, if needed.

The major fear in the western world remains the rocket, especially a missile launched by a 'rogue state' designed to deploy state-of-the-art chemical or biological weapons. One major threat to world peace lies in the notion of anti-missile missiles, because people argue that if the USA has them, it can order missile attacks on perceived enemies without fearing retaliation. Like the crossbow in mediaeval times, the anti-missile missile is seen as unsporting or even ungentlemanly.

The rocket has changed our society forever by bringing instant communication to the world, and it extends well beyond news. 'The people I dealt with in Irian Jaya [West Papua] are just one generation from head-hunting cannibals,' a geophysicist told me in Washington a few days after I flew in. 'Now they watch *Seinfeld*,' he added, 'and they want to know why they can't have the same goods and wealth.' In the early 1960s, the then President of Indonesia, Sukarno, suggested that the films of Hollywood were a grave danger to the West, as they depicted an idealised lifestyle that gave people of the Third World an exaggerated set of expectations and hopes.

That was then; now we can see dish-antennas all over Indonesia, bringing English-language films to the homes of the rich, with subtitles in idiomatic Malay and Indonesian. Even in the smaller villages of Sumatera and Java, away from the tourist trail, there are communal TV sets, bringing similar images to the people. The social impact on Indonesia is immense: eventually it will impact on us as well, and it is an impact that stems from rockets, flying into space.

It stretches beyond there: in Turkey, central Europe, and many other developing parts of the world, there is a mythical developed world of TV-land. It is depicted in tabloid journalism, tabloid television, amoral soap operas and trailer-trash reality shows as they are carried to a largely uncomprehending world by satellites put in place by rockets. Over time, better communication may lead to better understanding, but in the short term, what is being absorbed and understood should be a worry to those in the developed world who value their way of life.

Can the rocket be an effective weapon in the hands of a terrorist? In all probability there are easier ways of delivering a biological, nuclear or chemical blow than by rocket. For a start, long-distance rockets are complex items, not just hollow tubes filled with propellant. Simple rocket motors can be bought, and more expensive rocket technology is by no means out of reach, but a serious rocket requires complex control systems, guidance systems and even engines, if it is to hit a distant target or even get close to it. While a developed nation can develop, build and operate complex missiles, the knowledge base is just not there for terrorists, who are more likely to use suicide bombers or planted bombs, or ships to introduce weapons into coastal cities.

You don't need to be an Einstein to work it out but, curiously enough, Albert Einstein was the first to predict delivery of atomic bombs on a freighter, writing to President Roosevelt on 2 August 1939 to urge that work commence on the atomic bomb that he knew then was at least feasible:

> This new phenomenon would also lead to the construction of bombs, and it is conceivable—though much less certain—that extremely powerful bombs of a new type may thus be constructed. A single bomb of this type, carried by boat and exploded in a port, might very well destroy the whole port together with some of the surrounding territory. However, such bombs might very well prove too heavy for transportation by air.

Any nation can build rocket weapons good enough to attack a neighbouring country, but building, testing and calibrating an intercontinental ballistic missile takes a large range of skills, and while these might be purchased and hired, they are likely to leave a trail that intelligence organisations and snooping satellites will spot. We are left with the hope that the good things that rocket-based science and technology can offer will eventually outweigh the evil, but it will be a near-run thing.

When you come down to it, what has rocket science really given us? The major plus for science would be the knowledge we have of what lies beyond our atmosphere, from the instruments that have been sent into space. We know far more than we could ever have known without rockets, but it is doubtful that this has changed the world greatly. Two things, though, have changed our lives forever: the satellite, and the way in which photographs from space made us see the world as a single unit, bringing us to a more responsible attitude to the ecosystems we were rapidly destroying.

It is probably no coincidence that Rachel Carson's *Silent Spring* was such an instant success in 1962, coming at a time when we could for the first time see the view that Tsiolkovsky had predicted would be 'so magnificent, alluring and infinitely diversified'. Nothing brings home more effectively our isolation than something like that.

Since that time, satellites have tended to increase our awareness of our world, with GPS measurements being used to establish the actuality of movement in tectonic plates, while remote sensing assists in protecting crops, dealing with floods and tracking loose icebergs. Even the weather pictures that we take for granted on television at night have been there for less than a generation.

But the great spin-off claim seems to evaporate into nothing when you get down to it. Velcro (1948) and Teflon (1938) may have found uses in space, but they were not invented for that. Space blankets are a genuine spin-off that has benefited human-ity, but space pens, freeze-dried foods and all of the rest of the claimed benefits do not amount to much. There is little for the accountants to gloat over, but humanity as a whole is much richer for what we have learned by sending rockets into space.

# 14
# THE
# ALTERNATIVES

For the most part, the rockets we read about and think about today are rockets that use chemical energy, and for getting to the moon, or maybe even Mars, that seems to be enough—but it could easily have been otherwise. When John F. Kennedy was elected President, the US space lobby was hoping to see Lyndon Baines Johnson in the White House, because Johnson was 'very well-informed about space', and Kennedy no more than 'informed'. Having been elected, Kennedy hung back from making any commitment to space, but when Yuri Gagarin went into space on 12 April 1961, things changed. On 19 April LBJ was given the task of coming up with a space program plan.

If the decision had been made to follow the Goddard dream of going to Mars, things could have gone very differently, with atomic rockets coming to the fore, but chemical rockets took us to the Moon instead. The nuclear rocket program was far more than a pipe dream, however. As we saw earlier, Goddard had contemplated the use of atomic power as far back as 1907, and he returned to the notion in 1913, but until an effective nuclear reactor was available no real work could be done in this direction.

Nuclear energy takes two forms: nuclear fission, where a heavy nucleus breaks down into smaller nuclei; and nuclear fusion, where two light nuclei combine to form one heavier nucleus (although its mass is lighter than the sum of the two original nuclei). So far, only fission, the sort of reaction that happens in 'atomic bombs' has been tamed in reactors. Fusion is the sort of reaction that happens in the sun and in hydrogen bombs and, so far, has proved impossible to control.

In each case, the resultant nuclei weigh slightly less than the nuclei they were formed from. This difference, known as the mass deficiency, is the 'm' in Einstein's famously misquoted quotation, $e = mc^2$', where 'e' is the energy produced, most of it as heat. In a nuclear reactor, the products are used to trigger more nuclei to break down, so that quite a lot of heat is produced. The nuclear rockets used fission heat to give hydrogen large amounts of energy, so it would drive the rocket forward as it roared out of the nozzles.

The nuclear rocket program was put under way in 1954, and the first test rig, the aptly named Kiwi-A (after the New Zealand bird, since this test rig would never 'fly'—the stand weighed more than the 5000-pound thrust) fired a spectacular jet skyward in 1959. (The Kiwi-A was an earthbound rocket that jetted its exhaust to the skies, a common way of testing rockets.) There were tests of Kiwi-A and Kiwi-B until the end of 1961, but the scheme went no further, although a great deal of data was gathered.

In the post-Chernobyl world, we may wonder at the idea of nuclear powered rockets even gaining consideration at a political level. But atomic energy was seen differently in the 1950s, and Egon Larsen, a popular science writer, could blithely inform his readers that:

Within a few years isotopes will turn up in many more expected or unexpected places—perhaps the slogan 'Gamma Washes Whiter', will become quite familiar to us when our ultra-sonic washing machines are equipped with some gamma source to sterilize shirts and socks and napkins.

Egon Larsen, *Atomic Energy*, 1958

Waste was no problem either, said Larsen:

Solid wastes can be disposed of by incineration, closed storage, open burial, or drainage out to sea. Incineration is especially valuable for treating animal carcases and as a means to reduce the volume of the solid waste, but it gives rise to active gases and ash. The discharge of the gases should be clear of windows. Burial may be used on permanently enclosed sites at levels depending on the rainfall so that local groundwater is not contaminated. Even highly radio-active solid wastes can be disposed of safely in the sea provided all relevant factors are kept in mind: movement of the surface water, the breeding and migratory habits of fish, and the possible hazard to seaweed where it is harvested for food, fertilization, or industrial use.

Of course, nobody expected fission to be around much longer; fusion was just around the corner, offering clean, cheap energy, and Larsen quotes Sir John Cockcroft as saying:

We are now at the same stage as fission research was in 1940 when the possibility of a chain reaction was well understood but many uncertainties remained, and a further fifteen years elapsed before large-scale nuclear power was developed.

The Kiwi nuclear rocket was powered by liquid hydrogen at $-253°C$ going to gas at $2000°C$ in the space of a metre and a half; this carried, as James Dewar notes, 'severe thermal stress, thermal expansion and structural integrity problems'. This sort of situation is worth keeping in mind when 'rocket science' is mentioned: it isn't really the science that is a challenge, but the engineering.

The next stage, the NERVA (Nuclear Engine for Rocket Vehicle Application) scheme hung on for some years but in the absence of a mission that demanded a nuclear rocket and as its main supporter, Democrat Senator Clinton Anderson, about to retire, the program was shut down in by a Republican administration in 1972. It is possible that the nuclear rocket idea may be revived at some future date, perhaps for a Mars mission or a mission beyond our solar system, but given the protests that have been made at far smaller packages of plutonium going into space, this would have to be considered a relatively unlikely event.

In fact, these objections have been rather excessive. The plutonium at the centre of the most recent fuss, the Cassini mission, is contained within several layers of insulation which were tested and re-tested using explosives. In no test case was the plutonium exposed to the atmosphere. The plutonium itself was packaged to break into chunks if the worst happened, rather than dissolve into dust, so it could not be inhaled or carried on the wind. Ignoring this, the protests were based on a worst-case scenario, where all of the plutonium would be pulverised and then breathed by humans. All the same, it is unlikely that people will ever welcome any attempt to get fissile material into orbit so that it may be used to power a rocket, and that may prevent a Mars mission ever happening.

There is theoretically a way around this problem, and understanding it may help to explain why there is so much enthusiasm for identifying whether there is water close to the surface on Mars. The standard biological symbol for 'male' is a circle with an upward arrow. The symbol, derived from the spear and shield of Mars, the God of War, is also the astrologer's symbol for the planet Mars, and the alchemists' symbol for iron. By an odd coincidence, the planet's soil contains between 14 and 55 per cent iron oxide, making it almost ore-grade material, and this iron oxide may be the key to humanity opening up the rest of the solar system.

The trick is to transfer rocket manufacturing work to the moon or to Mars. In short, the plan is to make iron on Mars, which could be used to make receivers able to generate electricity from radio waves beamed from a mother ship in Mars orbit. This notion would allow non-nuclear power options for space bases on Mars and further exploration into space.

Because Mars is further away from the sun than Earth, an orbiting solar power source would need to be larger than a similar device orbiting Earth giving the same power. A solar power source on the surface of Mars would need to be even bigger, because of the energy losses through the thin atmosphere; when scientists realised they were talking about an area the size of several football fields, which would need to be backed by fuel cells for cloudy days and night-time, the option of generating power in space became tempting again.

This would require an unmanned propellant factory that could be set up before any humans left Earth. It would refine the Martian carbon dioxide atmosphere and mix it with hydrogen (brought along or better still, electrolysed from water ice) to make liquid oxygen and methane to power an expedition's return from Mars. This factory would get its power from microwaves beamed from an orbiting station at a rectifying antenna, or 'rectenna', which converts them into direct current.

The problem: you need metal, and lots of it, to make the dipole antennas that gather the energy. While iron is too dense a metal to be much use in space flight, Mars has only 38 per cent of Earth's gravitational pull, and hardly any oxygen to rust the iron when it is made. Better still, using water to convert carbon dioxide to methane also yields carbon monoxide, a reducing agent that reacts with iron oxide to produce carbon dioxide and free iron.

So a reactor could process Martian soil and air into both rocket propellant and iron for more rectenna parts. The iron would be rolled into strips to make the dipoles, or formed into wire to make a mesh reflector, while the waste, or slag, would be used to make insulator strips going between the dipole pairs. The solar collector would need to be in an aerosynchronous orbit 17 023 kilometres above Mars to allow it to deliver continuous power to the ground station.

On current plans, the Mars lander would carry enough materials to make a 1.5 kilometre-wide rectenna array that would provide 150 kilowatts of electricity to power the refinery. It would then grow to 20 kilometres in diameter, enough to provide 7 megawatts; growth beyond that point would only be limited by shipments of small, lightweight rectifier circuits from Earth.

Where solar arrays on the planet would need regular cleaning and dusting, space arrays would not have this problem, and tiny dust particles would have no effect on radio waves. The rectenna would work year-round, night and day, with the exception of short eclipses during the Martian spring and autumn equinoxes.

Of course, there may be other, better forms of rocket for space use. The curious pulsed plasma thruster rocket, or PPT, uses an electrical charge accumulated on a capacitor to ablate tiny amounts of Teflon to produce forces in the micronewton to millinewton range. PPTs have actually been in space for almost 30 years, used for attitude control on satellites where only very small forces are required, and even the smallest blast from a conventional rocket is likely to over-compensate.

Rather than carry fuel, oxidiser and pumps into space, the satellite carries a solid slug of Teflon and solar cells. Six units under computer control, are required to manage the orientation of the satellite—the reader may recall how many jets Tsiolkovsky envisaged around his pressurised barrel! At the right time, a capacitor is discharged, producing a spark which releases a tiny puff of Teflon as reaction mass, and as the Teflon slug wears away, it is advanced by a spring.

No spacecraft will ever fly far with a PPT, but perhaps there are other answers out there, better ways of making rockets that we have yet to consider. Perhaps ion rockets, again using solar cells, will prove effective, sending ionised xenon (or maybe mercury) out as reaction mass. This is effective because the ions can be accelerated to speeds far higher than gas molecules can be accelerated using heat, and is no longer just theory.

In 1998, *Deep Space 1* was successfully launched, but the first test of its ion engine was halted after just 4.5 minutes. The problem appeared to be a small short-circuit of the accelerating grids caused by a tiny piece of loose metal. Repeated attempts to restart the engine must in the end have evaporated the piece, as the engine eventually restarted and ran successfully until it was shut down in late 2002. The problem here is that there is always a risk that the ions will be deposited on the solar panels and as the craft's solar panels were found to be degrading, there is some speculation that this may be the reason.

One thing is certain: even if we get scramjets to lift more and more of us into space, we are going to need some other method to get to other planets or to the stars.

Back on earth, people remain keen to get off the ground in a number of ingenious ways—not all of them scientific, or even remotely practical.

There is a certain charm in the stories of those who attempt to do odd things with rockets and have mishaps. Some of the tales are apocryphal, others are wildly exaggerated, but all have elements of extreme accuracy about them, and these alone probably tag them as untrue. Take the earliest case we know about, said to come from a Chinese folk tale about a man called Wan Hu, who somewhere around 1500 sat on a chair to which 47 rockets were attached.

We must assume that Wan Hu was very rich, because the 47 rockets were lit simultaneously by 47 servants who rushed forward with torches and who must, we assume, have then hurriedly retired from the scene, because we hear no more of them, or any harm that might have come to them. There was little more to report about Wan Hu either, who is said never to have been seen again.

We will gloss over the improbability of 47 servants being able to gain access to the 47 fuses, all at the same time, which can be tested easily enough by asking a smaller number of people to crowd around a chair. At least Wan Hu (if he existed at all) had the courtesy to destroy only himself, but others were less considerate.

In fairness, though, we need to keep in mind that the first rocketeers had to educate themselves as they went along, and the clever ones survived. Congreve might have been able to tap into the wisdom of generations of pyrotechnicians, but Oberth, von Braun, Goddard, Truax and others all had to learn by doing and discovering, sometimes the hard way. All the same, the select group of people willing to investigate rockets seems to have included a number who could be classified as overly optimistic.

In 1806, Claude Ruggieri is said to have been launching small animals into the air with rockets, landing them with parachutes, and had got as far as to recover a sheep from an altitude of about 200 metres; the authorities stepped in when he planned to launch a small boy using a rocket cluster. In this case, the lack of exquisite detail suggests that this was indeed what Ruggieri had in mind—tall tales are generally much better fleshed-out.

Then there is Kibalchich, whose vision of a platform where the pilot hurls loads of gunpowder into some sort of furnace shows us something even less stable than Wan Hu's chair. When we compare this with the emphasis on stability and control that we see in the works of a Tsiolkovsky, a Goddard or a von Braun, we see the difference between amateur idiot and competent person bent on becoming a professional.

Next in our parade of people depriving some village somewhere of its rightful idiot comes stuntman F. Rodman Law. On 13 March 1913, Law tried to launch himself into the air with a giant skyrocket built near a New Jersey marsh. His exploit was reported in *Scientific American* on 29 March, where we learn that Law was, perhaps, not quite the idiot he appears, though the journal starts by noting that 'F. Rodman Law, known for his foolishly daring feats in the air, surpassed himself in recklessness on the ominous 13th inst'.

Law, the journal notes, had previously jumped from the Bankers' Trust Building and the Williamsburg Bridge in New York, and 'from a biplane at a height of a mile'. The parachute he used in his rocket attempt, of Japanese silk, weighed just 6.5 pounds (3 kilograms) but was said to be capable of carrying a 170 pound (77 kilogram) man. Law sat in the nose of a cylinder 3 feet in diameter, 10 feet long, with 50 pounds of slow-burning powder, enough to lift him to 3500 feet, or so people thought. Instead, there was a 'terrific explosion'. The badly burned pilot was thrown from the rocket and ended up in a hospital, lucky not to be badly broken as well.

*Rodman Law prepares to settle down under his nose cone.*

Of course, some of the 'idiot' impressions have been created by the experimenters themselves, telling a good yarn in later years. Homer Boushey was certainly highly regarded by the people I interviewed; while he was daring and took risks, so does everybody when there is a war on. He got his start as the test pilot flying a small Ercoupe aircraft to test the first JATO units. He agreed, out of curiosity, to try flying the aircraft using rockets only, but it needed a tow to get it moving—and the propeller had been removed to reduce drag. The Ercoupe, by the way, was a 753-pound low-winged monoplane, which would have made the towing easier. Boushey wrote of this escapade:

> As a foolproof method of releasing the rope, I volunteered to stick my arm outside the open cockpit window and hold the rope as long as I could during the tow. It was surprising how much pull force was exerted on my arm. It will never be known at what distance or speed the tow rope was released, but the point of release was somewhat below that wherein the arm-bone would have been pulled out of the shoulder socket. The 12 rocket bottles were then fired resulting in a take-off and marginally controlled flight for perhaps a distance of one mile. We should have anticipated some control difficulty. Removal of the propeller and consequent loss of prop-wash over the elevator, combined with the up-moment of the 12 thrusting rockets, caused the airplane to climb sharply. This pitch-up was promptly followed by pronounced pitch-down when the rockets stopped burning, since they and their racks were mounted well below the wing and created considerable parasitic drag. Also, the absence of the drag of an idling propeller mounted above the center of gravity added to the problem . . . . So the first U.S. flight of an airplane powered solely by rockets was brief but exciting.
>
> Homer Boushey, 'A brief history of the first US JATO flight tests'

He observed at the end of this account that their main mistake was to have treated the aircraft as a toy, the sage remark of a man who not only survived, but retired as a Brigadier-General in an age when promotion was based on competence. We should be grateful that he was so honest in one sense, though it was not as bad as it sounds—the Ercoupe rose only to 20 or 30 feet, and touched down further along the runway. Of course, most of the test pilots were made of the 'right stuff', but that did not stop any of them telling a good yarn.

On 14 October 1947, Chuck Yeager broke through the sound barrier in the X-1 rocket plane, doing so with two ribs broken in a horse-riding accident. He had his ribs strapped, kept quiet about the injury, and used a broomstick to close the X-1's door, since he had limited mobility. As well, to stop the windshield misting Yeager had rubbed it down with a wetting agent, shampoo. This is why you will often read something to the effect that 'Chuck Yeager became the first person to break the sound barrier with two broken ribs, a broomstick, and shampoo on his windshield'.

Perhaps the main difference with these two tales is that Boushey and Yeager knew what they were doing, both during their exploits, which they survived, and afterwards, when they told the true story. Where the flier did not survive, or did not exist, the chances of getting to the truth are less promising.

The greatest 'amateur idiot' yarn of all is the sadly untrue, completely fabricated, tale of the unnamed man who provided his car with a jet engine, a man usually described on the Internet as a Darwin Award winner. (These awards are given to those who improve the human gene pool by eliminating themselves from it, but nobody who ever gained the award did it as thoroughly as this.) The origin of this yarn may just lie in an occasion of unspecified date, but attested to by Aerojet workers, who recall a DeSoto convertible being accelerated to 100 miles per hour in 14 seconds (without taking off) when a new Chrysler proving ground in Michigan was being dedicated.

The story opens with the Arizona Highway Patrol finding

smouldering wreckage embedded in the side of a cliff rising above the road at the apex of a curve. It looks like a plane crash, which is a little bit correct, but it turns out to be the remnants of a motor vehicle, and a most unusual one at that, a Chevy Impala fitted with a JATO unit. A former Air Force sergeant had taken the vehicle to a long, straight stretch of road, where he attached the JATO unit to his car, then accelerated to a high speed, and fired off the rocket.

Various forms of the legend exist, most of them dwelling with almost necrophiliac delight on the remains, consisting as they do (with some minor variations) of small fragments of bone, teeth, and hair that were extracted from the crater, and fingernail and bone shards removed from a piece of debris believed to be a portion of the steering wheel. This detail adds a careful air of truth to the whole thing and lulls us into believing that:

> The operator was driving a 1967 Chevy Impala. He ignited the JATO unit approximately 3.9 miles from the crash site. This was established by the location of a prominently scorched and melted strip of asphalt. The vehicle quickly reached a speed of between 250 and 300 mph and continued at that speed, under full power, for an additional 20–25 seconds. The soon-to-be pilot experienced g-forces usually reserved for dog-fighting F-14 jocks under full afterburners.
>
> The Chevy remained on the straight highway for approximately 2.6 miles (15–20 seconds) before the driver applied the brakes, completely melting them, blowing the tires, and leaving thick rubber marks on the road surface. The vehicle then became airborne for an additional 1.3 miles, impacted the cliff face at a height of 125 feet, and left a blackened crater 3 feet deep in the rock.

Not all of the tales can be eliminated. This next one, also to be found around the Internet, is either an excellent legpull, or proof that rocketeers are still a breed with different ways of looking at survival, but it appears to have large amounts of truth in it. The hero, described as controversial rocket engineer Steve Bennett, was supposedly denounced for his daft scheme to win the X-Prize for being the first private individual or company to get into space. This is a prize of US$10 million, which may or may not be paid to the first such individual: at the last report, the amount promised by supporters had only reached US$5 million. The craft has to reach a height of 100 kilometres with two passengers, and repeat the flight within a fortnight, to prove that the first effort was no fluke.

According to reports, Manchester-based Bennett planned in 2001 to undertake an action denounced by others as suicidal, and likely to destroy British amateur rocketry forever. His Thunderbird capsule, said critics, was actually a converted cement mixer, containing sheets of hardboard and a few computer joysticks. And there would be no tests, either: Bennett was quoted in news reports as saying, 'We are not planning any tests such as wind tunnel or vibration tests before we launch it. That is what the test flight is for.'

(In case this does not sound alarm bells, Tsiolkovsky designed a wind tunnel in 1897, and a wind tunnel was seen as essential for Peenemünde. Wind tunnel tests don't kill people, but avoiding wind tunnel tests either kills people—or the claim of avoidance indicates a high level of fiction.)

Bennett's first shakedown flights would be in a capsule with a number of commercially available rocket motors strapped together. Each of these would have a burn-time of six seconds, and if they all fired together would subject him and his capsule to high g-forces, maybe enough to make the capsule (or the pilot) fall apart, say the critics.

The story has a number of holes in it—for starters, Bennett claimed to have used the NASA centrifuge in preparation. In fact, the centrifuge NASA uses is not theirs, but belongs to the US Army, and is not where Bennett said it was. As if that wasn't enough, NASA say they have never heard of him (Bennett, on the other hand, claimed NASA as one of his official sponsors, until the BBC news service reported the odd discrepancy), and his own colleagues say there has been no centrifuge training. In short, it sounds as though Bennett is preparing to rush in where angels dare to tread—if, that is, he is actually planning to rush in.

The BBC report also revealed that Bennett had announced plans to test a liquid fuel rocket motor at a military site, even though he had 'been banned, and caused all other rocketeers to be banned from military launch ranges, after he set fire to one when a rocket failed on launch a few years ago'.

Bennett claimed to lead the field, a claim that was hotly contested by other rocketeers, one of whom, John Bonsor, said, 'It is ridiculous to claim that he leads the field, except in the number of crashes.' And responding to Bennett's claim that he was the leading contender for the X-Prize for being the first private person in space, Bonsor snorted, 'Only if he reinvents the laws of physics.'

Clearly Bennett is one of a long traditional line. But is it the satirical line of Lucian, Swift and Munchausen, or is it the line of English eccentrics, or is he from the same mould as Wan Hu, Claude Ruggieri, Rodman Law and the unnamed JATO sergeant? We will let Bennett have the last word: 'Just watch me. "Seeing is believing", I say to my critics'.

No doubt we will. Of course, people laughed at Goddard, but Carl Sagan used to have an answer for people who used the 'they laughed at Einstein' ploy. He conceded that claim as true, but noted 'they also laughed at Bozo the Clown'.

It would be a shame to end the story of rockets with a bunch of people who seem to be contenders for the Darwin Award when there is a healthy and sensible bunch of amateur experimenters out there, testing assumptions and exploring the gaps. These are not idiots, they have all their fingers, and they may well end up as professionals, or in teaching the professionals a thing or two.

We have to recall that amateurs in Germany and the USA founded rocketry, certainly that using liquid fuels. Goddard began as an amateur, and so did Robert Truax. Goddard was originally a little disdainful of the American Interplanetary Society (later the American Rocket Society) and its first rocket, which conscripted to greater duty, among other things, a cocktail shaker and a saucepan, along with off-the-shelf components; he came around later as more engineers joined the ARS, as it now was.

The amateurs still have a contribution to make, and John Carmack is a case in point. As one of the founders of Id Software, he is well able to fund his experiments, and he documents everything, even the crashes, offering MPEG movies on the Web of various successes and less-than-successes, and explaining why things were as they were. According to my informants, Carmack is a real contender for the major prizes for amateurs, including the X-Prize.

Where Goddard in the 1920s was isolated in America from German and other rocket workers, the new rocket culture is more international, with Internet lists that discuss safety, fuels, rocket careers, control methods and mundane issues like cleaning the mixing bowls used to prepare solid fuel mixes. Other lists are used to plan major projects, and to announce test firings.

Of course, just as von Braun's team at Peenemünde would have had little to say to rocketeers in other countries in the 1930s and 1940s, there are also the military rocket makers, but everybody has to get their start somewhere, and people wanting to enjoy fancy fireworks can also do so.

In the same way, the University of Queensland people who assembled the scramjet have tended to refer to it as a 'scrounge jet' because they have scrounged and scrimped, using off-the-shelf components to build a complex machine. In some ways, their work is more reminiscent of the ingenuity and skill of Goddard and the amateurs of today than of the brute force methods of the great powers' industrial-military machines. The difference is that they have a clearer view of what they want to do, and how they should go about it.

# POSTSCRIPT
## ON THE
## FUTURE

And just where does that leave us with the scramjet, now we know the trial was a success? The 50-year clock has only just started ticking for this new form of propulsion, and it could go anywhere. Judging now what the scramjet might do for our future society is like trying to make judgments about an integrated urban public transport system based on extrapolations from a glimpse of Mulga Bill's bicycle on a mountain track on a stormy night.

We cannot really tell what contingencies will arise, any more than Alan Kay could do, and he was the man who gave us the graphic user interface or GUI (which for most of us just means a mouse and Windows something-or-other). Kay is credited with saying: 'Don't worry about what anybody else is going to do . . . The best way to predict the future is to invent it. Really smart people with reasonable funding can do just about anything that doesn't violate too many of Newton's Laws!'

One thing we can be certain of: the changes wrought by rockets and rocketry will come from young minds, and they will take a long while to be achieved—unless some of the youngsters are given a free hand to act as they see fit. That was what happened when the V-2 was being developed, and that was what happened in the American part of the space race, where staff numbers were growing too fast for the older men to establish empires and impose their world view on everybody.

There is a moral there, I think, but old Konstantin Tsiolokovsky deserves the last word: 'Earth is the cradle of humanity, but one cannot remain in the cradle forever'.

# ACKNOWLEDGEMENTS

Research on books is not what it once used to be, a matter of solitary seekers after musty facts scuttering through libraries, perhaps aided and abetted by one or two others. I have been in many libraries, but I also belong to an Invisible College of a new kind, the fellowship of the Internet, and that gives me access to experts all over the world.

Philip Olleson (Nottingham) and Michael Kassler (Sydney) gave me the benefit of their knowledge of Samuel Wesley, while Robert Radford filled me in on some of the family history of the Duke of Wellington, in which matter he was marvellously helpful. John Seonac pursued Samuel Wesley's 'Skyrocket Waltz' at great length, and gave me the leads I needed.

Theta Brentnall got me access to the Aerojet plant in Sacramento, and to the collected wisdom of Jerry Lewelling and his colleagues, Bill Campbell, Bill Sprow and Howard Williams, as they inducted me into an understanding of what is involved in filling a 15 metre tube, 1.5 metres across, with high explosive in a continuous pouring operation. In US terms, that is 50 feet long and 5 feet across, but either way it is a potential big bang.

Stephen Berry, Wayne Browne, Dan Collingbourne, Toby Fiander, Chris Forbes-Ewan, John Holmes, Donald Lang, Chris Lawson, David Martin, Paul Williams and Zero Sum on the ABC 'Science Matters' list all helped out on aspects of escape velocity, especially Marco Badaracco and Donald, who reminded me about some delightful pieces of Verniana.

Amateur rocketeers on the ERPS and Arocket lists helped me with technical detail, and I have to single out Russell McMahon in New Zealand for special mention, but there were many others who helped as well.

In Canberra, Tim Bonyhady found me the right place to look to learn more about Burke and Wills.

As usual, the libraries of the University of Sydney and University of New South Wales, along with the State Library of New South Wales, provided many of the most needed resources. At Worcester, Massachusetts, Mott Linn assisted me signally in finding unusual information at the Goddard Library of Clark University, and the people of Worcester amazed me with their friendliness. At the Library of Congress, volunteer Phyllis Cahan got this foreigner oriented promptly, and Fred Bauman in the manuscripts area was courtesy itself.

In Perth, Graeme Rymill at the University of Western Australia showed me how to track down old stories in *The Times*.

At the Smithsonian Air and Space Museum in Washington DC, Richard Dixon and Nancy Nett in the shop showed me great courtesy.

Then there were the friends who sent me books, clippings, snippets and URLs, including Christine Donnelly in Tasmania and Margaret Ruwoldt in Melbourne,

Other librarians helped as well, and in ways well beyond the call of duty. Kim Klein from the *Washington Post* contributed a day of her life to take me down the Beltway to see Baltimore,

Fort McHenry, and why it counted that the flag was still there.

I owe indirect thanks also to Karl Klager. He was one of the Paperclip scientists, and worked at Aerojet. My copy of the history of Aerojet came to me from his estate. He invented the technology that allowed solid ICBMs, and using polyurethane chemistry, he came up with a fuel with a higher specific impulse, and able to stand the temperature ranges. More importantly, he kept his book, which passed to me from his estate.

And then there were the retired Aerojet people themselves. At a time of heightened security concerns, they got me into as many areas as they could, showing me motors, motor parts, facilities and more. In one day they fed me more than enough information for a whole book, and I was lucky that they and their colleagues had already produced such a book, *Aerojet: The Creative Company*. Better still, Jerry Lewelling had a spare copy, one that came from the estate of the late Karl Klager.

My thanks, in alphabetical order to Bill Campbell, Jerry Lewelling, Bill Sprowle and Howard Williams, but especially to Jerry, who provided me with transport, welcomed me into his home and his church and who kept Karl Klager's copy of the history of Aerojet safe against the day when a foreign writer would come around, needing it.

Many friends suggested ideas for a title before we decided to keep it simple. For helping to keep me sane, I have to thank my wife Chris. At Allen & Unwin, Emma Cotter and Ian Bowring put up with me; but my greatest thanks go to Penguin Watson—and all the people who dreamed of space.

## Picture credits:

www.napoleonic-literature.com (pp. 61, 80, 96); Denisse, Amédée, *Traité pratique complet des feux d'artifice*, 1882 (p. 119); National Air and Space Museum 1992–0020, 979E (p. 123); Ordway, F. I. (ed.), *History of Rocketry and Astronautics*, volume 9, 1989 (p. 149); NASA 74-H-1065 (p. 175); NASA 74-H-1195 (p. 179); JPL photo 381–33 (p. 182); Crouch, T. D. and Spencer, A. M. (eds), *History of Rocketry and Astronautics*, volume 14, 1993 (p. 188); *Aerojet: The Creative Company*, 1995 (p. 205); Cornett, L. H. (ed.), *History of Rocketry and Astronautics*, volume 15, 1993 (p. 218); *Scientific American* (p. 234).

# REFERENCES

Aerojet History Group, *Aerojet: The Creative Company*. Los Angeles: Stuart F. Cooper Company, 1995, printed digitally on demand, ISBN 0-9659769-0-4.

Akhavan, Jacqueline, *The Chemistry of Explosives*. London: The Royal Society of Chemistry, 1998.

Anonymous, *Gentleman's Magazine*, June 1814, pp. 612–9, 'Diary of the Proceedings of the Allied Sovereigns'.

Babbage, Charles, *Reflections on the Decline of Science in England, and on Some of its Causes*. London: B. Fellowes, 1830.

Baker, David, *The History of Manned Space Flight*. London: New Cavendish Books, 1981.

Baxter, James Phinney III, *Scientists Against Time*. Cambridge, Massachusetts: MIT Press, 1946.

Becklake, John, 'British rocketry during World War II', in T. D. Crouch and A. M. Spencer (eds), *History of Rocketry and Astronautics*: AAS History Series. San Diego: American Astronautical Society, volume 14, chapter 11, 1993.

Bethell, Colonel H. A., *Modern Artillery in the Field*. London: Macmillan, 1911.

Blagonravov, A. A. (ed.), *K. E. Tsiolkovsky: Selected Works*, translated by G. Yanovsky. Moscow: Mir Publishers, 1968.

Bonyhady, Tim, *Burke & Wills: From Melbourne to Myth*. Sydney: David Ell, 1991.

Boushey, Homer A., 'A brief history of the first U.S. JATO flight tests of August 1941: A memoir', in T. D. Crouch and A. M. Spencer (eds), *History of Rocketry and Astronautics*: AAS History Series. San Diego: American Astronautical Society, 1993, volume 14, chapter 12.

Brodie, Bernard and Brodie, Fawn M., *From Crossbow to H-bomb*. Bloomington: Indiana University Press, 1973.

Bryant, Arthur, *The Great Duke*. London: Collins, 1971.

Burrows, William E., *This New Ocean: The Story of the First Space Age*. New York: Random House, 1998.

Caesar, Gaius Julius, *The Gallic Wars*, translated by W. A. McDevitte and W. S. Bohn, etext located at http://classics.mit.edu/Caesar/gallic.html

Callwell, Major-General Sir Charles and Headlam, Major-General Sir John, *The History of the Royal Artillery from the Indian Mutiny to the Great War*. Woolwich: Royal Artillery Institution, 1931.

Cavendish, Henry, *The Scientific Papers of the Honourable Henry Cavendish*, edited by James Clerk Maxwell. Cambridge: Cambridge University Press, 1921.

Chamberlain, Peter and Gander, Terry, *Mortars and Rockets*. London: Macdonald and Jane's, 1975.

Clark, J. D., *Ignition! An Informal History of Liquid Rocket Propellants*. New Brunswick, NJ: Rutgers University Press, 1972.

Clarke, Arthur C., 'Can rocket stations give worldwide coverage?', *Wireless World*, October 1945, reprinted in Arthur C. Clarke, *Greetings, Carbon-based Bipeds*. London: Voyager (Harper-Collins), 1999.

Clune, Frank, *Dig: The Burke and Wills Saga*. Sydney: Angus & Robertson, 1937.

Cockburn, James, *Memoir on the Preparation and Use of Rockets*. London: J. Harinell, for Her Majesty's Stationery Office, 1844.

Coil, Suzanne M., *Robert Hutchings Goddard: Pioneer of Rocketry and Space Flight*. New York: Facts on File, 1992.

Cornett, Lloyd H. Jr (ed.), *History of Rocketry and Astronautics*: AAS History Series. San Diego: American Astronautical Society, volume 15, 1993.

Cowper, H. S., *The Art of Attack*. Wakefield: EP Publishing, 1977 (reprint of 1906 edition published by W. Holmes, Ulverston).

Craufurd, Quintin, *Sketches Chiefly Relating to the History, Religion, Learning and Manners of the Hindoos*. London: T. Cadell, 1790.

Crouch, Tom D. and Alex M. Spencer (eds), *History of Rocketry and Astronautics*: AAS History Series, volume 14. San Diego: American Astronautical Society, 1993.

Crouch, Tom D., *Aiming for the Stars: The Dreamers and Doers of the Space Age*. Carlton, Victoria: Melbourne University Press, 1999.

Crowe, Michael, *The Extraterrestrial Life Debate, 1750–1900: The Idea of a Plurality of Worlds from Kant to Lowell*. Cambridge: Cambridge University Press, 1986.

Darwin, Charles, *The Voyage of the* Beagle. London: John Murray, 1845.

DeVorkin, David H., *Science With a Vengeance: How the Military Created the US Space Sciences after World War II*. New York: Springer-Verlag, 1992.

Dewar, James A., 'Project Rover: the United States nuclear rocket program', in J. L. Sloop (ed.), *History of Rocketry and*

*Astronautics*: AAS History Series. San Diego: American Astronautical Society, 1991, volume 12, chapter 9.

Dick, Steven J., *The Biological Universe*. Cambridge: Cambridge University Press, 1996.

Duberly, Fanny (Mrs Henry Duberly), *Journal Kept During the Russian War*. London: Longman, Brown, Green and Longmans, 1856.

Edelson, Burton I, 'Communication satellites: The experimental years', in J. L. Sloop (ed.), *History of Rocketry and Astronautics*: AAS History Series. San Diego: American Astronautical Society, 1991, volume 12, chapter 8.

Fang Toh Sun, 'Early rocket weapons in China', in T.D. Crouch and A.M. Spencer (eds), *History of Rocketry and Astronautics*. AAS History Series. San Diego, American Astronautical Society, volume 14, chapter 1.

Faris, Alexander, *Jacques Offenbach*. London: Faber & Faber, 1980.

Garlinski, Jozef, *Poland, SOE and the Allies*. London: George Allen & Unwin, 1969.

Garlinski, Jozef, *Hitler's Last Weapons: The Underground War Against the V-1 and V-2*. London: Julian Friedman, 1978.

Gillmor, Lt C. (RN), quoted in Turvey, P.J., 'Congreve rocketry revisited', in L. H. Cornett (ed.), *History of Rocketry and Astronautics*: AAS History Series. San Diego: American Astronautical Society, 1993, volume 15, chapter 2.

Gleig, G. R., *The Campaigns of the British Army at Washington and New Orleans in the Years 1814–1815*. London : John Murray, 1836.

Gleig, G. R., *The Subaltern*. London: Leo Cooper, 1969.

Glover, Michael, *The Peninsular War, 1807–1814*. London: David & Charles, 1974.

Goddard, Esther C. and Pendray, G. Edward, *The Papers of Robert H. Goddard*, three volumes. New York: McGraw-Hill, 1970.

Golas, Peter J., 'Chinese mining: where was the gunpowder?' in Li Guohao *et al.* (eds), *Explorations in the History of Science and Technology in China*. Shanghai: Chinese Classics Publishing House, 1982.

Gronow, Captain Rees Howell, *Reminiscences of Captain Gronow*. Project Gutenberg file grnow10.txt.

Guedalla, Philip, *The Duke*. London: Hodder & Stoughton, first printed 1931, reprinted 1974.

Hale, Edward Everett, 'The Brick Moon', written in 1870, reprinted in *The Brick Moon and Other Stories*, 1899, available as a Project Gutenberg file brkmn10.txt.

Hall, R. Cargill (ed.), *History of Rocketry and Astronautics*: AAS History Series. San Diego: American Astronautical Society, 1986, volume 7, part I.

Harding, James, *The Duke of Wellington*. London: Morgan Grampian Books, 1965.

Harris, John, *The Recollections of Rifleman Harris, as Told to Henry Curling*. London, Century Publishing, 1970. (Annotated by Christopher Hibbert.)

Haythornthwaite, Phillip, *Napoleonic Source Book*. London: Arms & Armour, 1995.

Hickman, Clarence, *Clarence Nichols Hickman, Electrical Engineer*, an oral history conducted in 1973 by Julian Tebo and Frank Polkinghorn, IEEE History Center, Rutgers University, New Brunswick, NJ, USA.

Hordern, Marsden, *Mariners are Warned! John Lort Stokes and H. M. S. Beagle in Australia 1837–1843*. Melbourne: Melbourne University Press, 1989.

Johnson, Stewart W., 'Reaching for the planet Mars: humankind's evolving perspective', in T. D. Crouch and A. M. Spencer (eds), *History of Rocketry and Astronautics*: AAS History Series. San Diego: America Astronautical Society,

1993, volume 14, chapter 8.

de Joinville, Jean, *The Life of St Louis*, translated by René Hague. New York: Sheed & Ward, 1955.

Jones, R. V., *Most Secret War: British Scientific Intelligence 1939–1945*. London: Coronet Books, 1978.

Kassler, Michael and Olleson, Philip, *Samuel Wesley (1766–1837): A Sourcebook*. London: Ashgate, 2001.

Larsen, Egon, *Atomic Energy*. London: Pan Books, 1958.

Lawrence, T. E., *The Seven Pillars of Wisdom: A Triumph*. London: Cape, 1935.

LeConte, Joseph, *Instructions for the Manufacture of Saltpetre: Electronic Edition*. Originally published Columbia, South Carolina, Charles P. Pelham, State Printer, 1862; electronic version by the University of North Carolina at Chapel Hill, 1999, http://docsouth.unc.edu/lecontesalt/leconte.html

Lent, Constantine Paul, 'Jet propelled dirigible' *Astronautics*, Issue 56, December 1943, pp. 14–15.

Lindbergh, Charles, *Autobiography of Values*. New York: Harvest Books, 1993.

Lord, Walter, *The Dawn's Early Light*. Baltimore: The Johns Hopkins University Press, 1994.

Lubbock, Basil, *The Arctic Whalers*. Glasgow: Brown, Son & Ferguson, 1937.

Lubbock, Basil, *The Nitrate Clippers*. Glasgow: Brown, 1966.

MacCurdy, Edward, *The Notebooks of Leonardo da Vinci*. London: The Reprint Society, 1954.

Macinnis, Peter, 'Fraudo the frog', in *Ockham's Razor 2*, introduced by Robyn Williams. Sydney: ABC Books, 1988.

McDonough, Thomas R., *The Search for Extraterrestrial Intelligence: Listening for Life in the Cosmos*. New York: Wiley Science Editions, 1987.

McKinlay, John, *McKinlay's Journal of Exploration in the Interior of*

*Australia (Burke Relief Expedition).* Public Library of South Australia facsimile (1962) of the original: Melbourne: F. F. Baillière, Publisher in Ordinary to the Victorian Government, no date (*circa* 1863?).

Mercer, Cavalié, *Journal of the Waterloo Campaign, Kept Throughout the Campaign of 1815.* Published 1870, 1927 and Cambridge Massachusetts: Da Capo Press, 1995.

Mikhailov, V. P., 'Some features of lifesaving rocket development in the 19th and early 20th centuries', in T. D. Crouch and A. M. Spencer (eds), *History of Rocketry and Astronautics*: AAS History Series. San Diego: American Astronautical Society, 1993, volume 14, chapter 3.

Miller, Ron, 'Speculative Spacecraft, 1610–1957', in Lloyd H. Cornett (ed.), *History of Rocketry and Astronautics*: AAS History Series. San Digeo: American Astronautical Society, 1993, volume 15, chapter 8.

Montgomery, Field-Marshal Viscount, *A History of Warfare.* London: Collins, 1968.

Moore, Patrick, *The Astronomy of Birr Castle.* Offaly: The Birr Scientific and Heritage Foundation, 1991.

Moorehead, Alan, *Cooper's Creek: The Opening of Australia.* New York: Atlantic Monthly Press, 1987.

Morris, Thomas, *The Recollections of Sergeant Morris* (edited by John Selby). Gloucestershire: The Windrush Press, 1998.

Napier, William Francis Patrick, *History of the War in the Peninsula and in the South of France, From the Year 1807 to the Year 1814.* London: Routledge & Sons, 1878.

Needham, Joseph, *Science and Civilisation in China*, volume 5, parts 1–7, esp. part 7. Cambridge: Cambridge University Press, 1954–2000.

Needham, Joseph, 'The guns of Khaifêng-fu', *Times Literary Supplement*, 11 January 1980, pp. 39–42.

Nepos, Cornelius, *Hannibal*, translated J. Thomas, 1995, http://129.186.40.170/THOMAS/netscape/hannibal.htm

Neufeld, Michael J., *The Rocket and the Reich: Peenemünde and the Coming of the Ballistic Missile Era*. New York: Free Press, 1995.

Olleson, Philip (ed.), *The Letters of Samuel Wesley*. Oxford: Oxford University Press, 2001.

Orange, Claudia (ed.), *The Dictionary of New Zealand Biology*, volume 2, 1870–1900. Wellington: Bridget Williams Books, 1993.

Ordway, Frederick I. and Hervé Moulin, 'Nineteenth century rocketry in France', in T. D. Crouch and A. M. Spencer (eds), *History of Rocketry and Astronautics*: AAS History Series. San Diego: American Astronautical Society, 1993, volume 14, chapter 2.

Ordway, Frederick I. III (ed.), *History of Rocketry and Astronautics*: AAS History Series. San Diego: American Astronautical Society, 1989, volume 9.

Ordway, Frederick I. III, 'The legacy of Schiaparelli and Lowell', in Lloyd H. Cornett (ed.), *History of Rocketry and Astronautics*: AAS History Series. San Diego: American Astronautical Society, 1993, volume 15, chapter 3.

Parkinson, C. Northcote, *Trade in the Eastern Seas Between the Years 1793–1813*. London: Cass, 1937.

Partington, J. R., *A History of Greek Fire and Gunpowder*. Cambridge: W. Heffer & Sons, 1960.

Plutarch, *The Complete Works Volume 3: Essays and Miscellanies*. Project Gutenberg, pluta10.txt.

Public Library of South Australia facsimile, *The Burke and Wills Exploring Expedition*. Facsimile (1963) of an original published Melbourne: Wilson & Mackinnon, 1861.

Rauschenbach, Boris, 'Scientific and technological prerequisites for the first manned spacecraft', in Lloyd H. Cornett (ed.), *History of Rocketry and Astronautics*: AAS History Series. San Diego: American Astronautical Society, 1993, volume 15, chapter 5.

Rosen, Edward (trans.), *Kepler's Somnium*. Madison: University of Wisconsin Press, 1967.

Sänger-Bredt, Irene, 'The silver bird story: A memoir', in Hall, R. Cargill (ed.), *History of Rocketry and Astronautics*: AAS History Series. San Diego: American Astronautical Society, 1986, volume 7, part 1.

Scholes, Percy A., *The Oxford Companion to Music*, 9th edition. Oxford: Oxford University Press, 1955.

Sharpe, Mitchell, 'Operation Backfire: England launches the V-2', in E. T. Ordway III (ed.), *History of Rocketry and Astronautics*: AAS History Series. San Diego: American Astronautical Society, 1989, volume 9, chapter 10.

Sloop, John L. (ed.), *History of Rocketry and Astronautics*: AAS History Series, volume 12. San Diego: American Astronautical Society, 1991.

Stroud, William G., 'Early scientific history of the rocket grenade experiment', in F. I. Ordway III (ed.), *History of Rocketry and Astronautics*: AAS History Series. San Diego: American Astronautical Society, 1989, volume 9, chapter 16.

Suetonius (Gaius Suetonius Tranquillus), *The Twelve Caesars*, translated by Robert Graves. Harmondsworth: Penguin Classics, 1957.

Talbot, Hugh, *The English Achilles: The Life and Campaigns of John Talbot, 1st Earl of Shrewsbury*. London: Chatto & Windus, 1981.

Templeton, Nicholas (ed.), *Works for Pianoforte Solo by late Georgian Composers, Volume 7: Samuel Wesley and Contemporaries, The London Pianoforte School, 1766–1860*. New York and London: Garland, 1985.

Thoreau, Henry David, *Walden*. Harmondsworth and New York: Penguin Books, 1983.

Truax, Robert C., 'Liquid propellant rocket development by the U.S. Navy during World War II: A memoir', in J. L. Sloop (ed.), *History of Rocketry and Astronautics*: AAS History Series. San Diego: American Astronautical Society, 1991, volume 12, chapter 5.

Tubridy, Michael, *Reconstruction of the Ross Six Foot Telescope*. Birr Castle, 1998.

Turvey, P. J., 'Congreve rocketry revisited', in L. H. Cornett (ed.), *History of Rocketry and Astronautics*: AAS History Series. San Diego: American Astronautical Society, 1993, volume 15, chapter 2.

Wells, H. G., *The World Set Free*. London: Collins, 1926.

Wilkins, John, *The Discovery of a World in the Moone*. London: 1638.

Winter, Frank H., *Baron Vincenz von Augustin and his* Raketen-batterien: *A History of Austrian Rocketry in the 19th Century*, in R. Cargill Hall (ed.), *History of Rocketry and Astronautics*: AAS History Series. San Diego: American Astronautical Society, 1986, volume 7, part 1.

Winter, Frank H., *Rockets into Space*. Cambridge, Masssachusetts: Harvard University Press, 1990.

Woolley, Richard van der Riet, 'Interplanetary Travel' (book review). *Nature*, 14 March 1936, p. 442.

I had finished writing this book when I discovered Simon Garfield's *The Last Journey of William Huskisson*, Faber & Faber, 2002. This is not a reference, but a recommendation.

# INDEX